ARCTIC SPRING

ARCTIC SPRING

Potential for Growth
in Adults with Psychosis and Autism

Laura Tremelloni

Edited by
Judith Edwards

KARNAC
LONDON   NEW YORK

First published in 2005 by
H. Karnac (Books) Ltd.
6 Pembroke Buildings, London NW10 6RE

British Library Cataloguing in Publication Data

A C.I.P. for this book is available from the British Library

ISBN: 1-85575-314-6

10 9 8 7 6 5 4 3 2 1

Edited, designed, and produced by Communication Crafts

Printed in Great Britain

www.karnacbooks.com

To my parents
With love and regret for all that was left unsaid

CONTENTS

PART II
Case studies

ACKNOWLEDGEMENTS

First of all, I would like to thank all my patients for the precious contribution they gave in shaping the hypotheses put forward in this work and for the trust they placed in me even during periods when there was no analytic improvement. By sharing their psychic torment, I was able to enhance my personal and professional knowledge. I would like especially to thank the patients who gave me permission to publish the work we did together. They were aware of the fact that it might be useful towards an understanding of others in helping them to realize their full potential.

I would like to thank all the authors mentioned in this book, since I obtained support and clarifications from their works.

I would like to express my gratitude to my colleagues and supervisors, who, during different periods of my training, helped me through individual analysis, seminars, or supervisions and patiently accompanied me during the long process of personal and professional individuation. Their original contribution and passionate interest in research were important elements of support and stimuli for my daily analytic work.

I would like to thank my supervisors who helped me during the early stages of my career. Due to the initiative and courage of Pierfrancesco Galli, in the mid-1950s a psychotherapy study group was set up in Milan, where Gaetano Benedetti (Switzerland) and the late

Johannes Cremerius (Germany) were asked to start up some seminars and supervisions. They helped me during my initial work in psychoanalytic psychotherapy, and their experience as analysts interested in applying the psychoanalytic method to clinical studies, in cases both of psychosis and of psychosomatic disorders, was crucial to my initial training. I am also grateful to the Swiss psychoanalysts Réné Henny and Bertrand Cramer, who supervised my first cases of infantile psychosis.

My thanks to Salomon Resnik, Argentine analyst who, after having completed his professional training in London with Klein, Winnicott, Bion, and Rosenfeld, settled in Paris and, in the 1970s, created an international work group in Venice (Italy) directed at infantile autism and psychoses. The originality of his thoughts, his broad culture, and his enormous generosity in transmitting to the seminar group represented the basis for creating a school that was highly stimulating and not dogmatic or, as he says, "a research laboratory like the workshops of the Renaissance craftsmen".

My debt of gratitude to Salomon Resnik is due to the fact that he made it possible for the group members to express their clinical experiences, thus leading to further observations and research. This way of working always started from clinical situations unhindered by preconceptions tied to rigid ideologies, without, however, neglecting to take into consideration the modern theoretical developments of psychoanalysis. This continual exchange of ideas with colleagues helped me to learn and develop the sense of my own professional identity. Through Resnik, it also became possible for me to meet foreign scholars, and this enabled me to extend my professional training. One of these scholars was Francis Tustin, with whom I subsequently began a long period of supervision of cases of autism. She offered me her personal experience of working with autistic children.

I am very grateful to Joyce McDougall, since it was her analytic and supervisory capacity, together with her creativity and generosity, that led me to write about my clinical experiences.

My warm thanks go to Anne Alvarez, a brave and sensitive child psychoanalytic psychotherapist who, for many years, supervised some of my cases of autism and threw light on some of my own unknown parts, similar to those of my patients. It was she who encouraged me to collect the material for this work.

I must also mention the valuable help given to me by Tommaso Senise, and thanks to all my friends and colleagues who have read the rough drafts of my work, especially Giuseppe Maffei, Graham Music,

Luciano Fornari, and Isabella Shiappadori. My thanks also go to Giuliana Di Gregorio, who supervised the English text with patience and enthusiasm.

Judith Edwards' patient and careful revision in clarifying some of my obscure or unexpressed ideas was of fundamental importance, as was her encouragement to carry out and finish the work.

I am grateful to my children Francesco and Fabio for their support that made my work easier and helped me overcome some obstacles.

Finally, I must thank Al Alvarez for his precious advice.

A NOTE ON THE SUBJECT OF CONFIDENTIALITY

The description of the clinical cases in the second part of the book refers not so much to the overall picture of each individual but, rather, to my interpretation of their reality and to the kind of relationship we established. I, too, therefore, am involved in the description of the analytic process. In my opinion, the therapeutic alliance with the patient represents the attempt to emerge from a common human condition of uncertainty and suffering, which everyone experiences, more or less, during certain phases of life.

The clinical cases described show the development of each analysis, which was long and complex due to the underlying difficulties that each case presented. Clinical discussion with colleagues is what enables knowledge to increase and new therapeutic approaches to evolve.

In order to protect the anonymity of each of my patients, I have modified or omitted some biographical details, even though this means risking being misinterpreted and misunderstood by the reader. Fantasies, dreams, and symptoms can belong to any human being and are the elements that represent the material that can be used in the scientific discussion.

* * *

For simplicity of exposition, in general discussions male pronouns are used for patients and female pronouns for analysts.

PREFACE

During one of my trips to Alaska I came across a small book of memoirs by the English geographer Roy Sylar (1987), in which he described the four years he had spent there. He wrote the book primarily to acquaint his grandchildren with his experiences in Alaska.

Sylar had been sent there, together with some other colleagues, to draw the map of the northwest coastal region, between the Bering Strait and the Yukon border, which up to 1949 had not been explored in detail. The area was vaguely referred to as the region of the Northwest Passage. After the first attempts of exploration in the seventeenth century, little was added to the maps of this region before the nineteenth century, and the map of the Arctic between Icy Cape and Baffin Bay showed a vast blank space marked "parts unknown". At that time, no one knew anything about the depth of the ocean, the currents, passages that were free of ice, the fiords, the refuges, dangerous areas, and other useful navigation information.

During their four-year stay in Alaska, these geographers were able to study the climatic and environmental conditions of this region and carry out their research projects with the modest instruments of the time, with their spirit of adventure and observation and their ability to overcome enormous obstacles.

It seemed interesting to use these geographical phenomena as a metaphor to introduce my research in the psychoanalytic field when attempting to reach the uncharted autistic parts of autistic patients. The autism we find in certain children or adult patients represents a frozen area, apparently without emotions, in which life seems to be asleep. What we try to explain to ourselves in the psychic field can be reflected in the geographical phenomena observed in this remotest corner of the world.

In order to map the coast, the geographers came up against their first hurdle: the conditions of the weather and the terrain. During winter, the ground froze hard, and the coast and sea blended in featureless white. Everything looked as if a sheet had been spread out, and, until the ice melted, it was impossible to distinguish the mainland from the Arctic Ocean.

In the late spring when the snow and ice began to melt, the ice broke up and created crevasses, the rivers began to fill, and the region became inaccessible for several months. In fact, the existence of mud, pieces of floating ice, and water made it impossible to reach the area by any means because there was not enough snow for skis, not enough water for ships, and not enough solid ground for wheels. Therefore, these areas could not be reached by airplane, ship, vehicle, or dog-sled, and the boundaries between land and sea could not be recognized. A period of patient waiting was thus required before the two elements of earth and water could be clearly distinguished and shapes and borders recognized.

Waiting for the unknown and the new, which is implicit in every journey including analysis, is made up of hope and reverie. But in the case of patients with more or less extensive autistic parts, the therapist's hope has to be very strong to accept the long period of waiting without any emotional responses. This allows us to see what lies buried beneath the ice. In Alaska, the period of waiting is rewarded by a sunrise-to-sunset burst of colour as the flowers bloom, basking in the 24-hour sunlight.

In the same way, emerging from the frozen condition of autism coincides with the blossoming of feelings in the transference.

Another phenomenon that is similar to autism and is well known to Eskimos is called "whiteout". It is a climatic condition in which, during the daylight season, when the light is particularly bright, large clouds sometimes come low so that everything looks white, with no shadows or colour. It is impossible to distinguish between the sky and the frozen land or to see the horizon. In such a situation, walking is difficult since one has the sensation of being suspended in space, with no points of reference. Besides the compass, the only instrument people had at that time were their senses, almost entirely limited to nerve endings in the soles of the feet and the leg muscles, which could tell if the surface they walked on was irregular or if there were dangerous inclines. It is no wonder that on one occasion the Arctic explorer, Admiral Peary, wrapped himself up in the American flag so that those who followed could have a reference point that was coloured and therefore visible.

The situation in which there are no reference points—that is, no emotional contact between individuals—can be the situation that exists during the therapeutic work with patients who have autistic features in their personalities and who are difficult to approach and get to know. That is why it is always necessary for the therapist to be on guard during the journey and remain in touch with her own inner world and sensitivity in order to intervene at the right time. Only then can one hope to avoid the dangers of freezing and melting, the unexpected falling into the holes of depression, the initial coldness and emotional numbness, and the subsequent explosion of emotions in the deflation of the delusional omnipotent world.

ARCTIC SPRING

Introduction

This work aims to bear witness to the existence of autistic states in adults and their integration following an intensive period of psychoanalytic psychotherapy. Although it takes into consideration the seriousness of the pathology and the initial imbalance between the autistic and the healthy part of the personality, this work attempts to give reason for hope to both patients and analysts who are interested in tackling the psychogenic elements in autism.

What kind of autism?

The word "autism" gives rise to immediate pessimism. It is easily associated both with the idea of the closure characteristic of the autistic world and with the enigmatic aspect of children with autism.

Since it is difficult to understand their strange behaviour and to communicate with such individuals, a sense of mystery and impotence is created in people who approach them, so that the term "autism" has been given an absolute meaning of chronicity and gravity. However, during the last decades autism has aroused great interest in medical and psychological circles, and both theoreticians and clinicians have begun to focus more specifically on this developmental disorder, attempting to look for the links with the child's early stages of development.

Compared to early descriptions of autism, what has recently emerged is recognition of a wide spectrum of autistic manifestations, with different degrees of gravity and features, as well as different sub-groups. Studies have focused on the possible causes in the constitutional and genetic make-up of each individual, or on the unfavourable meeting between subjective factors and environmental conditions. Generally speaking, these studies have led to the idea of multiple causality, with different levels of intensity and therefore of different prognoses.

In spite of the many questions this disorder poses to researchers, the hope is that the studies and the efforts made in different fields can gradually uncover significant elements for a greater understanding of autism, which might lead to new prospects for therapy.

In this book the term "autism" needs to be differentiated from the meaning, which is generally attributed to the infantile syndrome. In the adult patients described, autism is represented by the residues of an archaic defensive psychological organization that functioned during the early phase of their life. During the psychotherapy, autism emerged in the transference through the avoidance of an emotional relationship with the analyst and could be reconnected to primitive experiences of anguish that reappeared in the symptoms. Unlike the autistic child, who manifests an almost complete avoidance of the other and does not respond to outside stimuli, the adults avoid emotional relationship and, since their autism is less intense and less widespread, it is less evident.

Research focused on the earliest postnatal developments in order to study the very early modes of organizing experience and developing a sense of being. These studies consider that the most archaic, pre-symbolic experience is represented by the sensory-dominated period. Under ordinary circumstances, this early experience of sensory continuity associated with caretaking rhythmicity represents the background of intersubjectivity from which object relationships are formed (Bick, 1968, 1986; S. Klein, 1980; Meltzer, Bremner, Hoxter, Waddell, & Wittenberg, 1975; Ogden, 1980, 1982a, 1984; D. Rosenfeld, 1992; H. Rosenfeld, 1987; Tustin, 1972, 1980, 1981a, 1986; Winnicott, 1960a).

Psychoanalytic research has moved not only in the direction of observing the autistic child's behaviour but also in monitoring the mental states of the observer in relation to the child's mimic or motor reactions, in the attempt to discover the emotional links between the child and the outside world.

The perceptive and elementary data available to the infant initially refer to skin surface and represent the first sensory impressions, which are pre-symbolic. The object, initially identified through sensory impressions, receives meaning and gradually organizes itself by means of relationship with the nascent self. A relationship of closeness and contact is established which contributes to the fantasy of unity between mother and child and, at the same time, gives the sense of boundaries and separateness. When the mother–child couple is not harmonious, the child may withdraw from the experience of connection with the other, and therefore the process of integration of the sense of self does not take place.

If, due to constitutional or environmental factors in both mother and child, the experience of sensory containment cannot occur in favourable conditions and the attribution of meaning to the child's experience does not occur, the child's anxiety can become unbearable. Autistic defences become hypertrophic and rigid, determining more or less extensive forms of pathological autism. Autistic vestiges may also remain in neurotic subjects.

The connection between the vitality and subjectivity of the mother and those affects that are developing in the child will give rise to a specific relationship in which the newborn will experience continuity of his existence, his own bodily boundaries, and the double condition of unity and separateness.

If the early relationship lacks vitality, serenity, and interest due to different factors in either mother or child, a deficit might emerge in the child's representation of self and of object representation (Alvarez, 1992). In fact, the autistic child seems to lack curiosity or a desire for interpersonal relationships.

The theories of both Bion (1959, 1962b) and Stern (1985) have shown us a newborn who is less static and who is much more willing to receive from his experience with his mother the stimuli needed to develop his thinking capacity. The mother's alpha-function—her capacity to help the newborn by thinking about his experience—will not only serve to alleviate the child's anxiety and frustrations but will also help him to experience vital aspects of joy, pleasure, and hope. Both mother and child play a vital role in developing the child's capacity to think and his emotional equilibrium.

In an analogous way, in the psychoanalytic relationship with autistic patients, the interest and vitality that emerges from the analyst's personality will be of vital importance.

What are autistic capsules?

The term "autistic capsules" refers to the presence of vestiges of primitive experience that remain buried in the psychic organization of children or adults, neurotic or borderline, or of patients presenting psychosomatic symptoms (Tustin, 1986; S. Klein, 1980; D. Rosenfeld, 1982, 1990, 1992). These autistic cores can remain dormant in the personality until they become manifest through the explosion of psychic or psychosomatic symptoms. Autistic capsules seem to preserve sensory, non-conceptualized primitive experiences and represent a pre-symbolic condition, not the more severe a-symbolic condition of infantile autism.

These capsules are silent witnesses to traumatic experiences. Freezing these experiences in the depths of the personality may result in the persistence of incomprehensible fears of death or extinction and the formation of a widespread sensation of depression or mistrust in interpersonal relationships.

In these patients, anxiety has assumed the characteristic of a terror that cannot be expressed in words, or a sensation of being dissolved into nothingness, somewhere between a bodily or psychic symptom, so that they lose cohesion of their personality. Anxiety may manifest itself even as a fit of depression or a vague sense of an underlying depression or through psychosomatic disorders.

If we consider that the type of defence, which occurred in the early phases of life, was that of withdrawal into oneself or the freezing of a vital experience, we can hypothesize that the autistic capsules can contain, in embryo, potential parts of vitality and emotional richness and not only pre-symbolic sensory experiences or fears of falling forever. This leads us to hope that by recognizing and sharing those primitive experiences in the psychoanalytic relationship, it will be possible to recover the vital part that had been frozen and hidden for such a long time and thus enrich the entire personality.

My beginnings

I began practising psychiatry in the late 1950s. At that time, the wards of psychiatric hospitals were full of chronic patients, and I quickly realized that the therapies adopted did not consider the patient as "a person" who, despite serious problems, was pursuing his own existential path. Since psychotic patients certainly do lose the cohesion of their personality, they present different masks that are difficult to decipher. In those days, it seemed to me that the medical staff did not show any interest in understanding the patients' emotional experiences.

Drug therapy at that time was inadequate, the hospital staff were untrained, and the hospital wards were in appalling conditions. The therapeutic attitude was sometimes marked by coercive or violent behaviour towards the patients, such as electroshock, insulin or acetylcholine shock, or even leucotomy. This was supposed to bring about a change in the patient's social adaptation called "recovery". On the other hand, the patients were left to their own devices and were prey to their passivity and degradation. However, as a young therapist with a rigorous training in internal medicine where the search to identify the meaning of the symptoms was crucial in determining the therapy, I could not help but remain disconcerted by such a situation and found it difficult to maintain my scientific curiosity and lively interest in the field of psychiatry.

In that period, the discovery of psycholeptic drugs raised great hopes, since their introduction modified the approach to the patient and made it possible to develop psychotherapy techniques for each specific case. Consequently, there was an improvement in socialization and the organization of the hospital environments. Despite the improvement of therapeutic tools with the discovery of psycholeptic drugs, they assumed the role, although in a less violent way, of previous psychiatric treatment: they brought about modifications in the patient's behaviour without considering the psychological problems underlying the symptoms. The intervention of the therapist often became arid and mechanical, so that even variations in the prescriptions of drugs were given over the telephone! In this way, a situation is created in which the patient makes a fetish of the drugs, which do not require him to think. These can be a resort to the patient, but this fetish makes him potentially addictive. Thus this solution denies the need for a therapeutic relationship that can help the person understand the significance of the crisis within the general framework of his life. When the drug could not eliminate the symptoms and dashed the patient's expectations, his passivity and existential solitude re-emerged unchanged and contributed to making the disorder chronic.

During the last decades of the twentieth century, research and advances in theory enabled psychoanalysis to be used in professional training and applied as a therapeutic tool in psychiatry. It thus became an important instrument in the attempt to understand the patient's inner world.

When I began working as a psychiatrist in Italy, traditional psychiatry was experiencing a period of transition, and there was a crisis in the theoretical reference points of the previous century that came to be considered obsolete. In this context, the application of psychoanalysis in clinical cases seemed utopian. Psychotherapy was considered marginal and of secondary importance, a kind of religious consolation rather than a codified therapeutic tool with a scientific rationale. It was evident that it would be extremely difficult for the ideologies of the past to give way to a more democratic vision of the interpersonal relationship and to attribute to psychoanalysis the function of helping the individual reflect on his existential condition and overcome inner obstacles in order to obtain a more complete realization of the self.

Few people believed in a therapeutic tool that could take into consideration unconscious mechanisms, which could bring about, over time, a permanent transformation in the structure of the personality, both in neurotic and also borderline or psychotic cases. It was more reassuring to defend one's own "psychic normality" from the "psychic abnormality" of others and to make a clear distinction between the two groups.

At that time, many questions arose regarding, on the one hand, how to reconcile the theoretical principles of psychoanalysis and the previous clinical perspective and, on the other, how to reconcile "the wish to understand" and "the need to cure" required by the therapeutic role.

During the 1950s, the effects of provincialism and the cultural isolation of Italy during the Fascist period were still felt, even though psychoanalysis had aroused great interest among intellectuals, as demonstrated by the numerous works inspired by this cultural movement. At that time, in both universities and psychiatric hospitals, the study of psychoanalytic techniques was denigrated since it was regarded as banal and unimportant. In fact, it was hindered because it expressed a different social and political approach in the field of psychiatry. Moreover, the prevailing interests of academic research seemed to be more related to satisfying career objectives than to opening up new perspectives in psychotherapy. Due to the lack of institutions that could provide training, it became difficult to learn about these perspectives.

In this cultural context and also due to my own personal experience I felt the need to resort both to groups led by foreign psychoanalysts who held seminars in Italy and to psychoanalytic study groups abroad. This is why, despite a modest knowledge of foreign languages, I trav-

elled all over Europe, my only baggage being the cases to be supervised, my questions related to the course of the therapy, and my lively
interest in the patients who came to me.

I was fortunate to come into contact, in this way, with people of
different cultural backgrounds. My professional development was extended by these personal contacts, which added a deeper dimension to
theoretical discussions. I was always moved when I found that my
feelings regarding the course of the psychotherapies coincided with
those of my colleagues from different cultural and ideological backgrounds. The need to understand and appreciate different theoretical
models of interpretation with an open mind was an important stimulus for me, together with the continual concern of remaining close to
the patient's clinical situation. This allowed me gradually to shape my
own professional identity, combining the role of psychiatrist and psychoanalytic psychotherapist.

The period I spent working in hospitals allowed me to observe
cases of psychosis in children and adults. Faced with patients I could
not understand through my current patterns of thought and professional training, I began to fathom what the patient's thoughts and
feelings were and how we could understand each other in order to
form a therapeutic alliance. My attempts were prompted particularly
by observing cases of infantile autism, which made me look for what
was behind their isolation or silence: what could be done to transform
isolation into a relationship and silence into words? I did not want to
give in to the idea that the effort to create a human relationship between two individuals could be useless. Neither did I want to give up
searching for the trajectory of the patient's thinking and feeling that
had led to his pathology and could be traced through the inner logic of
his symptoms.

It was therefore necessary to leave the position as an asymmetrical
observer and the seduction of certainties provided by medical classifi-
cations. It was, instead, necessary to consider the forms of pathological
mechanisms that exist in every person, even if they are not always
recognized. I began to see them as a response to difficulties encountered in the long-term process of individuation, as self-protective
mechanisms, which contain a potentially vital force. This experience
led to an increased determination to use psychoanalytic tools to search
for the underlying psychological mechanisms behind the symptoms.

I have always been aware of how important it is to be thoroughly
trained in the specific use of a psychotherapeutic tool when treating psychotic or autistic patients. This also requires a profound and

ongoing self-analysis and the support of a supervisor. I also realized that the relationship with the patient is a global process of interaction between two human beings which cannot be limited to specific and schematic phases. The persistence of my interest in my patients was sustained by an ongoing search within myself and was the fruit of an implicit sharing of the questions imposed by the patients' suffering. I was also interested in the potential technical modifications and the attendant danger of oversimplifications.

Psychotherapeutic work aims to create a different kind of interpersonal relationship. We can expect analytic work to transform anguish in a positive way, with no pre-established objectives. In the case of autism, we can hope that a human relationship might emerge to replace the patient's sense of emptiness so that he may make the best use of his life. The efforts put into these long psychotherapies were rewarded by the enriching emotional relationships that emerged.

The patients

Many years of psychotherapeutic work with autistic children and adults who were borderline or psychotic or were suffering from psychosomatic symptoms made me aware of common themes. The characteristics they shared included a more or less pronounced lack of profound emotional contact, an initial absence of dreams and material related to the unconscious, and a more or less serious depression. Persistent situations of impasse prolonged the therapy and prevented it from developing. Finally, there was my difficulty in conveying my thoughts to the patients and helping them sense my involvement in the relationship. In the countertransference, I often found myself directly feeling the same experience of "falling forever" or "non-existence" that has been described with autistic children by Tustin (1990) and Ogden (1980, 1982a, 1989).

The discussions of the four adult cases presented in this book mainly deal with the autistic part of the pathological picture and deliberately do not include the complexity of the specific pathologies— the complex intermingling of autism with obsessive or delusional thoughts or with psychosomatic pathology would require another book! This needs to be borne in mind when descriptions may seem too general with respect to the complex relationship. They aim mainly to demonstrate the path followed back to the autistic cores.

The adult patients underwent psychoanalytic psychotherapy privately with me three to four times a week, a frequency that was necessary because of their high level of anxiety and of the need for establishing a close relationship between us. During the most acute phases, the patients were also treated with drug therapy by a psychiatrist colleague. These four cases were selected from a larger sample because there was clear evidence in them of autistic retreats, and prolonged treatment over fifteen or twenty years allowed me to have an overall picture of how the pathological situation developed.

I noticed the alternating emergence of a sense of vitality and of psychic death in the intersubjective space formed by the transference–countertransference relationship (Ogden, 1997). What therefore seemed to emerge again in the analytic space were the patient's primitive, distressing experiences and the coexistence of healthy parts alongside the autistic ones.

I was unable to assign specific meanings to the material for a long time in the first phase, because of poor symbolic communication, the lack of dreams, and the presence of somatic symptoms. Many sessions were the same—monotonous and difficult to describe in symbolic terms.

For a considerable period, analytic work took place mainly within me, in the form of both containment of transference messages and analysis of the emotional changes in my countertransference. It was possible to work out these elements only by my own inner work, taking into account the vicissitudes of the relationship between my own internal objects and what the patient expressed.

These patients, who had reached apparent adulthood and managed to integrate within the community, intermittently experienced identity oscillations. Parts of their identity that were missing, and which could, for example, be traced to experiences of depersonalization, seemed to coincide, in my opinion, with archaic infantile fantasies of annihilation, hypothesized in autistic children.

I speculated that behind each of these cases (involving neurosis, psychosis, borderline, addictive behaviour, and psychosomatic disorders), there exists a specific pathology characterized by a partial freezing of emotions and feelings in the early phases of life. It is very difficult to establish an emotional relationship with such a patient. During early periods of life, these autistic capsules served to protect the child from unbearable fears, experienced in the face of dramatic events. The somatic symptoms and the absence of dreams and fantasies seem to indicate the memory of a period when life was experienced largely through bodily sensations, before the patient became fully aware of the existence of the self and of other minds. The experience I gained in treating these cases led me to realize the need to work step-by-step and to try to see what could be done at a particular moment of the therapy.

The need to spend some time preparing the ground in order to be able to communicate on the level of symbolization contributed to prolonging the therapy. Nevertheless, the disappearance of the symptoms, the gradual emergence of feelings in the therapeutic relationship, and the improvement in the patients' quality of life were surprising and moved me deeply. Their initial somatic and psychological symptoms disappeared over time, and the ego structure of each individual was strengthened. Long-lasting results were maintained many years after the ending of the therapy.

The patients' vital force—expressed by their tenacity, the trust they and their families had in me, their belief in the value of psychotherapy, together with the concrete availability of both time and money—made it possible to continue treatment under very difficult circumstances. While my medical training had directed my attention to making symptoms disappear, my aim in therapy was to try to find an approach that would allow these people to develop and regain that part of their personality that they had relinquished at a very early age.

Technical issues

When we deal with serious clinical disorders such as autism, psychosis, or psychosomatic disorders, our first hope and aim is to work to make the symptoms disappear and, second, to study in depth the patient's inner world. We have to keep in mind that our purpose is mainly a therapeutic one and not a confirmation of theoretical formulations. Our research must be focused on the study of the basic significance of all human conflict rather than upholding the reliability of specific theoretical principles according to the different psychoanalytic schools.

However, adapting psychoanalysis to psychiatric cases requires technical modifications that also respect basic theoretical principles. The development of psychoanalytic studies during the last century has widened the categories of treatable patients, and it was therefore necessary to introduce modifications, especially in the cases of autistic children and adults as well as psychotic and borderline patients.

Analytic technique needs to be somewhat modified in order to overcome obstacles during the work, to help the patient sort out the symptoms, and to fight against his tendency to consider the situation as chronic. One of the problems related to emerging from chronicity is that the patient may be drawn back to his early traumatic experiences by transforming the current relationship into a new edition of the past. For patients in whom the level of deficit goes back to an early phase of development, we have to adopt a cautious approach in order not to reproduce the same conditions that caused the initial withdrawal. In the analytic relationship, the patient has to be helped by the therapist to transform the primitive emotional experience into something more helpful.

The classic analytic tools of neutrality and "deprivation" may be felt by such patients as pathogenic, and the initial suffering may re-emerge. In these cases of deficit, it is important to substitute the analyst's neutrality with emotional involvement that takes into consideration the patient's extreme sensitivity and his tendency to avoid emotional relationships. Aggressiveness in the transference should be interpreted only when the relationship with the analyst is firmly established.

Alvarez (1992) considers that before making interpretations in very severe cases, the analyst must assume the function of containment and reclamation to life, presenting her own self to the patient. I experienced directly how classic psychoanalytic interpretation did not help the patient, but prevented him from establishing a therapeutic alliance, as described by Joseph (1985, 1988, 1989).

Because of the obstacles I came up against in the analytic work, I evolved a spontaneous method that can with hindsight be considered to be made up of three phases: a first phase of containment, a second one of elaboration, and a third of interpretation. This method has some similarities with Alvarez's (1985, 1992) in the treatment of autistic children.

The first phase was characterized by a period of waiting, observing, listening to the patient, and containing his projections. This was essential in order to allow the patient to develop an emotional bond with the therapist so as to allow an emotional exchange. During this phase, communication mainly took place through physical channels, with signs such as crying or psychosomatic symptoms, or through actings-out rather than symbolic communication. Only then—often some years after the first phase—could my attention turn to the second phase of working out the elements provided by the patient and those derived from my own countertransference. Not until the third phase did I attempt an interpretation about the exchange between transference and countertransference provided by the material.

The anguish that the patient demonstrates and the absence of more usual emotional exchanges make the therapist move away from a position of detachment and neutrality. The method and timing of the interventions will vary for each psychotherapist, depending on personality and experience. When coming into contact with patients who present more or less extensive areas of autism, we sometimes come across confused areas of our own inner world, in which primitive undifferentiated experiences prevail. These existential fears or feelings of loneliness are unrelated to the process of imagination. Felt in the countertransference, they might demonstrate that the suffering that determined the original autistic withdrawal might date back to a very early period.

The analytic setting will help the patient to internalize certain characteristics of continuity and stability. The analyst will, however, have to adopt a flexible therapeutic approach and adapt the way she interacts with the patient by reference to her countertransference. She tests the ground to see if an approach to the patients' emotional world is possible without risking the increase of autistic defences. The functions of containment, transformation, and symbolization must take priority in order to allow projective exchanges and a bond to develop. Interpretation will then act as ego support.

The main therapeutic factors consist, in my opinion, of a cautious approach, the ability to tolerate non-symbolic communication, being able to wait in the hope that the patient will finally find a way to communicate his emotions, and the courage to face obstacles or frequent disappointments.

I noticed that these patients shared a common characteristic—namely, the experience of emptiness, connected to the lack of appreciation of self and of other people. The rejection experienced by the analyst in the therapeutic relationship will often be due to the continuation of a primitive attempt to transform the object into nothingness. The refusal of contact with the therapist may be the result of the patient's conviction that he is worthless and unable to attract the attention and interest of others.

Through the analytic work, the discovery of having intrinsic capacities and of being able to make the most of them revitalizes the patient. This new vitality experienced by the patient replaces the primitive depression and creates the basis for a development previously considered impossible. The process of change is slow because the patient's convictions are extremely difficult to remove and can be used in a perverse way in the analytic relationship.

Overcoming autistic defences, internalizing the feelings that emerged from a frozen state, and reaching a healthy depressive position (M. Klein, 1935; Alvarez, 1992, 1997) can be revealed by different, premonitory signs. Chief of these is the beginning of the patient's self-analysis and his attempts to become more independent from the analyst. Other signs might include the awareness of his gratitude and, in the analyst's countertransference, a feeling of being empathetically attuned.

The therapeutic process can be considered terminated when the emptiness previously experienced by the patient has been transformed into the absence of the object and the emotional coldness has given way to feelings connected with the working-through of mourning. At the end of the analysis, both patient and analyst can become aware of the results that have been achieved during the analytic journey and agree that the level of integration obtained is satisfying. This allows both of them to preserve the memory of a warm, rewarding relationship. The most reliable verification of our work comes from the patients themselves, who become more aware of their inner world, overcome their symptoms, and improve the quality of their life.

The countless debates about changes in traditional psychoanalytic technique as applied to different pathologies demonstrates the concern of psychoanalysts about the possible emergence of an anarchic empiricism and the creation of arbitrary codes or, conversely, of the danger that psychoanalytic theory may become a rigid fetish (Brusset, 2002).

In this connection, based on clinical experience derived from the cases described here, it seemed useful to alternate "psychotherapeutic moments" in which the empathic approach prevailed, "first-aid" interventions when there were more evident signs of disintegration (what Alvarez, 1992, calls "reclamation"), and "psychoanalytic moments" in which the interpretative method prevailed. These different approaches became intermingled in a complementary way according to the patient's pathology and as the specific phase of the therapy developed (Goijman, 1984). While we must not regard psychoanalysis as a panacea to use in all pathological situations, what this book aims to do is to affirm the validity of analytic treatment even in the most difficult cases. The analyst needs to find a personal inner equilibrium between experiences of impotence and fantasies of omnipotence which emerge during the therapy with those patients who are *"apparently impossible to treat"* through psychotherapy.

Obviously, any account of psychotherapeutic treatment includes not only those objective elements that can be traced back to the patient's personal history or emerge from the exchanges during the sessions, but also latent traces of observations, experiences, and theoretical references made by the therapist. This account cannot therefore but be incomplete with respect to the whole of these experiences and the underlying, unconscious mechanisms of both participants.

Structure

Some readers may prefer to begin with the case material later in the book before turning to the theoretical issues with which I open my account.

In the first part of the book, chapter 1 deals with the theoretical hypotheses related to autistic capsules in adults. This is followed in chapter 2 by a discussion of the analogies between the symptoms present in the cases of adults and of infantile autism and the importance of the vicissitudes of the countertransference in the therapeutic work. Chapters 3 and 4 deal with the development of the concept of transference and its application to autistic patients. Chapter 5 discusses the obstacles to the treatment of the autistic parts, and chapter 6 deals with the factors that proved useful in the therapy.

The second part of the book includes a detailed description of a case with predominantly obsessive and psychosomatic symptoms (chapter 7); a second borderline case with predominantly psychotic and psychosomatic components (chapter 8); a third case of psychosis-hysteria (chapter 9); and a fourth case of infantile autism of the Asperger type treated at irregular intervals over a period of twenty years (chapter 10).

In all four cases, the therapy took place intermittently over a period of fifteen to twenty years, with interruptions varying from one patient to another. These cases were chosen among other similar cases because they are particularly significant in relation to the hypothesis in question and because they were observed for a long period of time.

PART I

THEORETICAL ASPECTS

CHAPTER ONE

Autistic capsules in adults

Ne pas pouvoir joindre la vie antérieure à la vie présente, ne pas pouvoir la raconter en entier à quelqu'un, pas même à soi, telle est la solitude. Elle en étouffait plus d'un. Je savais que moi-même je faisais partie du lot.

["Being unable to link one's past life to the present one, being unable to narrate all this life to someone, not even oneself, this is loneliness. And this loneliness has stifled more than one life. I knew that I myself belonged to this group.]

F. Cheng, *Le dit de Tianyi*

Autism

In 1911, Eugen Bleuler introduced the psychiatric term of autism, later taken up by Eugène Minkowski, in 1954, to indicate a fundamental symptom in schizophrenic adult patients. "Autism" signified losing contact with reality, introversion, and loss of initiative. It was accompanied by other symptoms such as bizarre behaviour and hostility to the outside world. These patients had abolished all social relationships and lived in a strange, impenetrable world.

This term was subsequently taken up by Kanner (1943) and Asperger (1944) to indicate a psychiatric syndrome characteristic of childhood, and it was later widely adopted to define a certain type of personality. In psychoanalytic terminology, it was adopted to describe a state, position, or defence.

Infantile autism is a serious pathology of the child's development in the first years of life characterized by a triad of symptoms (Kanner, 1943; Wing & Gould, 1979): serious social impairment; the lack of verbal and nonverbal communication; the lack of imagination and, therefore, the inability to play, which is replaced by repetitive, bizarre, and senseless behaviour.

Autistic children are completely cut off, or cut themselves off, from reality. Since they are incapable of imaginative thinking, they are unable to imagine new experiences. Since they are unable to form symbols, they cannot play, and since they have no social skills, they cannot relate to others. Their behaviour is rigid and repetitive. It is as if an early trauma has frozen the child in a primitive defence mechanism so that his attention has become focused only on the inside and on the surface of his own body. Fraiberg (1982) described this most primitive survival mechanism. The child does not respond to outside stimuli and tends to act as if he were deaf. Such children do not listen; they seem indifferent to physical pain and are only concerned with their bodily sensations and their peculiar idiosyncratic world. Autism seems to represent an excessive defensive reaction towards an early unbearable event.

The characteristics of the children described by Kanner and Asperger are similar only in part, although the pathology is the same. Both authors underline the symptoms of social isolation, egocentrism, and lack of interest in feelings, as well as a higher incidence of the disorder in males than in females, and they describe the unusual forms of nonverbal communication that characterize these children, such as their fixed gaze, their avoidance of direct contacts with others, and their strange posture. Autistic children may also show an excessive interest in some banal or abstract subject. Today, Asperger syndrome is considered to be a "high-functioning" state of autism, and Asperger himself emphasized a particular form of intelligence involving logical and abstract thinking (Barrow, 1988; Frith, 1991).

In the last few decades, theoretical interest in autism has continued to develop not only in order to understand and overcome the difficulties in therapy, but also to study the links that autism has with the child's primitive mental states and his development (e.g., Baron-

Cohen, Allen, & Gillberg, 1992; Frith, 1989; Parks, 1983; Trevarthen, Aitken, Papoudi, & Robarts, 1996; Wing, 1996). Geneticists, neurologists, psychologists and psychoanalysts focused their attention in their respective scientific fields to finding an aetiological or psychodynamic explanation (e.g., Baron-Cohen, 1988; Bettelheim, 1967; Dawson & Lewy, 1989a, 1989b; Di Cagno, Lazzarini, Rissone, & Randaccio, 1984; Frith, 1989; Gillberg, 1990; Hobson, 1989, 1990, 1993; Leslie, 1987; Miller, Rustin, & Shuttleworth, 1989; Murray, 1991; Perry, Pollard, Blakley, Baker, & Vigilante, 1995; Schore, 1996; Trevarthen et al., 1996). They discovered that there exists a wide range of clinical cases, with different levels of gravity and variable developmental prognosis, which differ from one personality to another (Alvarez & Reid, 1999).

Although the psychoanalytic point of view does not exclude the presence of other possible scientific interpretations and the efforts made by scientists in different fields, it continues to focus on considering autism from the point of view of a two-person psychology rather than that of a descriptive, personal psychology. Psychoanalysts stress the importance of the internalization of the relationships with the object and the fantasies that emerge from the experience of the relationship (e.g., Bick, 1968; Bion, 1962b; Bollas, 1989; Meltzer, 1986; Meltzer et al., 1975; Ogden, 1989; Resnik, 1986; H. Rosenfeld, 1987; Tustin, 1986; Winnicott, 1960a, 1971).

Despite the differences of opinion, there is today a general consensus in considering the variety of factors—including, for example, constitutional, genetic, organic, and psychological factors—that may determine the autistic state. The interaction between innate and environmental factors cannot be reduced to a unilateral vision when interpreting the cause of such a puzzling and complex disorder. Even psychoanalysts who have studied autism, such as Tustin or Meltzer or Alvarez and Reid (1999), consider that many causative factors—both organic and psychogenetic—interact and overlap in determining consequences similar to a chain reaction. The general consensus is that this disorder is caused by a number of factors (Edwards & Lanyado, 1999).

Surveys conducted in Europe, Japan, the United States, and Canada report that the incidence of autism ranges between 4 and 10 in every 10,000 births (Sigman & Capps, 1997). A particular research field directly concerned with the newborn has emerged that focuses on the sensorimotor behaviour correlating with the emotional relationship between mother and child. The subject of study is how the newborn becomes a person and how the codes of communication with the family members function. Some criteria have been suggested for early screening to recognize autism during the first year of life in order to intervene in the early mother–child relationship (Bailey, Phillips, & Rutter, 1996; Delion et al., 1998; Haag, 1985; Haag et al., 1995).

Clinical studies have shown that there are many factors that can trigger psychogenic autism. They can be represented by different events in the story of the newborn, including the mother's physical diseases or psychic disorders during pregnancy; premature delivery requiring invasive treatment and long periods in the incubator; diseases of or birth defects in the newborn that require invasive surgery and long hospitalization. Other causes might be pathological brain-damage, sensory deficits such as deafness or blindness, early physical or sexual violence, psychic disorders like psychosis or depression in either or both parents, and situations of serious environmental danger like wars or genocide.

It is important to point out that when I speak of trauma as a possible factor that triggers autism, I am referring not to a determining factor but to a set of environmental conditions that does not provide for that particular individual sufficient well-being or sense of safety, both of which are indispensable during the child's early phase of development (Bion, 1962b; Winnicott, 1965a).

Tustin (1986) maintains that the break in continuity of the sensory experience might represent a threat of interruption of the sense of self and might be responsible for catastrophic fears in what she calls "agony of consciousness". These interruptions in the mother–infant relationship might determine some holes in the fabric of the "emergent self" (Stern, 1985), which could cause an unbearable sense of bodily separateness ("non-experience": see Ogden, 1980, 1982a).

As can be seen from the great number of research studies carried out during the last decades, understanding autism has considerably improved on earlier descriptions, but the aetiological and pathogenic questions are by no means resolved. As Newson (1987) has written, it is easier to describe autism than know how to deal with it.

Since the inability to communicate and relate to other people is one of the principal symptoms of autism, the psychotherapeutic approach aims to represent a model of human relationship on which to work. Although in the past the cognitive impairment in autism was traced back to organic causes and was considered to precede the impairment in affects, today the concept that is gaining ground is that emotional factors influence cognitive development. Surely mental impoverishment that becomes chronic during the development of a child must give rise to a cognitive deficit.

In her work, "A Contribution to the Theory of Intellectual Inhibition" (1931), Melanie Klein points out that, from a psychoanalytic perspective, the child's ability to explore the surrounding world and assimilate knowledge depends on the intensity of his persecutory fears regarding the inside of the mother's body. Winnicott (1948, 1949) underlined the existence of apparent stupidity in cases of psychosis, and Bion (1959) has pointed to the importance of affective factors in the mother–child relationship for the child's intellectual development. Tustin (1986) has pointed out how the fear of threat represented by the "not-me" has a great impact on cognitive development and emotional intelligence. Meltzer (Meltzer et al., 1975) considered that the learning capacity implies the ability to relate to others. Other authors (Alvarez, 1999; Rhode, 1997) have reconsidered and analysed in greater detail the concept of intellectual inhibition reported in cases of autism. If the possibility to communicate improves due to the therapy, it is evident that even learning, at the cognitive level, will improve and allow the child to become more socially integrated.

Autistic capsules

The concept of autistic capsules in adults grew out of studies on infantile autism in the 1980s and signifies a more or less extensive part of autistic experience in the personality.

When I refer to autistic capsules, I mean encapsulated parts of the personality that remain hidden under a neurotic or borderline organization in adult patients and which bear witness to the presence of autistic experiences (S. Klein, 1980; Ogden, 1989; Tustin, 1986). These capsules are cut off from the rest of the personality and remain silent until they emerge during the analysis through the patient's strong resistance to any attempt to change, and there is an absence of any emotional contact in the transference.

Autistic capsules (or cores, nuclei, or remnants) contain the experience of a sensory-dominated world where it is impossible to use symbolization and elaborate bodily sensations. They keep a part of the self frozen and preserve all the patient's potential for emotional life and symbolic thinking. The capsules were created to preserve a primitive sense of identity, which for some reason felt under threat. These capsules may be isolated and allow the rest of the personality to develop normally, while continuing to be chronic and rigid, thus representing an armour of bodily sensations that prevent direct contact with the outside world. This armour disguises, however, very fragile, emotional parts that are undifferentiated but that also contain, in embryo, vital and emotional potential. Interpretations in sessions with patients possessing autistic capsules must therefore be carried out very carefully and with the right timing, so as not to cause unbearable anxiety. I shall illustrate this later in the clinical material.

The term "autistic capsules" contains a concept of space to define a psychic area, which is more or less extended in the person's overall personality. Depending on the size of this autistic area, the relation between the part of the self where emotional feelings are frozen and the rest of the personality that seems to function normally will vary. Since these proportions vary, the autistic capsules can be more or less masked by an "apparently normal" behaviour and lead to a mistaken diagnosis.

Different authors have suggested the existence of autistic cores in neurotic, psychotic, or borderline patients (S. Klein, 1980; Rosenfeld, 1992). In his seminal work published in 1955, Bion had already developed the concept that in schizophrenic patients a non-psychotic part of the personality coexists alongside the psychotic one. In serious neuroses, the psychotic part of the personality is hidden under the neurosis, just as the part of the neurotic personality is masked by the psychosis in the psychotic patient.

Winnicott (1965a, 1974) pointed out that in neurotic adults, breakdowns were evidence of a very early primitive trauma. According to him, certain adult patients are afraid of breaking down due to the anguish they experienced at an early age. The memory of these experiences was linked to a time when conceptualization was impossible but which could emerge during the analytic work by means of the anguish experienced in the transference. During the analysis, the patient might tend to attribute to the analyst's mistaken understanding the original failure of his facilitating environment. During the transference, he experiences something from the past which he can recognize for the first time.

Tustin (1986, 1990), who mainly devoted herself to studying psychogenic infantile autism, has pointed out that autistic cores are also present in neurotic adults, especially in patients suffering from phobias or obsessions. In neurotic children during the period of latency, the autistic capsules that persist can subsequently lead to disorders such as phobias, anorexia, learning impairment, and psychosomatic disorders. According to Tustin, the hidden part of a personality becomes encapsulated at an early age in order to protect the self from early, traumatic inner experiences.

Autistic children and adults with autistic cores avoid entering into emotional relationships, and when they manage to communicate they express their inner sensation of emptiness. They lack a sense of self and a precise identity or are anchored to psychosomatic symptoms. These more or less active autistic capsules might even be responsible for chronic cases of psychosomatic disorders or hypochondria since the body expresses primitive body experiences that occurred in a pre-symbolic phase. Psychosomatic disorders may be an attempt to convey the existence of these autistic cores in the body.

Tustin found that, as patients in therapy began to emerge from their protective autistic shells, they began to manifest psychosomatic disorders. This finding has also been confirmed by other research studies. In fact, seriously affected autistic children who never became ill began suddenly to suffer from the most common childhood illnesses once they emerged from their autistic states. They became more human and more vulnerable.

The awareness of separateness from the mother that they experienced too early in infancy can represent a traumatic breaking away, which remains hidden and can reappear in particular situations in the course of adult life. Although autistic cores may represent reactions to vestiges of terror experienced during early infancy, which remain frozen and buried in the deepest layers of the personality, they do no rule out the potential for the self to develop. Tustin believes that this space contains models of primitive reactions that make the patient withdraw from contact with reality, replacing it with a personal world dominated by sensations that can be kept under control.

Elements regarding early phases of life usually remain unconscious and only emerge when certain psychic situations require psychological help. The analyst who finds herself faced with signs of suffering related to pre-conceptual or preverbal periods of life can only understand them through her capacity for empathy or intuition. The analyst will use these insights, which are particularly present in the mother during the first months of the baby's life and then gradually taper off when the communication becomes verbal.

Autistic capsules serve as a protection from experiences of pain and confusion caused by the relation to the outside world. This protective armour breaks when the subject can no longer maintain his isolation and self-sufficiency and therefore allows the emotional hypersensitivity to emerge.

Neurotic adults with autistic capsules may have psychopathic tendencies covered over by obsessive reaction formations. Although they seem to be normal, they are hard, impenetrable, overbearing, and presumptuous and tend to be manipulative, exploit people, and fanatically support certain ideologies (Tustin, 1986). They often seek perfection since they have not allowed themselves to experience the disappointment of separateness and have therefore continued to seek for the ideal relationship. Such patients suffer because they feel that there is something they have missed in life. They do not know what it is, and this fills them with resentment. Sometimes they use the therapy situation to protect themselves from experiences in their life that they find intolerable.

Referring to adult patients who lead a brilliant social life, Grotstein (1980, 1981) describes adult patients who resort to encapsulation in order to escape from what they experience as a stifling maternal relationship. He considers them to be quite fragile when faced with dangerous situations because they lack a "background of safety" (Sandler, 1960). Grotstein points out that inside the hard and apparently insensitive autistic capsule, there is serious depression. As regards psychogenic autism, Grotstein speaks of a connection with somatic diseases, defining it as "psychosomatic illness in statu nascendi" (1983, p. 491).

Sidney Klein (1980) points out the presence of autistic cores in adult patients who have developed normally around a core of psychotic depression. He agrees with Tustin that these autistic cores can reappear during periods of unbearable stress or biological changes during the course of a lifetime. This is a hidden part of the patient, which remains suspended until it can be recognized and analysed. His study provides a good description of the characteristics and effects of these autistic capsules. He noted that in some cases of adult patients who were particularly intelligent and well integrated in their family and social life, there existed a part of the personality that could not relate to the analyst and was rather similar to that of autistic children.

He compared these observations to Winnicott's concept of the false self (1960b) and Herbert Rosenfeld's psychotic islands (1978), but he also suggested a difference. The autistic capsules represent a cystic part of the personality which is encapsulated and cut off from contact with the rest of the patient's personality, and with the analyst. The existence of this encapsulated part emerges during the analysis, when the patient's feelings are fragile and flat. The patient demonstrates a silent and unrelenting resistance to change and regards the analyst with suspicion. What lies hidden beneath this appearance are feelings of fear, pain, disintegration, and a sense of death. On the unconscious level, such patients become very attached to the analyst, although they expect the analyst to be hostile and to be lacking in understanding. On the conscious level, they continue to idealize the analyst and regard her as being omnipotent and omniscient.

The patient pays more attention to the analyst's tone of voice or facial expressions rather than the content of her interpretation; this can be compared to the impression the newborn has of acquiring an ally, who will act as a support for his life. At the same time, however, the patient is always on the alert for signs of supposed hostility.

One of the characteristics of these patients is that they make little progress since they are unable to hear and introject the meaning of the interpretations and continually talk about their complaints and symptoms. In addition to a tendency to cling to others, these adults, like autistic children, tend to attack the bond between their most needy part and their hope for help from the analyst, so that she can do nothing to help them. They adopt compulsive and repetitive behaviour patterns that are resistant to any possible change.

Paroxysms of suspicion become an alternative to placing trust in the analyst: since the interpretation of hostile feelings cannot be accepted and instead triggers persecutory feelings, the process of development is blocked. As a result, the analyst feels helpless to continue her work. All the hostility, envy, and jealousy that are projected into the analyst are not seen as belonging to the patient, nor does the patient think he is capable of elaborating thoughts. The fear of separating from the analyst arouses terror of death and disintegration, corresponding to the very primitive experiences that were at the origin of the autistic states. The need for support is similar to that which an infant needs from the mother. Closeness is of fundamental importance and is an expression of the need to cling.

According to Sidney Klein, some patients are unable to put together the words they require in order to express themselves in a comprehensible way because they attack the connection between internalized objects and thus can no longer repair them. In this connection, Bion (1959) attributes the fragmentation of the ego and of the object in psychotic patients to the attacks on linking they make in order to liberate themselves of the experience of perceiving a reality they hate or fear. One can wonder whether in these patients the lack of links between words come in part from the absence of links rather than from the attacks on linking.

Sidney Klein believes that the autistic defence, primitively created to avoid pain, is the result of an intense fear of death or disintegration following the loss of the breast. These defences reappear during the analysis when the patient has to separate from the analyst. These anxieties are sometimes avoided by the patient through projective identification, by imagining that he is not yet born and is living inside the therapist. Anxieties can also be avoided by means of introjective identification with the analyst, who is incorporated as a hard, shell-like object. This avoidance can also be achieved by means of adhesive identification (Bick, 1968)—that is, by becoming attached to the analyst as if she were an object similar to the placenta, which nourishes and detoxifies the patient.

The analyst must pay careful attention to how the patient expresses himself and how he changes the way he expresses himself. These patients usually love to talk, but the premature development or the hypertrophy of language can be considered as a defence against feelings of emptiness or non-existence (S. Klein, 1980). Sometimes these children talked before they started walking, perhaps to overcome the anxiety caused by the fact that their feelings were not understood or contained. In fact, in the case of a depressed mother, her child can be used as a container for her own anxieties. The endless chatter of such patients serves to keep the analyst tied to them and, at the same time, to keep her at a distance rather than reveal the feelings of their inner world.

Sidney Klein was able to recognize in his patients a "communication level of non-communication" that corresponds to the mute phase of the autistic child, where aggressive feelings are not communicated alongside loving feelings. This occurs because the child is acutely aware of separation from the object and of being responsible for the relationship between the self and the object. This may represent the infant's difficulty in sending his mother messages regarding the state of his body, his primordial sensations and feelings, and, finally, his sense of solitude in an unknown, silent world.

If the therapist can recognize the existence of these encapsulated parts of the personality as remnants from an early age, the analysis will become more effective and subsequent breakdown can be prevented. These patients commonly oscillate between omnipotence and impotence, activity and passivity, being an adult and being a child, psychosis and neurosis, and thoughts that are simple or complicated. If these oscillations between opposite poles can be slowed down and analysed, these patients will have a firm foundation on which to maintain future psychic equilibrium.

David Rosenfeld (1976, 1992, 1997) considers autistic encapsulation to be a way of protecting the self against the fear of being hurt or annihilated. He found this phenomenon in adult patients who escaped from concentration camps. They had secretly been able to maintain the emotional part of their personality in order to survive when threatened with the prospect of death, but this then remained frozen and unavailable later. Rosenfeld has presented ample clinical material in which he has hypothesized the presence of an encapsulated autistic core in patients who are disturbed in their subjective identity. He has analysed the vicissitudes on the intrapsychic organization of object relationships in psychotic, psychosomatic, and drug-addicted patients. He considers a wide range of psychotic situations, with different clinical histories, in which it is possible to distinguish different types of psychic organization.

The formation of an autistic core in which the first object relationships are internalized may result in normal contact with reality in the rest of the personality but at the cost of the fragmentation and unavailability of any deep motional investment. He has described different types of psychic organization present in different pathologies such as neurotic, psychotic, and borderline conditions as well as perversions and psychosomatic disorders. He distinguishes three different types of hypochondria: one characterized by somatic delusions, another based on the primitive psychotic body image, and the third predominantly based on autistic mechanisms. The last type might include an autistic core that is often silent, hidden, and dormant until it emerges during the therapeutic exchange. This core, which has a defensive function against experiencing underlying conflicts with the object, is very rigid and seemingly cannot play a role in the analysis. It can be considered to be like an autistic object. The bodily scheme of these patients seems to contain an empty, hollow space, whereas in the other forms of hypochondria real elements of the body are always present in the patient's mind. This hypochondriac core is apparently hidden and kept under control, unlike the cases in which somatic delusions predominate. It is similar to infantile autism because it appears self-sufficient and tends to perpetuate itself in a chronic way through the years (Tustin, 1981a, 1986).

In psychosomatic disorders, we find the paradoxical combination of normal contact with superficial reality and an impoverishment of interpersonal relationships. Emotional, intrapsychic, and interpersonal relationships can function at different levels. David Rosenfeld considers autistic encapsulation to be a way of protecting oneself against unbearable terror by encapsulating and thereby conserving early identifications, but without integrating them into his inner psychic world.

He maintains that although encapsulation is a form of closure, it also serves to protect the trace of potential vitality that can thus be hidden away and preserved and subsequently found again under more benign conditions.

The psychic drama of patients who were subjected to violence in concentration camps (D. Rosenfeld, 1992) was the result of the coexistence of these two systems. One tended to preserve and shield the identification with the object and the other to lose significant identifications as a consequence of the terror. As in socially pervasive traumas like the holocaust or genocide, patients affected by early traumas lost the identifications with their family members and, at the same time, valuable parts of their selves. The withdrawal into the self represented a defence but also led to the loss of precious identifications.

Situations of loss provoke great anxiety in patients with autistic capsules since they are sensitive to re-experiencing the same feelings of panic attached to painful past experiences.

The concept of psychic retreats described by Steiner (1993) can in some sense be compared to those of autistic capsules. The psychic retreat refers to a defensive reaction in the pathological organization of the personality that provides relief in the face of unbearable anxiety by retreat into a sheltered place. This area represents a safe haven to which the patient can withdraw, where the pathological organization acts as a delicate system of defence and where the patient can remain with his paranoid or depressive anxieties.

Steiner believes that these states are experienced as if they are places where the patient can find peace and where he can escape from the unbearable anxiety from having emotional contact with others. This retreat might serve to control primitive destructiveness, representing both a receptacle of destructiveness as well as a defence against it. As a kind of compromise it is pathological, but it provides an area of temporary protection and isolation from contact with reality. On the one hand it apparently protects the patient, yet on the other it represents an obstacle to the patient's development. These patients have areas in which they can function fairly well, but when emotional problems arise they retreat into an area of isolation. In this way, the patient protects himself from feelings that reach him from the inner and outer world. The pathological organization serves to neutralize aggression and keep it under control.

The area of psychic retreat hampers psychoanalytic work from developing, and in order for the therapist to withstand the pressure the patient puts on her, it requires great patience and perseverance on her part to minimize this pressure and understand the defensive organization. Treating a patient such as this is difficult since he is out of contact and consequently the analysis progresses very slowly. Attempts to reach the patient are followed by his abrupt withdrawal.

These patients, cut off from contact with others, can offer a false kind of contact: their defensive system is very strong and represents a kind of armour they hide behind. They can be neurotic, psychotic, or borderline patients who in the analytic work demonstrate in various ways the need to defend this private area by means of either scornful rejection, or cold condescension, or a false kind of contact.

This hidden world full of fantasies of omnipotence attracts the patient so much that he manipulates it for his own perverse intentions. The retreat can also be experienced as an addictive experience that is difficult to abandon. Even the analyst can be entrapped in this sort of sanctuary. For a long time, therapeutic work remains marginal, until it becomes possible to help the patient detach himself from this situation. The therapist mainly experiences feelings of despair or impotence in the face of the patient's obstinacy.

Analogies between Steiner's concept of psychic retreat and that of autistic capsules mainly concern the fact that both of them can be viewed spatially, as an area of safety shut off from emotional contacts. In both cases, it makes any kind of emotional exchange between patient and analyst difficult and represents an obstacle to analytic work. Steiner's concept of psychic retreat represents the patient's permanence in the borderline position, where he feels protected from the depressive and paranoid–schizoid anxieties and tries to maintain his equilibrium outside these two positions.

Autistic capsules, in my opinion, represent an area that contains more primitive experiences. The capsules contain non-integrated stages rather than disintegrated ones. They were formed when the differentiation between self and object had not yet occurred, the bond with the subject was not yet established, and feelings had not yet developed. The autistic defence characterizes this part of the personality that has remained frozen with all its potential. Instead of representing a retreat, the autistic capsule represents the presence of an extraneous part of the personality that becomes manifest in the patient through chronic discomfort related to the sense of existing.

McDougall (1972) has described similar countertransference experiences with patients difficult to reach in the analytic relationship. These patients make the analytic situation ineffective by eliminating the presence of the analyst and blocking every attempt to make emotional contact. In this way, these patients also refuse to acknowledge that the other person is a sensitive, living being. She refers to these patients as "anti-analysands in analysis". They seem to be neurotic, but, in fact, they can be considered "hypernormal". McDougall has referred to them as "normopaths". Normal life crushes their imaginary life and the life of the emotions. She has introduced the concept of "disaffectation" to specify the psychic organization of subjects such as this, who seem detached from their emotions and unable to stay in contact with their psychic life.

These patients appear to have sought shelter from emotional storms brought on by intense emotions experienced at an early age which threatened their integrity and sense of identity. McDougall's hypothesis is that these patients, incapable of repressing the idea of suffering and projecting their disappointment in interpersonal relationships, eliminate their own emotions from their consciousness. The relationship with the analyst becomes cold, sterile, and crippling. When under stress, these disaffected patients are inclined to somatization, because their psychic organization wants to avoid psychotic anxieties since they cannot express them in words and so contain the underlying fantasies. Anxieties are expressed through their bodies in a pre-symbolic way.

According to McDougall, the defence mechanism used in "disaffectation" is that of "foreclosure", according to which fantasies, thoughts, perceptions, or psychological events are eliminated rather than being considered as causes of psychic pain. The use of mechanisms of expulsion of perceptions, thoughts, or remembered but unacknowledged fantasies can encourage the adult to regress towards somatic responses instead of psychotic reactions. This kind of defensive solution seems to be different from that of the neurotic, psychotic, or perverse patient and is shown in the transference as an avoidance of the relationship. The consequences of an emotional disinvestment are the reluctance to establish and use the analytic relationship even though they are attached to it.

Those who chronically use action as a way of protecting themselves against mental anguish run the risk of suffering from psychosomatic illnesses. The psychosomatic explosions are similar to acting-out and express a lack of symbolization. Body symptoms in psychosomatosis become equivalent to representations of things and cannot be put into verbal language. These patients often feel alone and empty and resort to substances or persons on which they become chronically dependent.

Corominas (1982, 1991, 1994, 2000), who deals with autism in brain-damaged children, hypothesizes the permanence, even in adults, of more or less encapsulated nuclei of non-integrated sensations that witness an early defence from catastrophic anguish experienced during the process of differentiation. These nuclei are not recognized as such by the patient but have to be traced back by the analyst in order to connect them to the crises of anguish that had remained unexplained earlier and had no apparent causes. Corominas observed in patients who presented serious, incomprehensible anxiety crises the existence of these cores of sensations that had not been worked through. These cores seem to exist at an unconscious level but are in some way connected to dramatic emotions experienced at a time when there was no possibility of a conscious memory. Subsequently these cores of sensations could remain hidden or contain elements that could trigger phobias or obsessional rituals.

It might be possible to compare the concept of sensory cores in the neurotic adult described by Corominas with the concept of autistic capsules. The partial persistence of primitive experiences in the adult personality might correspond to the presence of traces of a non-integrated capacity to experience sensations and the presence of the non-differentiation between object and subject. This primitive archaic stage, related to elaborating sensations and to differentiating between self and object, might also contain the experience of catastrophic anguish that has not yet been transformed into the depressive one because it is impossible to recognize the separation from the object. The patient lives partly at a level of non-integrated sensations due to a lack of connection with their emotional significance, and he is unable to understand interpretations at the symbolic level. If the analyst does not recognize this type of pathology, it might lead her to make some theoretical rationalizations and thus strengthen the patient's defensive armour.

In my own work with adults, I initially found some characteristics that were similar to those seen in autistic children and subsequently discovered the existence of autistic capsules representing areas that froze the remains of autistic experiences. In the countertransference I experienced a sensation of unease, because the relationship was devoid of feeling. This sensation led me to consider the existence of fragile, hidden areas, shut off from communication, that contained very primitive experiences of non-differentiation. These were responsible for profound, incomprehensible anguish in the patient.

Although often these patients say that they have always suffered from incompleteness and feeling undefined, they consider this as being a psychic characteristic and are unable to understand the causes. The fact that they cannot recognize this particular psychic structure makes them feel (and seem) superficial and rigid subjects incapable of emotional relationships. In the same way, they are unable to explain to themselves the situations of anguish they experience during moments of depersonalization and derealization.

By regaining their primitive parts during the analysis, the patients come into contact with their early experiences and give the analyst their own interpretation of why they feel detached from their own emotions and why they experience feelings of being incomplete. They usually lay the blame on some characteristic of their parents or relatives.

As analysts, we cannot know which elements are inherent in the subject (genetic, constitutional), and which in the environment, that contribute to the formation of autistic capsules. We can, however bear witness to our personal emotional participation with the patient and to the transformations of the transference–countertransference relationship during the analysis. The opening of autistic capsules not only enriches the patient's emotional life and gives rise to hope in the future, but also determines a new development of the patient's cognitive abilities that have been blocked by his autistic position. Since these cores have lasted for such a long time, as a defence against catastrophic anxieties, the relationship with the object and the development towards the depressive phase are difficult to reach. One part of the patient seems to live at the level of unintegrated sensations due to a lack of emotional ties and is unable to understand the interpretations at a symbolic level.

I hope to illustrate both the encapsulated states and the therapeutic process in the following chapters. If the therapist cannot understand these cores, theoretical rationalizations might be formulated, thus strengthening the patient's defensive armour.

CHAPTER TWO

Vicissitudes of the transference in work with autistic adults and children

"I have always been distracted and 'absent'. Now I understand the reason for this distraction: I wanted to run away from a relationship and reality. Even now, when I'm listening to the question I've asked, I sometimes find it hard to listen because I feel so far away from the other person as soon as I have asked it." *Irene*

This chapter describes similarities and differences in the course of psychotherapy as well as typical characteristics both of adult patients with autistic capsules and of autistic children.

If we start from the premise that autistic mechanisms are created to avoid pain and because of the fear of disintegration, during therapeutic analysis it will emerge that the patients with autistic cores have experiences that are analogous to their infantile traumatic situations. Just as in infantile autism it is impossible to establish a real relationship because of a lack of awareness of differentiation between "me" and "not-me", in adults we can see how the relationship with the analyst is either superficial or partially rejected.

Autistic encapsulation, as I have already indicated, immobilizes the part of the personality damaged due to a traumatic awareness of bodily separateness from the mother and isolates a set of primitive experiences that therefore continue to remain secret and undetected since they are buried in the deepest layers of the psyche.

The fear of annihilation—that is, the fear of losing the sensation that they exist and the fear of being separated from another human being who acts as support—becomes evident in the therapy of these adult patients. By coming to the sessions so diligently, they express their need to be protected from the fear of sliding into a desolate, loveless vacuum. Beneath the healthier parts of the personality which developed normally, there seems to be an encapsulated autistic core that was created in order to protect the self from painful or frightening situations.

During the therapy, these adult patients present characteristics that are similar to those of autistic children (Alvarez, 1992, 1996, 1997, 2000). Therapeutic treatment is slow with both groups, especially since such patients apparently do not relate to the analyst at all. The analyst often finds herself in a very difficult situation in which she seems to be the only one responsible for the therapy and interested in its outcome. The main differences between these two groups of patients are that the adults resort to psychotherapy not because of autistic symptoms but because of symptoms caused by different pathologies and that the autistic core is not initially evident to either the patient or the analyst.

If we consider how the request for psychotherapy occurs in the two groups of patients, we see that in the case of autistic children it is the parents who ask for help, since they are aware of the gravity of the situation. The passage of time and the normal teaching methods have proved ineffective and have had no impact on the child's development in terms of speech and sound development. In the case of adult patients, the psychotherapist is faced with different pathologies: neurotic, borderline, and psychotic patients or those with psychosomatic disorders. Psychotherapeutic treatment is primarily sought to eliminate the current symptoms rather than to understand the underlying causes of suffering. During the preliminary sessions with these patients, the secret autistic core is not immediately evident because it is masked by the different pathologies; only as the therapy progresses can it be recognized, especially through the countertransference. I shall illustrate this pattern in the clinical chapters, in part II.

Only gradually does the analyst become aware of the existence of these autistic cores. The analyst finds that she has to deal with patients who are extremely sensitive and vulnerable, even if they put on a mask of indifference or violence, and the emotional suffering is not expressed through verbal communication. These people are looking for a place where they can be understood and protected from their profound, unbearable anguish. They behave just like infants, who expect, without openly expressing it, the continuous presence of an adult: someone who will always be attentive to their needs so that they can continue to grow and develop. When the analyst is faced with the patient's silent plea for help, even though no real communication is possible, she finds herself trapped in a situation where she has accepted the patient but then finds it difficult to proceed.

In the case of psychotherapy with autistic children, the analyst can feel doubly uncomfortable, because the child is indifferent or refuses an emotional relationship and because the parents may put pressure on the analyst to bring about a rapid change in the child's behaviour. The analyst still has to deal with a double countertransference in the two therapeutic relationships—with the child and with the parents.

The adult patient's need to establish a close and prolonged relationship with the analyst, in which he can merge with the analyst without being aware of a real state of differentiation, appears to express not so much a symbiotic relationship—in the true sense of the word—but, rather, an adhesive or parasitic need. It seems that the adult patient is completely involved in the psychotherapy since it represents more a protective environment than a source of integration and hope. This leads to an unusually long therapy that is also difficult to bring to an end, because the patient does not seem to consider time as a real parameter. If the word "end" is mentioned, he pretends not to hear it or goes into a panic.

> I remember a patient of mine who, after each session, would go to the toilet to comb her hair and put on some make-up and remain sitting in front of the mirror, until I had to send her away. She considered such behaviour quite normal, since she wanted to postpone returning to the reality of the outside world.

The most significant bond seems to be the one between the patient and the analyst's room—which the patient regards as his place of refuge—rather than with the analyst herself. In fact, any change in the setting or position of physical objects can upset the patient, whereas the analyst can be treated like an insensitive object. In this connection, we must bear in mind that the primitive sensation of experiencing the nipple in the mouth brings us back to the experience of possessing objects rather than of forming a relationship between objects, and this is repeated in the analytic relationship. The distance is frustrating and unacceptable because of the feelings it triggers.

As regards the autistic relationship in particular, Resnik (1986) thinks that the autistic child's attempt to enter into a relationship comes about through a mechanism of expansion, the way an amoeba moves, and he thinks that it occurs much before the mechanism of projection. The child's self expands beyond its immediate space, controls it, and tends to incorporate the other person. This type of mechanism prevents him from establishing a relationship with the other, since such a relationship would contain in itself the concept of space and separation. This kind of defence is confirmed even in the case of adult patients if we observe the mechanism used by the autistic part of these patients who try to incorporate the analyst within themselves in order to feel safe from their life, without recognizing the real distance that exists between themselves and the analyst and that would allow the exchange of feelings and thoughts. In order to avoid profound human contact, these patients have cut off one part of the bond of dependency and thus avoid entering into a relationship. Their non-communication is a safety device that initially must be respected, otherwise the patient will flee and the therapy will fail. The technical difficulties encountered in such cases are described in chapter 5.

The sessions may, for a long period, be characterized by a cold atmosphere. In the past, this coldness has been idealized and become hypertrophic in order to protect the hidden autistic core. This absence of human warmth is projected into the analyst, and the danger is that the analyst's answers might be devoid of emotion and reflect this coldness. For example, the cold ambience that prevails as a result of the obsessive rituals might become chronic and paralyse the analyst's emotional reactions. The patient creates this atmosphere in order to protect himself from profound human relationships. He tends to keep the analytic situation static since it represents a special space that is relatively quiet and where he can find refuge from outside relationships.

For a long time, the material offered during the sessions might be repetitive due to the presence of rituals and obsessive thoughts, or it might merely be a list of physical complaints. At the beginning, there are few dreams and the patient does not always appreciate the way they are interpreted, since he thinks in a very concrete way.

For example, Irene (chapter 8) described a dream in which she had a headache but was unable either to make associations or to listen to any of my suggestions regarding the psychic suffering she experienced at that particular time. She could only talk about her migraine, her physical symptoms, and all the medical tests she had undergone.

The rigid thought patterns, repetitive behaviour, obsessive thoughts, physical complaints and the refusal of any emotional contact make the therapist feel alone, irritated and bored.

Since it is essential for these patients to feel protected, when they emerge from their emotional retreat, they experience the fear of falling into a void. Becoming alive and experiencing one's own feelings is frightening because one could be wounded, could suffer or die. The idea that the analysis might end brings with it the idea of psychic death. Feelings expelled from the analyst's mind might also repeat the rejection and annihilation experienced in the past.

The triad of symptoms in infantile autism compared to adults

Studies by Wing and Gould (1979) carried out on a large number of autistic children have confirmed the presence of three symptoms that characterize autism as described by Kanner (1943):

1. impaired social communication;
2. impaired verbal and nonverbal communication;
3. absence of symbolization and of imagination, which is replaced by repetitive behaviour.

If we consider these three symptoms of infantile autism and compare them with the characteristics of the autistic capsules in adults, we can see that, to a greater or lesser degree, these symptoms are present and integrated in the overall personality. There may, however, be both similarities and differences in the pathology and in the process.

Impaired social communication

Unlike autistic children, adult patients with autistic capsules (whether neurotic, borderline, psychotic, or psychosomatic) seem to be intelligent and can apparently interact socially, to a greater or lesser degree. We can thus hypothesize from the patient's anamnesis that during his childhood and adolescence the non-autistic part of the personality allowed the patient to socialize to a certain extent, to participate in school activities, to find a job, and to be involved in other activities.

Finding it difficult to interact socially might only be related to specific situations in which the patient is required to become more involved in a relationship. When the interpersonal relationships continue over a certain period of time and require an emotional exchange, anomalous socialization patterns might appear such as the inability to understand the feelings of others, tactless behaviour, and lack of interest in other persons. This is usually interpreted as manifestations of a bizarre personality and a tendency to manipulate others.

In the social sphere, the patient may ignore social conventions and can even break social rules, since he denies the existence of others. He may be also quite inflexible and stubborn. These characteristics can make interpersonal relationships unpleasant and difficult, even though relationships are not totally avoided. It is the emotional aspect of the relationship that is avoided, so the relationship then becomes superficial and anonymous.

A characteristic found in most cases is the tendency to establish a special relationship with one person, since forming a couple is reassuring to the patient and gives him a sense of continuity, even though it is not based on emotional involvement, common interests, or specific desires for physical or psychic contact. This type of relationship can be questioned and become unacceptable in the light of the analytic work, as past relationships were not formed because of personal affinity or feelings but represented a way of not feeling alone. For this reason, previous relationships that provided support may lose their meaning when the self is more integrated. We must remember that in states of greater undifferentiation, instead of looking for differences between himself and the other, the child tends to look for similarities that make him feel he belongs to the mother and can recognize himself in the other. Searching for differentiation in order to reach his own identity only occurs after he has experienced a solid fusion with the other to whom he feels similar.

It is clear that these patients suffer from impaired social communication, which can be pointed out only after prolonged and attentive observation. This kind of social interaction is especially evident often in the transference. In this context, it is therefore indispensable to establish a new interpersonal space in order to avoid creating a pathological "couple" or a defensive exclusion.

Impaired verbal and nonverbal communication

Verbal communication—impaired language

Unlike autistic children, adult patients can use language and for-mulate their thoughts in a syntactically correct way, even though for a long time there is no real communication. Their verbal capacity might be either scant or well developed, but in both cases this allows them to communicate and interact socially so that their social life may seem rather normal or even sophisticated.

Normally, language aims to convey information about the kind of person we are to the other person and to project ourselves outside our own body. However, words can also be totally unrelated to communi-cation and can be used to confuse, seduce, or avoid contact with an-other person (Bion, 1955). In order to understand the patient, it is more important to listen carefully to the emotional messages he sends out rather than to the content of the words. The analyst must learn to understand whether the patient is trying to communicate or confuse her, and this occurs only by means of emotional perception during the countertransference. Joseph (1985) stressed the importance of consid-ering transference as "a living relationship in which there is constant movement and change". She has pointed out that patients communi-cate more through the feelings they arouse in the analyst than by their words or associations. Joseph says that analytic interpretations would touch the more adult part of the personality, whereas recognizing feelings through countertransference means understanding the pa-tient's infantile part that was not understood in his childhood.

The role of the voice is of vital importance in early development. In early childhood, the child begins to introject the tone of voice of family members and associates the feelings that surround him with the musi-cal quality of the voices. In fact, relationship with rhythm and sound may also begin in pre-natal life. Maiello (1995, 1997, 2001) hypothesizes that the maternal voice heard by the foetus represents a proto-experi-ence of absence–presence similar to the way the newborn later experi-ences the absence–presence of the breast. She points out that the first experience of continuity and regularity that the foetus experiences is based on the constant stimuli from the body (breath, heartbeat). These represent the structuring elements of the experience of rhythmicity that is the prerequisite for the internalization of reliable temporal shapes and the development of basic trust. The rhythmical aspect of "sound-objects" might represent the precursors of the maternal object and might lead to experiences that precede listening to the maternal voice. The experience of perception of the bodily rhythm, partly auditory and partly vibratory and intertwined with a kinaesthetic and tactile level of experience, can provide the basic awareness of pulsating life (Erikson, 1950). Mancia (1981) considers that at a very early stage, the foetus can work out the experience of listening to the maternal voice and form inner representations that will subsequently allow the real meeting with the mother after birth.

Although words convey meaning, the resonance of a voice gives emotional significance to the message. In certain cases, however, there can be a dissociation between the symbolic message conveyed by the words through language and the emotional message conveyed by the rhythm, tone, and musical quality of the voice. The voice belongs to a more emotional and spontaneous register and can therefore give valuable information regarding the emotional sphere. By means of the voice, in the transference we can recognize elements that date back to the early "vocal" relationship with the mother and use this information in the work of interpretation.

One of the typical characteristics of autistic children is represented by a type of voice that can be flat, sing-song, or echolalic. Echolalia—which in the normal development of a child represents an early, transitory phase of identification through imitation—becomes permanent and replaces language. In the early phase, the child perceives more the quality of sounds in the maternal voice rather than the content, and he gradually internalizes the maternal model in all its complexity, thus moving towards his own individuality. The child goes from babbling to using language, and subsequently the voice represents a way of communicating his needs or his states of mind.

For a long time, Irene (chapter 8) spoke in a sing-song way and was unable to modulate the tone of her voice in relation to the content. Her voice was completely like her mother's. She was afraid of speaking in public, and this inhibition was related to her persecutory fears but also expressed her lack of identity. Irene repeated in an echolalic way the last words the other person said, and this seemed to represent the need to adhere to the surface of the other (Bick, 1968).

The sing-song way of speaking removed any meaning from the words and emptied them of any emotional content. It made the listener sleepy, and since it was an attempt to manipulate the other by means of the voice, it was also irritating. She spoke like a child because she was afraid to take on the role of an adult. She was always afraid that her words were devoid of meaning, showed her lack of intelligence, and therefore caused others to criticize her.

As the therapy proceeded, her sing-song way of speaking disappeared and her language became more meaningful and precise, so that she was even able to participate in theatrical performances.

Even the sounds that the patient inadvertently makes (expressions of preverbal communication) can be important signs.

For example, the loud, deep sigh Elisa (chapter 7) made as she lay down on the couch seemed to me a spontaneous sound associated with momentary relief. I thought that she was glad to be in a situation that allowed her to relax and seek emotional contact. However, once the session was over, the verbal communication conveyed just the opposite—namely, she denied having obtained any relief, minimized the therapeutic relationship, and refused any emotional contact. In this case, there was dissociation between the (unintentional) bodily and (intentional) verbal communication.

In all the cases I describe in the clinical chapters, the presence of the patient was dissociated from listening to me, and it was amazing to see how many times the patients repeated the same things or asked the same questions without responding to my remarks or reflecting on them.

Even though these adult patients participated in the sessions, they demonstrated their hostility and resistance towards me by acting as if I were invisible and non-existent, refusing to look at me and ignoring what I said. In this way, they also made any kind of introjective identification or change impossible.

Nonverbal communication and body language

Psychotherapeutic work with autistic and psychotic patients, both children and adults, benefits from observing the body. The most significant communication is made through the body rather than through language, since the former is related to the means of expression that occurred during the early, pre-symbolic period. Resnik (1987, 1999a) has stressed how much information we can obtain from observing the body as well as from verbal language. The body conveys more or less explicit messages regarding the patient's past and bears the traces of time and emotional experiences.

In addition to the absence of language, the most striking characteristic of the autistic child is that he avoids eye-to-eye contact and seems to look right through the person. His eyes are blurred or unfocused. In adults, eye-to-eye contact is fleeting, since they want to avoid a meaningful relationship. By so doing, the patient also makes an attempt (but in a less total way than a child) to exclude the other person in an unconscious attempt to deny the slightest sign of a transference relationship that could be an expression of dependency. The situation of dependence is reminiscent of the early dependence, which is too painful to be repeated in the transference. The eyes are sometimes expressionless or cold and indifferent or have a questioning look. This disconcerting expression gives the impression that these patients are aliens from another planet with whom it is impossible to communicate.

The image of one's body derives from primordial states or sensations. Autistic children live mainly in a sensation-dominated world. Primordial states and sensations are of basic significance in the development of the sense of self. When the body image has more consonance with the actual body, a greater sense of identity and existence develops (Tustin, 1986).

As Tustin (1986) described, children with autism maintain their body surface in contact with hard objects by clutching them in their hand, and they envelop the surface of real objects with their saliva. They have, however, no interest in the significance or use of the objects themselves. Similarly, adult patients seem to relate to their body and that of the other person in a formal, superficial way so that they can remain emotionally distant even though physically close.

Ambra (chapter 9) used to come to the sessions carefully combed, made up, and always wearing different clothes and hairstyle. She even changed the colour of her eyes by wearing tinted contact lenses. In this way, she managed to disguise herself so that she was unrecognizable. Her theatrical behaviour expressed through the body was meant to confound me as regards her identity. However, apart from the most symbolic meaning of such behaviour, our sessions were limited to the meeting of two bodies with no feelings, no memories. She would even go so far as to ask me if I recognized her, since she changed her outward appearance so often.

In this case, since there was no symbolic thought, the patient gave the body, the clothes, and the make-up the task of communicating her messages, and in the transference she reproduced the absence of a profound and meaningful relationship, as in her early years.

This particular kind of body language is a source of precious information hidden beneath insignificant and monotonous verbal communication.

Absence of symbolization; substitution of imaginary activities with use of autistic objects, rituals or repetitive behaviour, and acting-out

Absence of symbolization

The creation of symbols in the child's development is based on the capacity to use substitutes for concrete things or situations after becoming aware of the separation between oneself and the mother. Although symbolization is linked to the concept of loss, it is accompanied by the pleasure of experiencing once again, in the mind, the presence of an object that, in real life, has been lost and is no longer there. By bringing it back to mind, it can provide comfort.

When the newborn still does not realize that the world exists, the mother makes the activity of her mind available to the child and creates a special space where exchanges can take place. In this situation there is a meeting in the child's mind between expecting to have the breast—a preconception, according to Bion (1962b)—and having the real breast. This brings about a satisfactory experience that is necessary for survival. Both the preconception and the hallucination of being satisfied represent an innate tendency to form a mental representation, which bears witness to a human potential that is genetically transmitted. The mother's capacity for reverie and the rhythm between the satisfaction or lack of satisfaction of these needs represent the factors that trigger the process of symbolization. The failure of this propitious meeting between the child and his environment may be responsible for the absence of the process of symbolization which we find in autistic children.

In the case of, for example, birth defects that require surgery in the first weeks of life or cerebral palsy, which hinders normal neurophysiological development, a satisfactory mother–child relationship will be difficult to achieve. Since the child will receive from his body sensations of suffering and pain and his movements will be restricted, the mother will consequently experience strong emotional reactions to her child's handicap, with the result that the relationship may be disturbed (Tremelloni, 1988).

Bion adds that if the child's sensory and emotional needs are frustrated and not immediately satisfied, this will lead him to form his first thoughts. However, if the child experiences too much pain and is emotionally deprived, this can lead to a feeling of omnipotence and denial of reality. The child's early orientation towards narcissistic protection occurs when it is impossible to cope with excessive frustration. Alvarez (1999) points out that in the experiences of the child, when frustration becomes intolerable and desperation prevails, frustration no longer represents a stimulus in the formation of thinking but, instead, produces dissociation and cognitive disorders.

The mother's reverie, the fact that she is receptive to the child's motor, sensory, and emotional needs, her empathic responses, the way she can regulate satisfaction and frustration, when to be near or away from the baby—all these represent an early experience of a relationship that occurs before the baby can distinguish reliably between "me" and "not-me". As the mother gradually helps the infant with micro-separations, the notion of space in between and of a transitional area becomes internalized. A human bond is created, and the concept of otherness becomes acceptable. If this does not occur, the mother's absence causes a sensation of catastrophic anguish (Bion's "nameless dread", 1962a) characterized by a feeling of emptiness and fear of annihilation.

Autistic children, who mainly live within their body sensations and have not developed a space where they can develop their fantasies and imagination, have little ability to symbolize. Their lack of imagination and fantasy leads to an inability to play or enjoy inventing games and seems to be replaced by repetitive behaviour such as the use of autistic objects or stereotyped rituals. In the adult, the inability to use symbols might be partial, as demonstrated by the substitution of a symbolic thought with shapes or mental processes that are comparable to those of autistic children. A lack of curiosity about finding out about the meaning of both the outside and internal world can signify a more general difficulty in using symbols.

For example, Ambra (chapter 9) was unable to show any interest in any specific area and lacked any intellectual curiosity or creative capacity for any manual activity. Things simply existed in themselves but did not provide any stimulus that could arouse her interest. When she studied, notions became glued to her memory but were of no interest to her and did not give rise to any other thoughts.

Substitution of imaginary activities

During the analysis, these patients present fixed, repetitive thoughts with no symbolic value or repetitive behaviour patterns that are comparable to rituals or actings-out. More detailed examples are given in subsequent chapters.

Autistic objects: autistic thoughts or "autistic objects of the mind".   Autistic children manipulate objects in a repetitive way but do not use them for a specific purpose or to invent games. They are usually hard objects from which these children cannot part and which they consider part of the body. These objects have been called "autistic objects" (Tustin, 1980).

Autistic objects have been interpreted as acting as a kind of support to replace a human relationship. The child seems to have used the objects to replace a reassuring human relationship that could satisfy his physical and emotional needs. The objects are considered irreplaceable just because they make him feel safe and protected. They replace awareness of separateness from the mother and of the space that exists between the two.

There are a number of autistic objects a child may choose that may not be the hard objects usually described. These might be a book, illustrations, or films that the child repeatedly wants to look at or a particular kind of music that he always wants to listen to (Barrows, 2001). In these cases, the pleasure is no longer limited to touch but is closer to visual representations of situations that have become familiar.

In the adult, certain fixed thoughts are always present. These thoughts are extremely difficult to question or modify and are comparable to delusional thinking. In my opinion, these thoughts might represent the equivalent of autistic objects, since their hardness is psychic instead of physical. They are deeply rooted convictions that the patient refuses to discuss, question, or abandon. In this sense, these thoughts make the patient feel secure at an intellectual level—unlike feelings, which can change, disappoint, or cause him suffering.

> *For example, one patient continued investing his money as his father had done twenty years before even though he was aware that it would be a bad investment. He did not deviate from his father's old thinking and could not consider the present economic situation and his own doubts about his decision. The thought of his father remained unalterably fixed in his memory.*

* * *

Another patient of mine always wore the same colour at all the hours of the day because her mother had always maintained that a particular colour was the most fashionable for a woman. Despite the fact that she felt extremely hostile to her mother, she was unable to eliminate that particular thought or colour from her mind, because it was a concrete representation of her mother. Although this thought in itself had no emotional significance, it prevented her from changing her way of thinking: she was glued to her mother's thoughts.

In the context of psychiatric semiotics, these autistic thoughts differ from delusional, obsessive, or prevailing ideas. Autistic thoughts differentiate themselves (1) from *delusional thoughts* because they are not part of a morbid ideation included in a delirium and are not accompanied by hallucinations; (2) from *obsessive ideas* because they are not incessantly recurrent and not connected to *states of anxiety*; and (3) from *prevailing ideas* that have particular emotional significance and are recurrent with respect to a *specific subject* from which the patient cannot detach himself.

"Autistic thoughts" are cut off from emotional content and become attached to specific, apparently unselected subjects. In the case of autistic children, the preferred objects are those that give them sensations— for instance, tactile or acoustic. In the case of adults, I think that these objects are represented by a set of thoughts, or "pseudo-thoughts", since they imitate the thoughts of others. These thoughts seem to be a substitute for a human presence and give the impression of a core of identity that would make it possible for these patients to think. Autistic thoughts seem to be "glued" to their mind.

Some patients continue tenaciously to maintain visions of reality that are an exact copy of certain concepts derived from the experiences of their mothers. Although they persist in holding on to these visions as valid, they had in reality a great aversion for their real parents and the relationship with them. Given their hostility towards the relationship with the parents, these persistent thoughts represent the only element of safety they appear to have received from the family environment, a kind of model on which their thinking is based. These fixed thoughts do not allow any different interpretation or any elaboration based on their own personal experiences. They do not even seem to be the result of a process of symbolization but, rather, the result of having taken possession of one part of the maternal object which escaped them in the pre-symbolic phase.

These autistic thoughts can be compared to Joseph's (1982) concept "chuntering", which is a special kind of mental activity used by adult psychotic or borderline patients: they pick up something that has been going on in their mind and start to use it over and over again in "some circular type of mental activity". These patients believe that they are thinking but, instead, they are using this "chuntering", which is "the complete antithesis of thought". Just like the children who cannot part with their autistic objects, such adults cling to these stereotyped thoughts, thus making any hope of change and individuation impossible. Since the thoughts are always present, they provide instant gratification so that the patient does not have to wait and deal with emotional frustration. These autistic thoughts could be termed "autistic objects of the mind": a cyst-like growth in the mind that is used as a defence mechanism (the protective armour in the transference) to avoid emotional contact with the therapist and as an offensive mechanism to annihilate her mental functions. What these fixed thoughts have in common with autistic objects is, I think, that they function as a substitute for the attention and care these patients desire that would provide support, security, strength, protection, and a presence.

One of my patients always wanted to participate in family dinners even though he imagined first, and verified after, that he would feel sad and uneasy since he felt he would be misunderstood. However, he held on tenaciously to the idea that he had a warm and welcoming family as a solid reference point.

Because of these thoughts, the patients cannot experience separateness, loss, and reparation. It makes it impossible for them to become aware of their desire for comforting relationships. It prevents them from creating and using symbols and developing their individual thoughts, their fantasies, and their imaginative ability and condemns them to remain on the surface of concrete things. This would also explain how impossible it is for them to wait, to imagine, and to hope in personal development, and establish new emotional bonds.

Rituals and repetitive behaviour.   Some authors think that autistic children perform rituals in order to protect themselves against anxiety (Kanner, 1944). Kanner has pointed out that rituals represent the patient's obsessive desire always to look for things that are similar and identical (sameness). Meltzer (Meltzer et al., 1975) considers rituals to be related to a primary, catastrophic depression rather than to anxiety and thinks that these rituals are more primitive than the obsessive rituals of neurosis. In his opinion, they are the result of a dismantling process of the sensory apparatus, so that the senses become fixed on the most stimulating object of the moment and tend to make the real experience meaningless.

In Tustin's (1980) view, autistic rituals do not have a symbolic significance related to human figures; rather, they replace human figures. She believes they are used to ward off other stimuli from the real world and considers them more a protective mechanism than a defence mechanism. She thinks that the rituals are an attempt to control others and free themselves from unbearable experiences. Since the rituals can act as a substitute to make a person feel secure and help him relate to the outside world, they are difficult to abandon. It would be dangerous to eliminate them, since the patient might replace them with something else.

In this connection, Tustin (1981b) and Meltzer et al. (1975) add that these rituals can be explained as an attempt to overcome not so much anxiety as the experience of a catastrophic depression related to the sensation of falling infinitely.

Although the use of rituals is initially connected to a subjective cause, it subsequently assumes an addictive nature (Alvarez, 1992) and tends to enslave both patient and analyst. This concept was first pointed out by Kanner (1944) and then later taken up by Tustin (1981a) and by Meltzer (Meltzer et al., 1975), who related it to fetishism and perversion (Alvarez & Reid, 1999).

The persistence of the repetitive symptoms makes it impossible to reach the patient and contributes to the idea that the pathological situation is chronic. The quality of the rituals can be different according to the child's phase of development and can be a substitute for the normal activity of playing. They may be characterized by excitement, ecstasy, or avoidance of contact. In adults, repetitive behaviour patterns become fixed and are in no way modified by the analyst's interpretation regarding their original significance. Monotonous and unchanging rituals have the function of expressing great strength and power in the transference relationship.

Renzo (chapter 10) used to come to the session much earlier than his appointment, and he continued to maintain this ritual even after having discussed and cleared up the meaning according to the various phases of the analysis. This habit disturbed me. As the analysis developed, it gradually diminished but never entirely disappeared. In this way, he imposed his timetable on me and would not accept the timetable we both agreed on.

Acting-out: By using verbal communication through memories and free associations, analytic treatment ideally excludes any acting that attempts to avoid the psychic process. Acting-out consists of a tendency to express one's own emotions or conflicts through action, and can be present in all types of personality organization.

During the early phases of a child's development, his messages are mainly related to motor activities and the mother interprets them according to her reverie. These primitive exchanges represent the core of the process of symbolization, since the mother interprets the messages and tries to satisfy the child's needs. We should also remember that the first bodily movements of a child transmit his first attempts at projective identification. The mother sometimes cannot tolerate these messages related to motor activities or she may induce excessive motor stimulation herself, thus providing the child with a model of meanings for such activities. Movement thus becomes a means of expression which precedes psychic activity.

In adults with autistic capsules, the actings-out can reveal a degree of slight or partial symbolization. They can represent an easy way to give vent to feelings through motor activities, since the patients are unable to work out strong feelings like serious anxiety; alternatively, they can represent an attempt to eliminate the suffering represented by the relationship.

Given the few associations and dreams, the actings-out provide interesting and meaningful signals and must be evaluated in a different way from those in neurotic cases. This evasion of thinking has ancient roots, when movement meant receiving the attention of the other person in order to alleviate physical pain or satisfy needs. By means of its motor capacities and the force with which it can express itself, the body wants to show that it can prevail over thought.

It is very difficult to help the patients understand the meaning of their acting-out, since they are reluctant to abandon it. But we have to bear in mind that acting-out has two poles, a positive and negative one. The positive is that it provides the therapist with information about the unconscious; the negative is that it temporarily replaces the mental process. Actings-out are part of a complicated form of communication even if they reveal an impairment of psychic containment. With regard to borderline pathology, Godfrind (1993) indicates that actings-out can represent a valuable defence mechanism against depersonalization and the fear of falling apart.

> *Just after a crisis of depersonalization, Irene (chapter 8) called me without knowing what to say. Since she merely wanted to establish a contact and reassure herself that she really existed, the sound of my voice served to abate her anxiety.*
>
> *Rather than an acting-out, this seemed a way of letting off steam in the face of extreme stress in which her individuality was put to the test. In this situation, the analysis of the acting-out was not focused on the transgression of the setting, since the state of psychotic anxiety exceeded the patient's capacity to work out and contain it.*

In these patients, actings-out do not usually contain a wealth of unconscious meaning as in the case of neuroses, but represent the impossibility of working out thoughts. Although they should not be encouraged, actings-out must therefore be considered as a kind of temporary communication that will gradually be replaced with symbolic thinking. They may be important because they give rise to countertransference feelings that help the analyst understand the underlying unconscious meaning.

Conclusions

I have tried in this chapter to identify analogies between the most important characteristics of infantile autism and those of the traces of autism in adults. The similarities between some characteristics in the two groups of patients bear witness to the presence of analogous primitive experiences.

Since in adult patients the traces of autism are less evident and widespread than in infantile autism, they remain hidden for a long time and do not prevent the other parts of the personality from developing. Only when acute states of anxiety or depression call for psychotherapy do the autistic traces emerge in the psychoanalytic relationship.

CHAPTER THREE

Countertransference: an overview

"Once I didn't speak at all . . . then I spoke without thinking . . . now speaking for me means getting tired, because it's difficult to transform a thought into words and understandable sentences." *Renzo*

During the last fifty years the development of psychoanalytic studies has focused increasingly on the concept of countertransference. The initial interpretation of the countertransference as an obstacle to treatment was transformed into a useful and indispensable tool in understanding the patient. Since then, the countertransference has made the analyst more responsible for her verbal interactions with the patient, because she can no longer consider herself a detached observer but is involved in a complex relationship in which both actively participate in realizing their own self. In particular, the extension of psychoanalytic psychotherapy to also include autistic and psychotic patients has led to theoretical and technical modifications and consequently has determined additional changes in the concept of countertransference, which has taken on fundamental importance in psychoanalytic treatment.

Starting from Freud's (1912e) description of the concept of positive and negative transference to express the infantile feelings of love and hate that become ritualized in the relationship between patient and analyst, the concept of countertransference gradually emerged. It refers to the overall feelings the analyst has towards the patient.

According to Freud, successful therapy could only be achieved through instinctual–libidinal interpretation, especially with regard to personal development during the oedipal period. If the patient did not accept the analyst's interpretation, it meant that he had some resistances that would have to be overcome in order for the analysis to continue. Freud felt that the analyst should act as a mirror on which the patient could send his projections. Since the analyst was someone who had already been analysed and was healthier than the patient, a position of neutrality had to be taken by the analyst to avoid exercising some influence over the patient.

In his paper "The Future Prospects of Psycho-Analytic Therapy" (1910d), Freud excluded any consideration of countertransference from analytic work and advised his colleagues to remain completely neutral and as anonymous as possible in the analytic situation and to act like a surgeon in an operating theatre. In this way, however, the exploratory psychic activity was possible on only one side, and the psychoanalyst's own emotional reactions that emerged from the relationship, which were regarded as " a problem" rather than an analytic tool (Heimann, 1950), had to be kept in check. As for the patient, he did not have to take into consideration his own insights and observations regarding the analyst's emotional reactions: these aspects concerned only the therapist's personal analysis and were not to be expressed. The problem, though, is that communication is not just verbal.

The intentional exclusion of the countertransference in analytic practice did not eliminate its existence. In the subsequent years, the development of psychoanalytic studies prepared the way for the extension and modification of the concept of transference to include the countertransference. In the 1920s, Ferenczi and Rank considered the exploration of real experiences as being fundamental in the psychoanalytic meeting, since it gave great importance to the concept of the "here-and-now". This concept represented the beginning of a new view of the countertransference. Indeed, the exploration of the experience of a human contact becomes the centre of the analytic relationship.

Without rejecting the importance of the concepts of psychosexual development and the oedipal period, the concept of direct experience in the analytic relationship in the here-and-now and the conviction that communication does not only take place through the words of the interpretation made possible a new psychoanalytic conceptual position. From the absolutism of a single perspective there was a shift to a pluralism of perspectives based on direct experience.

These pioneer studies represented an unexpected driving force in the development of analytic thought in the following years. Reik (1937) maintained that the insights that come from the analyst's unconscious provide the best material to understand the patient, but he distinguished it from countertransference, which he thought represents instead the resistance of the analyst. In that period Anna Freud's (1936) work on the defence mechanisms of the ego, as well as that of Hartmann (1939), Sullivan (1940), and others, led to subsequent studies on the influence of interpersonal relationships in human experience.

Starting from the concept of projective identification (M. Klein, 1946), the countertransference has been considered as the analyst's reaction to feelings projected in him. These reactions can be partly attributed to the analyst's unsolved neurotic parts but can also be due to feelings that emerge from the intensity and nature of the patient's projections. The more the patient is regressed, the more the analyst is open to the projection; the more the countertransference reactions are intense, the more they can be used in analytic comprehension.

In the 1950s, after a long period of silence, many scholars began to consider the countertransference as inevitable, even if it did not necessarily have to be communicated to the patient. The patient and analyst became co-participants in the therapeutic relationship and could mutually observe each other. The countertransference could no longer be ignored and led to different interpretations. The resistances could be considered as useful material to evaluate as an expression of unconscious aspects. The analyst's feelings no longer had to be eliminated, and she had to experience a direct encounter with her patient in the field.

The traditional analytic type of relationship therefore changed into a new, more genuine situation, in which the two participants in the relationship were each capable of participant observation from his or her own point of view. The analyst consequently got closer to the patient in a situation of mutual observation, and as a consequence the patient got closer to the analyst. This made it possible to focus greater attention on the "problems" of countertransference.

Subsequently the works of Paula Heimann (1950) and Heinrich Racker (1957)[1] modified the concept of countertransference, and instead of representing a danger, it came to be considered a useful tool.

Heimann (1950) was one of the first analysts to state that the countertransference was important in understanding the patient. She writes:

> in addition to the evenly suspended attention which allows the analyst to follow the patient's free associations . . . to perceive the manifest and latent significance of his words, allusions, references to childhood events . . . the analyst needs to be emotionally sensitive in order to follow the patient's emotional responses and unconscious fantasies. Countertransference is an instrument of research into the patient's unconscious. [1950, p. 74]

Heimann considered countertransference as the analyst's emotional response to the patient:

> The emotions reawakened in the analyst are much closer to the crux of the problem than intellectual reasoning . . . the unconscious perception of the patient's unconscious is much more acute and rapid that the conscious one. [1960, p. 153]

The emotional response should serve as a criterion when the analyst selects from the material offered by the patient in making her interpretations, but the analyst will also have to recognize and process this response and not confuse it with her own unconscious material.

According to Racker (1957), the countertransference can be interpreted either as an obstacle (danger of blind spots), or as an instrument to understand what is happening in the patient, or as a space where the patient can have a new experience. Racker considers the analyst not only as an interpreter of the transference but also as an object of the transference.

Racker further differentiated countertransference into two processes: concordant identification and complementary identification, the first corresponding to the patient and the second to the patient's internal object. Concordant identification gives rise to what other authors refer to as an empathic relationship. With complementary identification, the analyst will be identified with the patient's internal object and will feel treated as such. In this case, the countertransference will provide useful information regarding the patient's inner world. The complementary identifications are closely connected with the destiny of the concordant identifications but if the analyst fails in the concordant identifications and rejects them, certain complementary identifications become intensified. It is important to remember that concordant identifications can more easily create a narcissistic bond and imply a greater degree of countertransference participation.

The analytic relationship thus becomes a complex, dynamic system in which the analyst differentiates himself from the patient because of her capacity to perceive her own inner emotional states as a result of the projections the patient sends her and to give them meaning.

Money-Kyrle (1956) admits that although the countertransference is useful and beneficial in understanding the patient, it also represents a hindrance. The feeling of being in contact with the patient in an empathic way represents the normal countertransference. Faced with the transference, which reproduces infantile experiences, the analyst assumes a parental role. Money-Kyrle believes that the countertransference properly begins through the projective identification of the analyst's infantile ego onto the patient and with the introjective identification of the parental figure. If the identification occurred only with the patient's suffering infantile ego without considering the parent-object, the analyst could use projective identification not just to understand the patient but, also, to get rid of her own infantile problems. Money-Kyrle has also made a distinction between a destructive projection and a desperate one and recommends not mixing them up, simply in order to make a "correct" interpretation. The analyst should not urge the patient to cope with his suffering before he has the capacity to do so.

In the 1960s and 1970s, the standard model of Freud's therapeutic technique was questioned and accused of being too rigid in the light of the profound cultural and historical changes of that period. The position of neutrality defended by Freud's disciples does not seem to have been rigorously followed and observed by Freud himself. In fact, what emerges from the description of his clinical cases is the importance of his values and even his own personal involvement due to his therapeutic effort.

German-speaking psychoanalysts (e.g., Cremerius, 1985, 1991) who continued in the steps of Ferenczi (Ferenczi & Rank, 1923, 1927) and Balint (1968) reconsidered the works of Freud and demonstrated that he was a much more active and spontaneous analyst than his first theoretical works made him seem. These authors reassessed the relationship between patient and analyst with respect to the classical analytic rules. These rules were no longer considered ideal instruments of a silent analyst, closed within himself, but were considered more relative and could be adapted to the final purpose of the analytic process.

In particular, Cremerius (1985), who carefully studied Freud's case studies and personal observations, demonstrated that the real method Freud used was far from the cold neutrality proposed in his early theoretical works. Cremerius (1991) agrees with Freud's approach that emerged from his documents and proposes a model of an analyst "vital, spontaneous, discreet, very personal, without any mean scruples, who can imagine something which might help the patient emerge from a difficult situation" (p. 108). The psychoanalytic relationship requires a progressive dialectical understanding, and in this perspective the concepts of transference and countertransference were re-evaluated.

The possibility of openly speaking of countertransference and self-analysis in order to understand the patient and the analyst has been considered by Symington (1983) as an "act of liberation" from the oppressive element of history, culture, and the psychoanalytic society of the early twentieth century. In the 1970s, the formulation of the concept of the self focused attention on this central element that presides over the perception of reality, the awareness of being, the perception of one's own body, giving the sense of tension at having attained self-fulfilment.

By extending the area of psychoanalytic treatment to include borderline and psychotic patients, the concept of countertransference was once more brought into question. Searles (1965), like other psychotherapists who have treated schizophrenic and borderline patients who present a weak, fragmented ego, has pointed out that "the therapist must be able to respond emotionally with a frequency and intensity which is greater than what Freud recommends". He goes so far as to say that the analyst must sometimes let the patient help her, since he can provide her with the lost parts.

When working with borderline patients, Searles (1988) hopes that the analyst's "professional identity is not allied with the forces of repression but more with the emergence of feelings, fantasies or anything else which the patient wants the therapist to understand so that the patient can identify with him". The analyst should use her own sense of identity as a real organ of perception in order to enter into the symbiotic therapeutic phase or to differentiate herself from the patient when the transference is too intense.

Winnicott (1947) distinguished between abnormal countertransference feelings, which require further analysis on the part of the analyst; normal feelings related to the usual experiences of analytic work, which is different from one analyst to another; and, finally, objective feelings such as love and hate, which are determined by the real behaviour of the patient. The analyst will have to keep the feelings she has experienced within herself until she finds the right moment to discuss them with the patient—Winnicott's concept of holding. His conceptualization of transitional phenomena made it possible to consider the analytic setting as the place where emotional exchanges can allow the process of symbolization to emerge. The mental availability of the analyst makes it possible to create a potential inner space where the patient can relive his childhood experiences.

Herbert Rosenfeld (1987) points out that the analyst must recognize during the analytic work psychic movements within herself and put them to the service of communication with the patient. Rosenfeld warns the analyst of the danger of a narcissistic collusion with the patient in receiving the projected feelings. He distinguishes empathy and insight from technical knowledge. The complex interplay between transference and countertransference can cause confusion in both analyst and patient. Therefore, it might be necessary for the analyst to observe the feelings experienced in situations such as her own personal analysis or in the case of supervision so that she can formulate therapeutic interpretations.

Bion (1962b, 1965) developed the concept of the containment of the feelings projected by the patient into the analyst and their transformation by the analyst. Just like the mother with her infant, the analyst has the task of containing and then giving back, in an acceptable form, what the patient cannot bear. He thus gives shape and meaning to the feelings experienced by the patient and makes thoughts thinkable. In his work with schizophrenic patients, Bion observed that they did not recognize the feelings they had awakened in the therapist through projection. This was due not to a defence mechanism but to the fact that they were unaware of that part of their personality that the analyst had to tolerate temporarily as the patients were incapable of doing so.

Resnik (1972) prefers to speak of a double transference instead of a countertransference and underlines the dual transmission of messages, hoping the analyst will assume the position of both analyst and patient. This means that when the analyst is working with seriously disturbed patients, she will have to get in touch with her own core of regression and with the vicissitudes of her own process of identification, all the while maintaining her role as a responsible professional. The transference experience can guide the analyst towards the understanding of herself, and, in its turn, the countertransference can modify the transference. In this way, both the analyst and the patient act by continually changing the relational field during the analysis.

Bollas (1987) studies the receptive capacity of the therapist and takes into consideration the position of the analyst as the second patient in the therapeutic relationship. By making herself available, the therapist finds room in her own inner world to receive the messages sent by the patient; however, she must accept as inevitable the ensuing period of uncertainty and confusion, since she must subsequently distinguish between the elements that belong to the patient and those that belong to her and then attempt to understand them and give them back to the patient. Therefore, she will have to face a period of uncertainty and realize that she might lose her way in a situation of suspended animation before being able to understand clearly the different feelings and meanings.

Benedetti (1980, 1992), referring to the psychotherapy of psychotic patients, distinguishes between the counter-identification of the analyst and the countertransference. He describes counter-identification as the capacity of the analyst's therapeutic unconscious to put itself in the place of the patient to furnish him with stimuli for identification. Benedetti considers countertransference, on the other hand, as intense impulses that are stimulated in the analyst by the patient's similar impulses, which are of a sexual or aggressive nature and are particularly intense in psychoses. The countertransference must be understood and worked out in order to understand whether it interferes too much by disturbing the counter-identification or whether it can be used since it expresses the patient's needs.

Benedetti distinguishes between the therapeutic fantasies (conscious and unconscious) and the real countertransference. The unconscious therapeutic fantasies might be a form of communication directed to the therapist herself since the patient's pathological processes can stir up a latent problem of the therapist that is symmetrical to that of the patient. These fantasies might also correspond to an identification with the patient resulting from the therapist's need to help him emerge from his pathological situation. Benedetti also underlines the importance of dreams about the patient.

According to Alvarez (1983), the countertransference includes the feelings that the patient transmits to the analyst, whereas empathic perception represents the comprehension of states of mind observed in the patient that are not projected into the analyst. Starting from Bion's concepts of containment and transformation, Alvarez suggests that, by means of the countertransference, the analyst hypothesizes the patient's answers to the possible interpretations before expressing them. By so doing, the analyst evaluates how the patient might accept them and tries to anticipate the possible reactions by trying to find the proper words with which to express them.

The conscious part of the countertransference might be related to the intensity, nature, and degree of the patient's projections and how they are integrated in the analyst's personality. However, there is also an unconscious part of countertransference, which must be found through the analyst's careful introspection.

Alvarez's concept of reclamation (1992) in serious cases of autistic withdrawal suggests that the analyst has to intervene more actively than in less serious patients, since in her countertransference she feels it is urgent and indispensable to revitalize the patient. Faced with the coldness in the transference, the analyst can remain bewildered, but if she carefully observes the parallel oscillations in her countertransference feelings, she can realize how the analytic relationship is developing. Only by listening to our own feelings can we give appropriate answers.

In the 1990s, the main representatives of the American Intersubjectivist School (Renik, 1993; Stolorow & Atwood, 1996) reformulated the concept of the analytic experience, and even countertransference. According to these authors, the analytic relationship creates a psychic field made up of the psychic realities of the two participants, who are considered as whole and real persons who interact.

Note

1. Although the contributions of Racker in Buenos Aires and Heimann in London were probably written at the same time though published at different dates, each did not realize the existence of the results of the other. Therefore, there is a tendency to consider the temporal coincidence of the two works which resulted from independent thinking (Etchegoyen, 1986).

CHAPTER FOUR

Use of countertransference in patients with autistic capsules

"Once I looked at myself in the mirror and saw the external shape of my body but I did not feel I existed. I was like a shadow. I remember the anguish of being unable to distinguish the mannequins in shop windows from real people. I felt I found myself in a terrifying unknown world."
Irene

The use of countertransference in work with adults with autistic capsules is of fundamental importance, since these people tend to avoid emotional relationships. Due to the absence of emotional messages from the patient, the analyst will have to pay constant attention to her own inner world in order to recognize the patient's different emotional positions through her own feelings, especially when the patient re-experiences early anxieties. The analyst will have to be in contact with her own regressive cores and connect her inner processes to those of the patient.

Because the transference relationship in cases such as these occurs on two different levels, the countertransference will also undergo similar oscillations. By analysing the countertransference, the analyst will be able to distinguish between the patient's different projections and intervene in an appropriate way where are signs of a primitive catastrophic anxiety.

Autism presents particular problems with using the countertransference. In the case of infantile autism, since the patient cannot express himself in either words, feelings, or symbolic games, the analyst is unable to play the role of interpreter as he usually does with neurotics. In this case, there is the risk of shifting the lack of emotion and of thoughts and the feelings of rejection onto the patient, thereby confirming his sense of isolation (see chapter 1). The countertransference thus takes on an extremely important role in the treatment of autistic children or adults with autistic capsules.

In this connection, working with autistic children serves as a paradigm, because the problems it presents are more evident and extreme. In the case of autism, there is apparently no form of communication that can be used. The sensation one experiences when faced with apparently senseless behaviour or the absence of a human relationship is disconcerting, whatever the situation, even though we can hypothesize that there exists in every human being the innate tendency to look for analogous bonds that mirror his moods or feelings (preconceptions). The fact that the autistic child does not differentiate between the animate and inanimate world explains why the observer is so disorientated. Only through the experience of personal analysis and supervision is it possible to focus attention on the countertransference feelings aroused by session material and come into contact with one's own deep-rooted regressive cores in order to initiate a dynamic process of interaction.

Child psychotherapists working in the field of autism have carried out some innovative research that maintains that the relationship between the autistic child and the therapist is a bi-personal one and not a mere description of the child's behaviour or characteristics (Alvarez, 1992, 1999; Bick, 1964; Bion, 1962a; Tustin, 1981a; Winnicott, 1960a). These psychotherapists, describing the feelings the observer experiences, stressed the boredom, sadness, and sensations of impotence when faced with the total lack of vitality or novelty. These feelings, made known by the analyst to the patient, represent the driving force that makes him realize how he can get in contact with other people.

Although we are unable to establish with certainty how these states of mind were formed in the patient and how we can attempt to modify them, we can analyse what they produce in ourselves, in the hope of giving them back to the patient in a new and constructive way. We cannot, of course, expect the autistic child to be a lively interlocutor, but we might be able to discover that he is extremely sensitive, though this sensitivity is masked by confused reactions and mechanical or meaningless behaviour. We must keep in mind that in all cases what the child needs is an interlocutor who is lively, intelligent and interested in him—in others words "live company", to quote Alvarez (1992).

Alvarez (1992) points out the importance of intervention based on countertransference response. Just as the mother must take care to keep the right distance so that the child can benefit from what is offered to him (breast and face), so too must the analyst reflect on this function of offering ideas that can be seized by the patient, thus promoting introjective processes rather than projective ones. The analyst must continually carry out a reconnaissance mission in her own inner world in order to discover analogous experiences and therefore give back to the patient the idea that she can share the same problem. Alvarez points out that the experience of the newborn in assimilating the messages transmitted by the mother "may have more to do with question of perspective than with question of projection" (Alvarez, 1992, p. 79). This marks the beginning of an introjective process rather than a projective one. The analyst has to respond to the patient in accordance with his capacity to listen and grasp new ideas.

Melanie Klein (1935) suggested that attention must be paid not only to the parts lost in the patient's unconscious, but also to those that are expelled through projective identification. Without diminishing the importance of the patient's biography, in the interaction with the present the analyst will be able to find precious parts of the patient's personality that have been abandoned. Therefore, in her interaction with the patient, the analyst must understand within herself why she feels the way she does. Not only does she represent the object in the mind of the patient, but "her own state of mind" will inform her of the patient's parts chronically projected into the others.

Alvarez points out that since autistic children are so isolated, they trigger "considerate attention". The therapist will have to find a way to communicate just as a mother does with her infant. Alvarez and Reid (1999) have stressed that, in order to give meaning to the puzzling behaviour, it is important to pay attention to the slightest change in the feelings of the analyst when she is with the patient.

Alvarez and Reid (1999) add that especially in those cases characterized by serious depression and passivity, the analytic work cannot just focus on the interpretation but must also rekindle in these patients an interest in life and related feelings. These authors admit that in these cases the therapist has to have the mind, energy, hope, and imagination of two. Close observation of the patient, the observation of one's own emotional reactions to any change, and the patient's response to the treatment will provide the basic material that will allow the therapist to give symbolic meaning to apparently inexplicable behaviour.

This type of approach obviously calls for an analyst who is more active, expressive, immediate, and able to use her own feelings as a tool in her work than the classic, neutral analyst. Working this way is essential, otherwise the analyst remains stuck in an unproductive, stalemate situation. For example, in the face of the autistic child's rituals, it might be useful to refuse to accept certain repetitive, meaningless behaviour patterns.

With autistic children who are particularly passive, introducing something that makes them want to play means coming into contact with their psychic state by recovering our own infantile world of play. We must look within ourselves to find new elements that can give rise to an interpersonal exchange. An interlocutor who is attentive and full of life must help these patients by giving them a sense of vitality, before retrieving the parts that have been dispersed (Tremelloni, 1988).

Adult patients with autistic capsules are initially different from autistic children since the non-autistic part of their personality as well as their interpersonal relationships are more developed. In part, they behave by assigning a role to the analyst and developing a sufficiently meaningful transference relationship, and, in part, they deny it due to the emotional deficit in the development of their personality. The analyst is faced with a patient who functions on two psychic levels: one is represented by the autistic core, the other is more integrated. One part of the patient is blocked and does not communicate, whereas the other is more in tune with the analyst and can express itself both by means of symbolic communication and by the mechanisms of projection.

As the therapy develops at a deeper level, however, the autistic closure becomes much more evident, thus leading to a complete stalemate, hindering the possibility of making any further progress. In these cases, it seems that the patient's task is to keep the object absent and refuse to acknowledge that the other really exists. When working with these patients, as I have said, the countertransference becomes more than ever an indispensable instrument.

The continual oscillation between these different modes of expression leads to different transference messages, which go from being isolated and desperate and on the brink of a catastrophic depression to feeling strong and aggressively shielded against the outside world.

The analyst must, for instance, distinguish between passive behaviour that expresses hidden opposition, behaviour caused by a weak or fragile personality, and behaviour that represents the beginning of a greater integration of the self.

In the more symbiotic phase of the therapy, Elisa (chapter 7) was obsessively present at the sessions because she was worried about not missing one of them, even when she did not feel like coming. In fact, she was afraid she did not exist outside them. At a certain point, she began to skip the sessions in order to avoid expressing her aggressive feelings that began to emerge but that she was unable to recognize.

When she subsequently emerged from the phase of catastrophic depression or non-existence, she decided for the first time to go on holiday and left her family, her job, and the sessions for a few days. At that point, the holiday represented the possibility of making a decision to separate herself from me and her realization of the need to take care of herself. Compared to the times that she had not come to the sessions, these absences represented a change in their meaning, and it was therefore opportune to interpret them in a different way.

Through the countertransference, I was able to unveil her different intentionalities about her presence or absence in the sessions and decide when and how to interpret them, according to the degree of structure of the self she had reached and her capacity to separate from me.

In spite of my attention to countertransference, I often realized that as soon as I thought I had understood the material, proposed a suitable interpretation, and felt close to the patient in an empathic way, the autistic defences intervened to drive away and deny any transference feeling. This way of proceeding prompts in the analyst a situation of countertransference which goes from hope and interest to uncertainty, disappointment, and confusion, like an alternately hot and cold shower, and this makes it difficult to understand and welcome the patient. It is therefore important for the analyst to resort to another relationship, with her supervisor, since it represents a space in which to reconsider and re-experience the analyst's own homologous parts implicit in the relationship with the patient.

An important point to bear in mind is that the therapist must realize that it is essential to maintain the "right distance" from these patients, since they alternate between periods when they need close emotional contact with the analyst and periods when they reject her or even deny she exists. If the analyst is too emotionally close, the patient feels trapped and flees, since he feels that she is not sincere and only wants to control him. On the other hand, he might fear that the therapist wants to persecute him; instead, if she is cold and aloof, the patient feels rejected or thinks his situation is hopeless.

When the transference is characterized by aggression and closure, the countertransference danger is represented by the analyst's boredom with the patient's rigid obsessive defences and her irritation at the patient's continual expressions of contempt or rejection.

Another disturbing element experienced in the countertransference is represented by the recurrent symptoms and rituals that imprison us in a situation of impotence, since they prevent us from using our analytic skills. Rigid behaviour and obsessive thoughts transform the analytic relationship into a kind of mechanical gear that has nothing human or new about it. Faced with repetitive actions and an expressionless void, the therapist must try to find a personal way of establishing contact in order to help a human relationship emerge. The patient will thus have the opportunity to experience something new happening in his inner world.

In my experience, when periods of obsessive repetition or hostility prevailed, I often wondered how I could create some pleasant or interesting moments during the session to make me feel comfortable in my relationship with the patient, so that the countertransference feelings of psychic death, boredom, rage, and expulsion would not prevail. If the patient experiences these unpleasant feelings of the analyst through projection, they can become iatrogenic.

The case of Renzo (chapter 10) describes the development of an analytic psychotherapy beginning from childhood. As shown by the details of the case, the work of interpretation could begin only many years later. To do so earlier would have been counterproductive, since it would have strengthened the patient's fantasies of persecution and hostility. Since the bond was very fragile, at the beginning it was considered opportune not to express personal evaluations but, rather, to provide containment.

However, this period when messages are absorbed by the analyst is not to be considered a passive phase but represents an important opportunity for her to observe and reflect in order to find meaning. Interpretations made too early might mean throwing back to the patient all the things he is trying to make the analyst understand, just as occurred in his first important relationships.

In the case of Renzo (chapter 10), the countertransference feelings were mainly characterized by uneasiness due to the immobility stemming from his repetitive thoughts and behaviour. For a long time, I had to discourage him from his tendency to maintain his obsessive rituals that made our work ineffective.

To demonstrate the usefulness of this period of containment and attentive waiting, one can see in this case that following this period of apparent incomprehension and analytic inactivity, the relationship changed until fertile thoughts emerged as well as emotional exchanges. I considered the blossoming of such a fertile relationship as a reward for the long period I spent inactive and waiting in a seemingly static situation.

Bion's view of containment refers to a dynamic situation that tends to maintain a balance of power (1962b, 1965). Alvarez (1992) describes this function of the analyst as a thoughtful emotion and an emotional reflection. Starting from Bion's concept, Alvarez divides the analytic process into four stages: the first is the receptive or containing stage; the second, the transforming work inside the therapist; the third, the interpretative work, which may or may not involve returning the projections to the patient; and the fourth, consideration of the effect of the interpretation on the patient. I, too, have found that this approach was the most suitable to make progress in the analytic work (see chapter 6).

McDougall (1982a, 1989) points out that even if the analyst uses constant self-analysis, she cannot but feel disappointed when her affectionate attitude towards the "disaffected patient" does not provoke even the slightest emotional response. The verbal exchanges become a mere set of words with no value whatsoever and devoid of any emotional bond or real meaning. As a result, a vacuum is created in the emotional life of the analytic work. The analyst has the impression that her therapeutic efforts are totally ineffective, as is her emotional closeness. In interpersonal relationships, these patients reproduce a kind of relationship in which they use others more as an object to satisfy his needs than as a subject that is a source of desire.

McDougall (1972, 1982a) describes these patients, who are far removed from their own psychic reality, as if they were relegated to a prison where they find shelter from the feelings that threatened their integrity during a very early stage of life. They got rid of the excessive emotions that could not be integrated by dispersing them, and when they became adults they lived their life in concrete terms, with action replacing feeling. The removal of unbearable psychic experiences would seem to favour the phenomena of addiction (alcohol, smoking, food, sex) and explosions of psychosomatic symptoms.

A recurrent feature of the patients I describe was that they regarded persons as being actually interchangeable. Indeed, the patients admitted that, in both social and emotional relationships, one person was as good as another as long as they satisfied the patient's needs. In the relationship, the particular characteristics of the other person were not taken into account. This kind of addiction to people created problems in their emotional life, although their partners continued to remain attached because of their own dependency needs. Even in the transference, the interchangeable nature of people emerges and tends to distort the analyst's real nature.

In this connection, I remember that for some time Irene (chapter 8) underwent therapy with two different psychotherapists at the same time (each unaware of the existence of the other) without feeling guilty since she felt she would benefit more from two therapists rather than one. Quite by chance, the two therapists came to know of this situation that the patient considered quite normal and an expression of goodwill. As already experienced in the countertransference, the patient used the analyst without attributing to the relationship any particular uniqueness.

The patients I discuss were, like those described by McDougall, unable to have mental representations related to feelings or communicate their experiences and therefore brought to the analysis their bodily sensations or somatic symptoms in the absence of fantasies or dreams. Given the regular analytic setting and the constant emotional attention, the analyst will have to adapt himself to the patient's different levels of communication. Even communication through acting-out can have different meanings, and it is necessary not to mistake signs of omnipotence for signs of the initial capacity for action.

The countertransference responses will continually oscillate according to the various levels of transference expression. The analyst will have to perceive the position of the patient at any precise moment of the session or therapy and will respond accordingly, relying only on countertransference feelings. In certain cases, if the request for an extra session coincided with the countertransference feeling of psychic danger and with the need for immediate assistance, I felt I had to provide it so that the patient could see that it was possible to experience an empathic human response to his desperate cry for help. In those cases, the patient needed another mind to think when he was not able to do so. However, if I felt that in the countertransference the request was an attempt to manipulate me and not a desperate plea for help, I would merely postpone discussing the meaning of the request until next session.

When one is faced with acute persecution anxiety or feelings of annihilation near to psychic death, the patient's requests for help will mobilize our feelings of understanding and assistance. The degree of understanding and identification with the patient will certainly differ from one analyst to another and will be proportional to her specific involvement in a certain pathology and related to her personal experiences. In this connection, it seems interesting to point out what Godfrind (1993) has to say about the double transference in the analytic treatment of borderline patients, since there might be analogies with the patients described here, in the sense that they function on two different levels. In her search, to make therapeutic work possible with borderline patients, Godfrind underlines the symbolic functioning of the analyst, which provides the patient with something he can hold on to and identify with since he can use symbolic thought only in part. However, this symbolic functioning, which is based on working out the problems linked to otherness, can alternate with periods of temporary regression, even on the part of the analyst.

When the symbiotic core of the patient emerges, he comes into contact with the homologous counterpart of the analyst, which preserves similar archaic remains in the inner structure of her own identity. The part of the analyst wanting to enter into a non-conflictual union with the patient tends to respond in a non-symbolic way. During episodes of violent transference manifested through expressions of love, hate, or desperation, the analyst's archaic, narcissistic core is stimulated and can be driven towards symbiotic collusion or can determine responses that may be acted out by the analyst. This may happen, for example, when there is a temporary change in the setting. The analyst's actions are sometimes immediate and aim to allow the therapy to continue, with the hope of returning to symbolic functioning, which has been interrupted due to an emergency situation. The symbiotic collusion can represent a danger if the analyst does not regain her symbolic functioning, even though collusion can sometimes represent a necessary, if temporary, condition in order to overcome a stalemate.

In work with adult patients with autistic capsules and faced with acute anxiety attacks triggered by episodes of depersonalization and derealization, I have found it indispensable to provide this emotional understanding. I also found it useful to intervene immediately at a verbal level—even in a non-analytic way—and thus underline my interest and involvement, which could be urgently provided. In such cases, it is useful to reformulate thoughts that were expressed by the patient in a confused or incomprehensible way, to give a precise name to vague feelings, or to give some advice in the form of a question. The therapist might also offer some words of encouragement or hope or describe symptoms in a comprehensible way, thus providing some kind of temporary support.

In this connection, I would like to point out the importance of the use of the analyst's voice and language, which is analogous to that used by the mother with her baby. The mother talks to the newborn to express her empathy, her presence, to identify feelings and needs, to protect him from bothersome environmental stimuli, without expecting any response. She uses the sonority of her voice to underline doubts, questions, projected events, in a way different from how she communicates with other persons and in other situations. She creates the notion of a harmonious couple by transmitting the idea that she recognizes the child's early experiences and by trying to explain them to him.

The analyst's capacity for reverie, which is transmitted through this type of verbal intervention, contributes to building up the patient's inner structure. The intonation of the analyst's voice will transmit her feelings such as acceptance, hope or even firmness and the suggestion to change. Alvarez (1992) points out that reverie is not just maternal but is due to the introjection into the mother's mind of a good paternal object combined in a proper way with a maternal object. This is, however, a matter of some complexity. According to Benedetti (1980), in the face of the psychotic ego that is dissolving, the task of the psychotherapist is to stay with the patient in his symptoms before it is possible to interpret them:

> The psychotic symptom has a double dynamic meaning, a double function, and a double interpersonal aspect of communication and defence. ... The symptom wants to tell us something that the patient cannot express in any other way, and, if the symptom is the only possible means of communication, staying with the symptom is the only way to stay close without making it dissolve and without being rejected. ... Staying in the symptoms, listening to them, and answering them means experiencing feelings and emotions with the patient who can only express himself through them. [pp. 171–173, translated by L.T. for this edition]

With her psychotic part, Ambra (chapter 9) wanted to prevail over me and drive me mad with her lies and her delusional ideas. With the autistic part, she remained frozen and inexpressive, completely detached. At the moment, I felt some emotional and intellectual void that she projected onto me.

The only countertransference feeling was one of extreme unease, which could only be eased by making some slight allusions to the desperation and solitude she had experienced as a child. These authentic forms of communication, which represented a crack in the autistic core, were sufficient to represent a spark of warmth in our exchanges and allowed me to create a warmer atmosphere in which we could relate, as well as some feeling of empathy. That was the time to intervene with what Alvarez (1992) calls "reclamation".

Because of the persistence of these alternating feelings, a long period of containment was required with no interpretations given before I could give her back the concept I had formulated regarding her suffering, since at the beginning she had been unable to understand my participation and my thoughts. However, even containment was difficult, because it mainly concerned aggressive and violent feelings, which were sometimes acted out against me and against everything in the analyst's room.

In his work on schizophrenia, Searles (1965) points out that in the phase of the therapy characterized by absence of contact, the analyst experiences a sense of non-involvement and alienation. He suggests the analyst maintain a calm attitude, demonstrating a personal, scientific and human interest in the patient, whose psychotic symptoms hold the key to his individuality.

Re-introjecting the projected and lost parts requires an ego that can function and introject. Communicating by giving back feelings experienced by the analyst can make the patient understand something he was unaware even existed before, since he had got rid of it. It would be a mistake to carry out this operation too soon, and untimely attempts to send back the projected feelings are immediately evident. As Herbert Rosenfeld (1987) suggests, the patient's projections have to be contained over a certain period of time and the analyst has to support her confusion and anxieties without giving back her replies too soon.

Another disquieting feature of sessions was the questioning gaze of some patients who were trying to find meanings within me but without knowing exactly what they were. What question were they asking me? Were they trying to find the identifications that they had avoided by withdrawing into their autistic core at an early age? What could my countertransference feeling be, faced with the patient's emotional void? Resnik (1972) has often pointed out that the analyst must tolerate his own ambiguity and uncertainty. He considers the analytic situation an adventure in which the analyst must let herself go, while never forgetting the responsible role she has to play.

In the analytic relationship with patients suffering from psychosomatic disorders, we must not forget the presence of the bodies of the two participants, which unwittingly communicate meanings that go beyond words. How is it possible to reply to these bodily messages through the countertransference? Somatic symptoms need to be tolerated for a long time because of the primitive level of the communication before the analyst can finally identify and interpret the sources of anxiety in a symbolic way. Children can kick and shove; they can remain passive and not move, or they can be incontinent; they can attack the objects in a room in a much more impulsive way than adults. Some adults use body language to communicate, or they only talk about bodily symptoms, so that the body becomes the principal interlocutor. The analyst, too, may use body language, by falling asleep or getting a stomach-ache when the inner meeting between transference and countertransference is blocked and cannot lead to the elaboration of a symbolic communication ("the block of the inner traffic": Resnik, 1999b).

This way of talking with the body or about the body signifies very primitive levels of communication. The infant makes his requests known or expresses his needs only through body language. For example, he can tell that the breast is near through his sense of smell before the sense of sight.

Ambra (chapter 9) used to put on a different perfume every day and expected me to guess the mood she was in according to the perfume she had on. Each perfume and its name were supposed to convey the feelings she had.

In this way she was actually forcing me to get close to her through the smell of the perfume, which I obviously could not escape. At the same time, however, she communicated hidden, regressive needs that were very primitive.

The development of the therapy and our own countertransference will show us the meaning of what the patient wants to communicate at a particular moment, and this will allow us to formulate an answer.

Although it might seem impossible to encode this approach as it might appear too individualistic, in my opinion it is the only approach that allows the therapist to be continually close to the patient's emotional communication and continue the analysis. The analyst must always remain in touch with her own fundamental questions and regressive areas of her own infantile ego which she utilizes in the work.

The fact that for many years such patients refuse to listen to others prevented them from learning. If it is possible to modify this apathy, information can reach the patient and change is possible. This gradual change is of great value to the therapist, since it represents a sign of improvement or trust and therefore strengthens the emotional bond, which paves the way for further development.

When we work with patients who present more or less extensive autistic parts, it is impossible to maintain the neutral position prescribed by classic analytic technique. Working with this kind of patient determines a situation of a real and primitive contact between two living human beings in which the analyst must shed her enigmatic or intellectual role and experience the vicissitudes of a relationship in which the fundamental instrument is her humanity, characterized by a vast gamut of feelings. We perceive a part that is delicate and suffering, hidden behind a harsh exterior, that requires particular attention until it can finally express itself in a symbolic way.

If we want to help these patients, we have to understand and deal with our own despairing parts that are similar to theirs. Coming into contact with these more regressive patients, we can find ourselves in a confusing, unknown region, with no hope of finding a way out. When we reflect on our own state of mind, we often experience feelings of solitude, inertia, and absence of meaning and fantasy. Remaining permanently in this region makes us understand the primitive nature of the autistic defence and the kind of solitude these patients experience, with no imagination, because we come into contact with the regressive, asymbolic, and narcissistic cores that are buried in our own personality. The analyst must therefore have a solid idea of her own identity so that she can remain in this pre-symbolic region as long as necessary and experience the confusion and lack of understanding. One comes into contact with the truer parts of the self while waiting to take up the process of elaboration.

One of the biggest problems I had working out the countertransference was related to the capacity to limit, fix, and memorize emotional states of mind in order to give them meaning. Although these emotional impressions brought about by the patients' projections represented my spontaneous, immediate response to the transference, they remained vague, quickly disappeared, and were replaced with more rational thoughts. I wondered whether these flashes represented rapid and sudden recollections of my own archaic experiences that corresponded to those of the patients, and whether, in this way, I was coming into contact with my most authentic and primitive experiences that had preceded my capacity for elaboration and symbolization. Only during discussions with colleagues and supervisors was I able to recover these impressions.

Bollas (1987) says that by working on the countertransference, the analyst can, in a certain sense, discover that he is ill. Therefore, treating our own illness becomes important so that we will be capable of treating the damaged parts of the patient, and by treating ourselves we can deal with the transference of the patient. If we connect our inner processes with the painful experiences of the patient, we can attempt a process of elaboration in ourselves that can be transferred to the other.

In the process of identification with the regressive parts of the patient, we are faced with a dilemma represented by the ambivalence of the requests from the patient's archaic part. On the one hand, he expresses the need for a symbiotic bond that allows him to experience a protective relationship, yet, on the other, he rejects otherness and even denies its existence. Again, on the one hand, he expresses the need to merge in an ideal union with the therapist, yet, on the other, he maintains his need to isolate himself, though this does not mean true separateness. The patient presents himself as being fragile but protects himself behind a strong armour.

The patient's needs for fusion may make the analyst attempt to satisfy them by offering him a model of similarity. This model might, however, reassure the patient but also reinforce his adherence to the analyst even more. For example, if the patient wants the analyst to accept him unconditionally, the analyst might feel obliged to comply with this request since she wants to offer understanding and facilitate the relationship. For the analyst, however, there is a danger in accepting all these requests for symbiotic fusion for too long or too intensely, since she is afraid of appearing as someone who rejects the patient or frustrates the patient's attempts to get emotionally close.

The autistic part stirs up in the analyst fantasies of having to represent either a good mother who accepts everything or an analyst who is profoundly empathic. In this way, she can be tempted to react in a special way to the patient's request and therefore emotionally collude with his pathology, thus hindering the process of differentiation. It is therefore necessary to be careful to register and analyse one's own feelings of irritation or anger in the countertransference related to the sadistic attacks of the patient.

It must be borne in mind that the symbiotic period of these therapies last a long time because the patient regards differentiation as a danger, since he fears separateness, which feels to him like expulsion. Losing the analyst can cause him to experience fear and panic due to his fantasy of wanting to control and possess the object. However, we must not forget that in this case, as I have already indicated, fantasies in these areas of omnipotence seemed to mask early feelings of annihilation.

With patients who remain blocked for a long time with no real contact, the therapist experiences oscillation between feelings of deep frustration and the desire for contact. She might be convinced that these cases cannot be treated, her self-esteem might diminish, and she might question the efficacy of the analytic method. She might become aggressive due to the constant refusal that might make her act and thus modify the picture, or she might give too many interpretations to explain the resistance of the patient.

Faced with the underlying presence of these hidden archaic parts and the obstacles they represent in the analytic process, one can wonder what hope the analyst has in continuing the relationship and how this is related to the commitment she has made. Both the obsessions and an apparently inability to think tend to make the analyst less confident in the usefulness of her work.

Although the patient wants to experience relatedness, at the same time he wants to remain detached and to preserve his state of isolation. He continues the analysis so that he can feel more protected and secure, but he has no intention of getting to the root of his problems. He only wants to be accepted and to get rid of his unpleasant symptoms. For a long time, he has difficulty introjecting the analyst's messages but finds it interesting to observe the effects his words have on the analyst's mind.

With many patients, the difficulty of bringing about changes is tied to the difficulty of separating from one's own childhood and so continuing to be chronically shaped by primitive defence mechanisms. In order to continue her work, as I have previously emphasized, the analyst will be greatly helped by self-analysis and supervision so as to avoid excessive identification with the patient's archaic parts and to discover her own unconscious defensive needs and therefore the blind spots in the relationship.

Bollas (1987) thinks that, in the relationship, the analyst should consider herself as the second patient and give room to her interior mental processes in order to be helped in understanding the patient. It is not always clear whether what we feel is due to the position in which the patient wants to put us or if it has always belonged to us. According to Bollas, this uncertainty gives us a sense of humility and responsibility in carrying out the analytic work.

In the long relationship with Elisa (chapter 7), I continually asked myself this kind of question. Elisa only considered me in my professional role as analyst and saw me as a cold, inhuman presence despite my intense participation in her crises of anguish and my keen interest in her as a patient. I often wondered whether she really felt that way about me by reproducing in the transference her relationship with her mother or whether she regarded me as unfeeling and cold by projecting into me her own coldness and rejection. However, I also wondered whether I was the one who had an armour made of hardness or professional coldness (of which I was unaware) and therefore was unable to express my warm feelings and maintained a distance between us.

Bollas suggests that in some cases the analyst should use her own subjective states, though in a very limited and careful way, in order to help the patient discover his own feelings. During certain periods of impasse, due to the autistic block, this attempt might be opportune since it demonstrates our empathy and produces an analogous emotional involvement on the part of the patient.

Conclusions

The countertransference is the indispensable compass that the analyst uses in his therapeutic voyage with the patient. The countertransference monitors the signs of change in the emotional atmosphere of the sessions and in the transference. Bursts of laughter, exclamations of surprise, or changes in the way of communicating can signal the beginning of a feeling of sympathy or the liberation of certain emotions that allow the patient to emerge from his autistic condition. In an analogous way, however, if the interpretation is mistaken, awkward, or untimely, the analyst in her countertransference immediately recognizes the patient's block or retreat.

In short, therapies with this kind of patient are characterized by the absence of emotional contact in the countertransference, attachment to the therapy and not to the therapist, and the presence of repetitive rituals and easy actings-out, resulting in extremely slow progress. This, in itself, leads to a chronic pathological situation. If the analyst, together with the patient, manages to recognize and work out the autistic part, the work of interpretation can subsequently proceed since the emotional relationship will be warmer.

CHAPTER FIVE

Working with adult patients with autistic capsules: obstacles to treatment

"When I was a child I learned to write in a mechanical way, just copying words. Only now, however, do I understand that my writing is like a sign that I exist. I used to read words without understanding the real meaning of the sentences. It made it so difficult for me to study." *Irene*

The duration of the psychotherapeutic treatments of the patients I describe was frequently extended due to many external factors (interruptions, illness, etc.) and to difficulties in the analytic work because of a certain deadness in the emotional communication between therapist and patient.

Sidney Klein (1980) points out that in these cases, since it is impossible to contact one part of the patient, which is unknown to both patient and analyst, the analysis fails to bring about any significant change. The social situation and the intellectual activities of the patients made it difficult for the analyst to imagine that such regressive parts existed. However, in the cases described here, the request for analysis was motivated by acute symptoms such as depression, crises of depersonalization or derealization, psychosomatic diseases, or psychotic episodes. The main topic of discussion was the patient's description of her or his symptoms.

I shall now attempt to analyse the reasons behind the impasse that arose frequently in my clinical experience.

Lack of emotional communication

The most obvious obstacle in such analysis (which is, at the same time, the diagnostic tool used to recognize autistic capsules) is represented by the lack of emotional communication in the analytic relationship.

This aspect of the transference, which is evident and more pronounced in infantile autism, has also been described by McDougall (1989) in disaffected and psychosomatic adult patients and by Steiner (1993). (See also chapters 1 and 4.)

In patients with autistic capsules, the therapeutic relationship is experienced not as a way to get close to another living and thinking being, but as a way to obtain a concrete support that must never be given up. In this situation, the patient only considers the superficial aspects of the other person and cannot consider either the personal ways of thinking or the differences that would comprise signs of differentiation and separation. This position recalls Bick's (1964, 1968, 1986) and Meltzer's (Meltzer et al., 1975) concept of adhesive identification, as well as Resnik's (1986) concept of expansion in autism. As I have already said, Meltzer points out that such defensive adherence to the object is intended to alleviate the anguish of disintegration.

Although the patients feel unable to leave the therapy, they do not trust the therapist, they remain aloof, and they are always on the lookout for expressions of hostility towards them. Although these patients never miss the opportunity to express their disappointment regarding the psychoanalytic method adopted, they never miss a session. In this situation of superficial and adhesive contact, accompanied by the refusal to establish a therapeutic alliance of which the patient is not conscious, the analyst becomes confused and may experience contradictory emotions.

In adhesive identification, there is no exchange with the object, since the analyst is considered to be merely the outward appearance of a person without depth and with no possibility of containment. Since both the analyst and the patient might not have a receptive space within themselves, the movements of introjection or projection cannot occur.

Ogden (1989), however, admits that:

psychological change can result from experience with external objects in an autistic-contiguous mode; such change is mediated in part by the process of imitation. In autistic-contiguous forms of imitation, the individual experiences a change in the shape of his surface as a result of the influence of his relations with external objects. . . . [pp. 73–74]

Ogden adds that the idea of internalization is linked to the notion of conscious and unconscious fantasies about taking parts of all of another person into oneself. Imitation might be the only available means to hold onto parts of the other (Gaddini, 1969).

In the autistic model, in which the terror of disintegration and loss of pieces of the self dominate in the inner psychic world, the adherence to the surface appearances of the other may seem reassuring. In the case of mimesis, the hidden parts of the self are not masked as in the case of the personality with "a false self"; instead, the person presents himself only as a surface, and imitation is an attempt to make the surface cohesive so that a self may be constructed.

Ambra (chapter 9), once she had emerged from the most serious phase of confusion, began dressing and combing her hair like me. She even dyed her hair the same colour as mine. She tried to discover what make-up I used so that she could imitate me and was convinced that I would feel gratified by her attempts to model herself on me.

She regarded the language of surface appearance as the most important, but her actions irritated me since I felt that in our relationship she was trying to rob me of that part of myself that was a living, thinking being, completely different from her.

At first, I did not realize that it was the only way that Ambra could establish any kind of contact with me, and that it could be the first step towards the beginning of a human relationship. I subsequently realized that I had felt irritated because I was especially discouraged by the adhesive situation, which made it impossible to achieve a projective identification that would allow the patient to develop.

Use of language

Another misleading factor—which might be a hurdle rather than a help—is illustrated through the use of language in such cases. Verbal communication, while it may be formally constructed, is often repetitive, mechanical, and rigid; rather than being a means of communication, it serves as a protective shell that can only be modified with difficulty. In one case, in which the cognitive deficit masked the autistic part, talking was characterized by fragmentation and lack of logical links between sentences and words, demonstrating the absence of symbolization.

In the early years of life, the acquisition of complete language is accompanied by a parallel process of differentiation, when the child can distinguish between "I" and "you" and the related grammatical structure is linked to the capacity for interpersonal and intrapsychic communication (Resnik, 1972). The grammatical structure may be poor, as may be the syntax, which points to a confusion at the level of the ego ("inability to communicate with oneself and the other": Resnik, 1972).

In my patients, talking throughout the session sometimes served either to relieve feelings of tension or excitement, to keep alive past traumatic experiences, or to talk about things the patient invented or distorted. The discourse seemed not a wish to communicate and be understood, but an attempt to invade and paralyse the mind of the analyst. No emotional link was thus established that would make it possible for the content to give rise to interpretations. The patient used words as hooks to feel linked to the analyst.

As Sidney Klein (1980) commented, the patient's words are simply used to establish a bond with the analyst, rather than to communicate. Resnik (1999b) asserted that "talking and communicating are not the same thing. Communicating means putting things together, establishing a relationship with the other, dramatizing a message and implies the existence of a subject and an object" (p. 90).

Although my patients for the most part had a lot to say, I often realized that what they said did not really communicate anything but was merely a list of memories or facts. Much more significant were the sensory aspects of what they said—the rhythm of the words, the tone of voice, the sound patterns, and the intention behind their verbal communication.

During the early phase of his therapy, in which autistic defences prevailed, Renzo (chapter 10) did not talk for months. He would sometimes utter short phrases with an imperative tone. If something did not coincide with what he wanted, his silence became a way of expressing his aggressiveness and refusal.

According to Resnik (1999b), the silence of autistic patients may convey a sense of emptiness, but this might be an emptiness full of meanings.

Even in the case of Renzo, this emptiness was so full of chaotic and painful thoughts that he had to deny their existence.

When he spoke, he used neologisms since he wanted to invent new words to represent private "shapes" that could not be shared with others. This, in fact, created a further barrier to communication.

According to Tustin (1980), bizarre words take the place of autistic objects and represent an autistic barrier.

When Renzo was about 10 years old, he began to communicate more directly in the sessions. He organized a game similar to a treasure hunt. He would write little cards indicating, "go right" or "go left". The words, however, merely repeated sounds he had heard and did not correspond to the usual concepts of right or left. This obviously led to some confusion when playing the game since the other player's concept of right and left did not "coincide" with his. This would cause him to fly into a rage because he felt misunderstood, and this in turn heightened his persecutory fears.

When he was an adolescent, his range of vocabulary widened and his syntax improved. When he spoke, he spilled out his words uncontrollably and would become sexually aroused. On these occasions, it was necessary to understand not only what he wanted to say, but the sensory signifi-cance and impact on the analytic relationship within the context of the session.

A most significant element of language is represented by the tone of voice, the sound pattern, the pauses that transmit the intention of the speaker. Adult patients with autistic capsules express themselves through the senses rather than through the intellect. Emotional signifi-cance must therefore be perceived more through hearing the tone than through intellectual understanding of the content. Communication occurs primarily at the level of the senses and thus can give us an indication of the patient's most primitive mental states.

Studies on prenatal auditory experiences of the foetus suggest that primitive mental states are linked to sounds and rhythms produced by the biological functions of the maternal body. In particular, perceiv-ing/sensing the mother's heartbeat might represent the auditory basis of the experience of rhythm and discontinuity, thus determining a primitive differentiation between presence and absence and a feeling of security since the pattern is always the same. Unlike these kinds of sounds, the maternal voice introduces a different sound, which is different from the biological rhythms of the auditory world of the foetus. The voice is unpredictable and variable due to the emotions. The quality and musicality of the maternal voice represent an early sensory basis of interpersonal relationship, which indicates presence and absence (Maiello, 1995) (see chapter 2).

For years, Elisa (chapter 7) talked incessantly, describing real facts or obsessively ruminating over the same things but with no emotional communication. Her words were like objects stuffed into a suitcase, only to be taken out and thrown away during the sessions (Rustin, Rhode, Dubinsky, & Dubinsky, 1997). Psychotherapy merely seemed to provide a setting in which someone would listen, accept, and contain her.

Elisa would tell me her boring stories in a loud voice, never pausing or allowing me to interrupt her. She spoke in a high-pitched voice so that I would listen and remember her words. Only towards the end of the analysis, when she no longer felt she had to control and prevail over me, did the tone of her voice become gentler and more modulated.

* * *

In a different way, Ambra (chapter 9) for a long time used the sessions to give vent to her rage and violent feelings or to make up crazy stories using a loud voice. Only when she abandoned the psychotic symptoms did she become as silent and detached as an autistic child.

At that point, she sat there wordless, her face devoid of all expression. Just looking at her made me experience the same: no thoughts, no feelings, no hope. All her previous outpourings that had filled the sessions proved to be a superficial armour made up of words stuck together "agglutinated" or unexpressed thoughts that instead of communicating something in the normal way were meant to confuse the listener even more.

During her more psychotic fits, Ambra would shout with rage and start screaming violently; during her fits of hysteria her voice became shrill and high-pitched until she lost it completely.

* * *

Irene (chapter 8) used words only to recount real facts or ask questions and would sometimes mispronounce or invent new words. She had created words that were halfway between language and dialect, which was the way her parents communicated. Irene used a "stupid" sing-song voice that engulfed the listener and made me drowsy; she had a childish tone of voice, which indicated her desire to regress. The musical intonation of her voice was the same as the tone of voice of the mother from whom she could not differentiate herself, and it evoked images of ingenuousness and frailty. This sing-song way of speaking seemed to envelop the patient like a protective armour that did not let the emotional part show through, because she had no intention of communicating.

When the analyst comes into contact with archaic areas, she must therefore consider the auditory meaning of communication. If, during the sessions, communication occurs mainly through the senses, it might make the analyst experience bodily sensations such as stomach-ache, migraine, drowsiness, joint cramps, or various superficial sensations such as pruritus. These phenomena demonstrate that the analyst is completely receptive to the messages the patient sends out. Only subsequently can these messages be interpreted in terms of symbolization by observing the transference–countertransference correlation.

Absence of dreams and imagination

The absence of dreams and imagination makes analytic work more monotonous because of the absence of elements other than those that are obsessively repeated. Dream life activity is disparaged, because it is not concrete and it is impossible to connect dreams with the process of symbolization.

In some cases, it was necessary to wait for a long time before there were dreams; in other cases, the dream stories were an obvious mass of confabulations and therefore produced confusion rather than a wealth of material. Sometimes dreams were not told, due to the fear of revealing secret feelings or impulses.

Body language

The existence of autistic capsules bears witness to the persistence of pre-symbolic states in which sensory experiences prevailed. Body language thus takes on a significance that replaces more symbolic avenues of analytic communication. The semiotics of movements, gestures, and the spontaneous production of sounds represent an important part of the therapeutic approach. It is a matter of deciphering bodily messages and connecting them with the verbal ones in order to understand the unconscious meaning of the communication.

Renzo (chapter 10) would avoid my gaze by closing his eyes; on those rare occasions when he did open them, it was only to observe and control the outside environment.

He had a heavy, passive body and expressionless face and slept during the session. His sound sleep may have meant that he could relax in a safe place or that in the session he felt wrapped up and contained in a second skin (Ogden, 1989). Once he emerged from the initial phase of complete closure, his face would express anger when he felt I didn't understand him or failed to fulfil his unexpressed desires, or he would adopt a comic mask. Acting like a clown and making jokes was the only way he could relate to other people, by making them laugh and entertaining them. This phase lasted a long time and gave way to a more natural form of communication only after many years of therapy. It was then that I was able to explain to him that his comic mask served to hide his violent and sadistic feelings.

* * *

Elisa (chapter 7) had regular features but a serious, fixed expression. She walked in a rather mechanical way, like a soldier, and always seemed in a rush. Her face betrayed no emotion. She expressed her aggression by actings-out such as arriving late or asking to change her appointments. Towards the end of the analysis, she would smile when she arrived and modulated her voice so that it was gentler. Elisa's harsh gaze initially made it impossible to get emotionally close to her and gave the impression that she wanted to keep her distance so as not to create an emotional bond.

* * *

I found Ambra's face (chapter 9) quite enigmatic. For a long time, she would put on a different "mask" every day by changing the colour of her hair and her hairstyle, make-up, and clothes. She would sometimes dress casually, other times quite elegantly, or she would transform herself into a vamp or, more tragically, into a child.

After this phase ended and she stopped hiding behind the different masks, her real face finally appeared. It was, however, expressionless and disturbing since it was devoid of all emotion and meaning. At times she would gaze at me with a questioning look on her face or with a look of defiance, but there was never any sign of understanding or alliance. This situation of emptiness and lack of human feelings coincided with the disappearance of verbal communication.

Ambra's gaze seemed expressionless. When our eyes met, I often won-
dered who she really was, whether she was a beautiful or a disturbing
presence, in which I was unable to detect the slightest trace of feeling or
meanings that would allow me to make some kind of contact with her. She
was only able to express her aggression and violent feelings in a high-
pitched voice, but her face remained impassive.

* * *

Irene (chapter 8) had beautiful, expressionless eyes, which she would keep
wide open as if to understand better what her mind was unable to grasp.
Her face was immobile except during anxiety attacks, when it expressed
fear. It gave no sign that she understood what the person was saying or
what was happening around her.

I was astonished when, towards the end of the analysis, her face became
expressive and pleasant; her smile revealed how glad she was to be with
me, while occasional tears were finally an expression of experiencing and
recognizing her emotions.

The emotional atmosphere of the sessions

If we consider the place and time of the session as what Baranger and
Baranger (1969, 1990) refer to as an "operating space" where the experiences, emotions, and thoughts of the two participants emerge and
intertwine, the result is that every therapeutic relationship occurs in a
particular atmosphere. The emotional atmosphere (climate) of the sessions becomes an important element that must be considered.

When we are there daydreaming over the next session with the
patient, our expectation is pervaded with the emotional quality of the
previous one. In patients with autistic parts, the emotional climate of
the sessions is characterized more by the monotonous repetition of
physical symptoms or obsessive thoughts than by emotional communication of the patient's inner conflicts. This is also true of psychosomatic patients who endlessly describe the same physical symptoms in
great detail. Therefore, the climate of the session is cold, the landscape
is grey and static with no movement.

At other times, the patient might be overwhelmed by great anguish
linked to the idea of dissolution of the self, falling into boundless
space, or not existing. This was borne out by the symptoms of depersonalization or derealization with sensations of imminent dissolution
or falling infinitely (Bick, 1968; D. Rosenfeld, 1984; Tustin, 1981b, 1986;

Winnicott, 1974). Other manifestations of anguish during the sessions were linked to bodily sensations. Due to the permanent autistic state, the subject is restricted to a closed system of bodily sensations that precludes symbolization (Ogden, 1989). Under such conditions, the analyst experiences alternating emotional states that are difficult to deal with and range from boredom to a state of alert attention.

Elisa (chapter 7) was continually preoccupied with her vital functions and had delirious thoughts that she would suddenly die.

When she lay down on the analyst's couch, her breathing was loud and noisy. She became convinced that it was a symptom of bronchial occlusion (cancer suspicion) and had some medical tests done. She refused to accept the idea that the way she breathed merely expressed the relief she felt at finding herself in a protective environment where she could relax and abandon her normal hyperactivity.

Since Elisa could not connect sensations or bodily acts to feelings, she was unable to attribute symbolic significance to bodily signs. She was so terrorized by normal bodily functions that she would refuse to accept or block some natural functions and even the existence of the body itself.

* * *

Ambra (chapter 9) suffered from tactile hallucinations regarding her whole body or the inner mucous membrane of her mouth or vagina. When she listened to me, Ambra experienced strange sensations in her head or felt that the limits of her body surface were endangered by the presence of external persecutors.

* * *

When Irene (chapter 8) felt irritated, she often suffered from migraines or such serious waves of nausea that she had to interrupt the session. The physical symptoms prevailed over any other kind of communication and forced us to only consider real bodily situation.

Obsessive rituals
and "autistic objects of the mind"

A further obstacle to analytic work is represented by obsessive rituals and repetitive autistic thoughts that I call "autistic objects of the mind", especially regarding the past. The repetition of this kind of behaviour lasts a long time because it represents a defence against primitive anguish and corresponds to behavioural rituals and echolalia in infantile autism. Those who study infantile autism interpret this behaviour in different ways: it might represent an initial defence against anxiety or depression. Once initiated, this behaviour takes on the characteristics of addictive behaviour and, as such, wields great power in the relationship with others.

Unlike neurotic patients, who are disturbed by obsessive rituals, autistic children enjoy their rituals and seem to take pleasure in them. These children take no pleasure in communicating or interacting with others or feeling loved and protected. The rituals might be used to make them feel less isolated, or they might become a friend they can control. Moreover, although these rituals have no rational explanation, they sometimes take on perverse meanings and are used as a means to irritate or challenge the other person.

Meltzer (Meltzer et al., 1975) believes that the repetitive behaviour of autism is the result of "a process of fragmentation of the sensory apparatus into its components". Ogden (1989) thinks that the autistic-contiguous mode is an important dimension of the obsessive–compulsive defences. He believes that

> this form of defence regularly serves to plug sensorially experienced holes in the individual's sense of self through which the patient fears and feels (in the most concrete sensory way) that not only ideas, but actual bodily contents, will leak. Obsessive–compulsive symptoms and defences have their origins in the infant's earliest efforts at ordering and creating a sense of boundedness for his sensory experience. [p. 67]

As already mentioned in chapter 1, Tustin (1980) believes that rituals have a protective function and that the obsessive use of autistic objects, devoid of symbolic meaning, are a substitute for human relationships. Alvarez and Reid (1999) believe that obsessive handling of objects, in the sense of adhesive attachment, makes them feel safe (adhesive identification).

Alvarez (1999) differentiates between the different functions of the autistic child's rituals: they can fill the sense of emptiness and uneasiness or represent the only thing the child can do. They can sometimes be used to reduce the level of inner excitement, and, in this case, they are an attempt to keep and elaborate anguish. At other times, they can represent a means of consoling oneself or the pleasure of masturbation. Because they are so persistent, they can represent a provocation towards the outside world. When the patient improves in the therapy, the rituals may change, become more vital, and take on meanings that are different from the primitive ones.

Alvarez remarks that when faced with the autistic child's repetitive rituals, the analyst experiences not only the quality of the obsessive repetitions but also some disturbing qualities attached to these rituals. The repetitive actions or words can make the analyst stop thinking and remain glued to fixed ideas. This is a danger in the countertransference. The analyst must therefore handle obsessive manifestations with the utmost care, since they represent early defences and are an integral part of the personality.

Even in adult patients with autistic capsules, rituals and obsessive repetitions create serious problems in the countertransference because these obsessive mental activities are set up to avoid separation and are a substitute for imagination, fantasy, and metaphors. Only when emotional exchanges are established can the analyst intervene and work together with the patient to find the origin of the rituals and to underline the countertransference effect of boredom or irritation.

During the first period of therapy when he was 10 years old, in addition to the initial lack of verbal communication, Renzo (chapter 10) continued to perform his rituals at the beginning and end of the sessions. He had to draw or open the curtains carefully, switch the light on or off, ask how much time was left halfway through the session, at a certain time prepare to get ready to leave. He would also repeatedly untie his shoelaces only to tie them again, and so on. Later on he used the drawing paper in a compulsive way, covering the sheets with scribbles or obsessively repeating the same sequences of a game. During this phase, no interpretation was possible and I could only be a spectator.

During the second part of the therapy, when he was a young man, new rituals appeared, including blowing his nose, coughing, sitting down and getting up, putting on and taking off his pullover, and other movements. All these bodily movements were exaggerated and flaunted in order to annoy me. It was evident, however, that these rituals were different and were designed to send messages to the other. They differed from the rituals of autistic children, who use them as an armour to isolate themselves. Up to that time, I had tried in vain to make him stop his repetitive rituals.

Subsequently, the rituals became less marked, and I was able to observe and interpret their unconscious meaning to Renzo since he no longer reacted in an aggressive way. At this point, Renzo was able to talk about these rituals and try to work out their meaning. He eventually abandoned them and began to assume responsibility for his actions.

When he became an adult, he used to enter the room and place on my desk his wallet, cell phone, and gloves on top of my diary or personal belongings so that I could not get to them freely.

This indicated, on the one hand, that he wanted to be near me but in a contiguous, sensory way (with sexual overtones) and, on the other, that he wanted to control me in an authoritative and possessive way. When he was able to accept my interpretation, the behaviour disappeared. He finally learned to express his feelings in the transference, but the communication still occurred through contiguous sensations expressed through our personal belongings, until by repeated interpretations he could let go of the behaviour.

* * *

For a long time, Elisa (chapter 7) initially manifested an obsessive ideation that was limited to certain areas, and she would spend a good part of the session talking about them. Many of these thoughts were secret and involved the continual repetition of numbers and calculations even when she was busy doing other things or studying. Other fixed thoughts were linked to her mania for horoscopes and predicting events. This not only prevented Elisa from creating an independent future of her own but was also a way of disparaging the analytic work.

The obsessive repetition of certain concepts or ideas, which came from her or her family, had the significance of "mental autistic objects". They served to assuage her fear of fragmentation and the fragility of the self and originated in her childhood. Even as a child, this secret psychic part served to console her and gave her the impression that she had a psychic life. It was like telling herself an interminable story, which she would repeat during the sessions. Despite a conflictual situation, she inherited these concepts from her family, and, in my opinion, they were preserved like concrete pieces representing the mother instead of an emotional relationship. The obsessive repetition of numbers represented an alternative to the transference relationship; when problems arose between us, the number reappeared and represented harmless and obedient friends. With the same meaning she made repetitive obsessive movements.

Elisa had a type of behaviour that was similar to the rumination of thoughts and sensations. She limited the analytic process to a controlled

*and controlling production in which she used her own thoughts to nour-
ish herself, blotting out my presence.*

These continual repetitions bring to mind "rumination" or
"merycism", which is a serious symptom in autistic infants who regur-
gitate partly digested food and then swallow it again, showing a condition of ecstasy (Gaddini & Gaddini, 1959). This symptom has been
interpreted as the infant's negation of the rudimentary awareness of
otherness. In this way, he seemingly attributes to himself the act of
nutrition and then engages in a close auto-sensory cycle of creating his
food (autistic shapes that act as a substitute for the mother). This paves
the way for an objectless self-sufficiency (Ogden, 1989).

Acting-out or acting-in

Attention must also be given to a disturbing condition of the transference in these adult patients as well as in children—namely, actings-out
or actings-in. They are part of an automatic means of expression that
short-circuits symbolic elaboration. As such, these patients evade the
formal analytic framework and impose a different means of communication, replacing thoughts with action. What always remains is an
inclination to express desires, emotions, and conflicts by means of
action rather than words.

If, on the one hand, the acting-in or acting-out can represent a
transgression of thought, on the other, the purpose is also to send the
analyst messages. Their origin is tied to experiences linked to the body,
and it must not be forgotten that the motor messages in the early
mother–child relationship represent the most direct vehicle to carry
messages as a precursor of projective identification. This primitive
exchange between mother and child will constitute the premise for the
process of symbolization. If we consider that in the preverbal period,
the baby's movements and the mother's motor responses play a very
important role in their relationship in place of language, we can say
that in the therapeutic relationship, the acting-out behaviour serves as
a vehicle of communication.

The patient finds it difficult to recognize that his motor manifestations have symbolic meaning, and this shows that he is resistant to
leaving his autistic condition. However, instead of continuing to interpret these manifestations as a form of resistance, it is more useful to
view them as nonverbal material that repeats old, unconscious sce-

narios in the transference. The behaviour sometimes contains a wealth of condensed meanings, even though it bears witness to an infantile aspect of omnipotence. Interpreting the meaning of the behaviour varies according to the context of the analytic relationship and the kind of action: from an action-discharge to the acting out of complicated scenarios, from actings-out to actings-in. The analyst's monitoring of her own countertransference reaction can help her understand the unconscious meaning of the behaviour.

If we consider the existence of a partial autistic state in the patient and his difficulty in reaching a depressive state, which is a necessary factor in developing the process of symbolization, we would consider these phenomena in a different way. We must bear in mind that the patient struggles to avoid reaching symbolic understanding, because he wants to protect himself against the realization that he does have an inner world and this would imply too much suffering. This does not mean that during the course of these therapies we must accept the behaviour as a normal means of expression, but it can be seen as expressive material while the analyst waits for the patient to reach a more integrated degree of mental functioning.

When he was a child, Renzo (chapter 10) wanted to act out physically on my body. For example, he would dig into me with his elbow as he closed a drawer, and if I asked for explanations he would become irritated, deny everything, and accuse me of making it all up. Or he would say I was the one who started it, projectively identifying me as the initiator of the behaviour.

In this case, it was an action rather than an acting-out. It could be interpreted in different ways: it might be the recognition that a relationship existed; or he could imagine a physical contact full of feelings, which had been lacking in his life. Or it could be an attempt to transmit the only type of relationship he had experienced so that I also could enter into his unconscious scenario and understand him. Or it could be a way to get rid of his rage by provoking it in me.

When he became an adult, Renzo's behaviour had a different degree of symbolization. At the end of the month he would hand me a post-dated cheque so that he could earn a few more days of interest on his current account. At this point, the acting-out had a more complex meaning that could be interpreted and discussed.

* * *

When Elisa (chapter 7) had transference problems she returned to her addictive behaviour and began drinking a little more than usual. She realized, however, that such behaviour was a substitute for thoughts that emerged during the analysis concerning separation and differentiation which made her take refuge in sleep and return to her passive state.

Another habitual obsessive behaviour was being continually late for her appointments. Although she would give a million different excuses, in my opinion the reason was quite obvious: the session became much shorter and then it was difficult to end.

On the one hand, the rituals demonstrated her need to keep her omnipotent power of control and, contrary to not coming at all, indicated the ambiguity of the transference. On the other hand, there was the desire to emphasize the situation of having someone wait for her, projecting into me the desire to see her. (What was always present was the suffering she had experienced as a child because of lack of affection). Coming to the sessions meant accepting being dependent, whereas the systematic lateness meant not being able to adapt to the analyst's schedule. The interpretation of her defence did not modify her behaviour but, rather, represented a pretext to consider me a persecutor since I was unable to understand the daily efforts she had to make.

The continuation of these behaviours, with no possibility of symbolic elaboration, made them similar to obsessive behaviour. The interpretations were superficially understood but not profoundly accepted. Up to what point did she want me to experience her feelings of affective deprivation that had never been satisfied?

She began to understand better the meaning of these phenomena when I expressed how I felt about them. After unsuccessfully attempting to provide different explanations for her delays, I openly talked to the patient of how her behaviour affected me, interpreting that the way she related to me was like her object-relation. She could thereby understand what kind of feelings she induced in me. I asked her how I could help her more in her attempts to change and integrate herself. In this way, I tried to focus more on my feelings rather than on hers and thus make my presence felt.

This type of intervention brings to mind what Bollas (1987) refers to as the use of the subjective state of the analyst. In this way, the patient was able to come closer to me emotionally and introduce me in her inner scenario in the role of a concerned mother instead of the rigid analyst who became irritated because the "right interpretation" was not accepted.

Absence of the time coordinate in the inner space

Another disturbing element can be represented by the absence of the time coordinate in the inner space of these patients, who act as if they could live forever. They consider the analytic relationship as something that will go on forever, and they cannot even talk about the duration since they are afraid of considering the word "end".

The analytic situation is not connected to a work project that has a specific time limit and end. The usual topics of discussion during the sessions concern an eternal present and, most of the times, a static past. This leads the analyst and patient to regard the situation as chronic and static. The concepts of differentiation and separation are avoided because they are at the origin of rituals and profound anguish.

In the countertransference, this state of affairs makes the analyst afraid that she might anticipate the process of separation too early, thus demonstrating little sensitivity, or encourage the symbiotic situation to continue for an excessively long time.

Once Renzo (chapter 10) emerged from his autistic state, he became obsessed by the death of the analyst and expressed his fear of remaining with no support during the course of the analysis. However, he was careful to express his fear so that I would not interpret it as a premonition of death or death wish. In this way, he shared with me his feelings of desolation at the thought of our separation. He was afraid that this thought would also upset me. He never pronounced the word "death" but used old-fashioned, formal expressions such as: "if you passed away due to natural causes" or "if you passed on to a better life". In those moments, the expression on his face expressed his feelings and revealed his terror of being left alone, even though, at times, he tried to conceal it with a mask of irony, which was his dominant trait. He would ask me with great determination to give him the address of a therapist who could replace me.

* * *

Elisa (chapter 7) was also afraid that the analyst might die. She feared that if I abandoned her, she would fall to pieces since she would no longer be physically "attached" to the other. That is why her fantasy of being inside the other and not just near the other, and continuing to consider herself a desperate, little child, was difficult for her to overcome. She desperately wanted to stay in contact with me, even outside the usual setting.

* * *

When Ambra (chapter 9) found herself faced with a real, unavoidable separation, she was able to understand in a more concrete way that the analysis might be coming to an end. She therefore accepted the time dimension but fell into a new psychotic crisis. She felt alone, and the thought of losing the analytic space created a dramatic situation in which she felt that the pieces of herself had dispersed, and she experienced a feeling of death that she could not overcome.

Conclusions

The obstacles in establishing an analytic relationship occur in a repetitive and constant way, thus giving rise to the idea that the pathological situation is fixed and chronic. In fact, the resistance against emerging from the autistic state is strong and is rooted in a very early phase of the individual's development.

The early modes of organized experience imprison individuals and often prevent them from accepting new ways of understanding reality. In patients with autistic capsules, we come up against persistent areas of early sensory experiences and fixed models of early object relationships full of anxiety. Therefore, in the analytic relationship, what can emerge are the early fears of dissolution of bodily limits as well as fears related to recurrent early relational experiences. A long period is needed to overcome the obstacles that prevent emotional closeness, since they were formed during the early period of life. Moreover, the idea of change in an individual's psychic organization also takes a long time to be accepted.

The analyst finds herself faced with a superficial level of communication and must patiently look for the communication that lies hidden at a profound level and needs to be listened to. In these psychotherapies, the significant elements are not so much provided by symbolic verbal communication, by dreams or fantasies, but by bodily expressions, actings-out, and repetitive behaviour. Therefore, faced with the patient's asymbolic way of communicating, the analyst must lend the patient her own capacity of symbolization. For these reasons, during the early phase of the therapy it is necessary to adapt psychoanalytic technique to the patient's level of communication so that there will be no misunderstandings between patient and analyst.

CHAPTER SIX

Therapeutic factors in the treatment of patients with autistic cores

"Once, when I acted in a play, I re-experienced my past feelings of being lost in the world like a tiny grain of sand. Now, however, when I experience the depth and fullness of living, I become dizzy with excitement." *Irene*

Despite the common denominator represented by autistic defences, each patient must be considered as an individual, just as each autistic child has his own particular personality (Alvarez & Reid, 1999).

How much is the autistic part of each individual related to the rest of the personality? We deal with the most archaic part of mental functioning, which does not use a symbolic language to come into contact with others, in addition to another, more structured, part that seems to relate to others in a more normal way. The analyst has accordingly to adopt a flexible approach so that she can adapt to the different levels of the personality structure as they are alternately presented.

For her part, the analyst has her own mental organization, which comes into play in countertransference responses where the experiences and projections of the two participants intermingle. Although the analyst has undergone a good analysis and is interested in doing analytic work based on symbolization, she always has some blind spots, especially with regard to the persistence of undifferentiated islands, which are functioning in an archaic, asymbolic way.

In this connection, Godfrind (1993) points out that a part of the analyst's own personality might aspire to non-conflictual fusion with the patient, and this represents a residual vestige of the symbiotic bond. This inclination might interfere with the patient's development and thus lead to the creation of a state of stagnant immobility, which represents a refuge and a way for both therapist and patient to avoid conflict. Resnik (1999b) refers to areas of unconscious influence, which act reciprocally in the analytic field. A dialogue is thus established between the patient's unconscious and that of the analyst in the form of emotional responses.

The verbal description of any analytic treatment is always limited compared to the actual complicated intermingling of conscious and unconscious processes that occur in the patient–analyst relationship, and especially in one that has lasted a few decades. It would be presumptuous to think that it is possible to find a way to retrace one's steps out of the labyrinth of a complicated pathology. While attempting to reconstruct the phases of the analytic work, I become aware that I am unable to testify to the various phases that made the patient change. It might be interesting for research purposes to find out from the patient himself how he was able to use my presence as analyst in his process of individuation and what he regards as the most useful and transforming intervention or the most significant moment that promoted change. Analytic work is a complicated affair, and there are countless lines of thought that can be followed. However, among so many of the analyst's interventions, some in particular trigger a specific insight and the recognition of parts previously misunderstood or completely unknown.

The advantage of such long periods of observation is that this allows the therapist to recognize the mistakes made in forecasting possible outcomes or in the timing of her interventions and to appreciate unexpected changes that occur and that validate her earlier insights. The study of these adult patients is particularly interesting since they bear witness to the existence of states of mind or sensory experiences that can be attributed to their having experienced an autistic state at a very early stage. Such experiences cannot be remembered through conscious memory, because they belong to a pre-symbolic period, as I have previously discussed, and only become manifest through sensory experiences, perceptions, and states of mind that are experienced again during the transference–countertransference exchange. The analyst's capacity to perceive and share these communications can thus represent the synthesis between her reception of the patient's projections, her own primitive feelings that re-emerge, and her degree of symbolization. This capacity can be compared to the mother's ability to focus on the child's asymbolic requests and to combine them with her own reverie and perception of the child's needs.

Cases of such adult patients are thus extremely important since they can provide valuable information about autism that autistic children cannot provide because of their immature mental development. Moreover, at the beginning of the therapy I also met these patients' parents, who related details of the clinical picture since the patients were too young or because of the seriousness of their symptoms.

The analyst is faced with two different parts of the patient's personality: an autistic part that is more archaic and a part that is more organized. The analyst must constantly be aware of where the communication comes from and how she can effectively intervene. She must therefore adopt a different approach depending on whether she is dealing with the more damaged infantile part or the more structured adult one.

We could consider the therapy as having three different phases. This division, which might appear schematic or arbitrary, emerged spontaneously due to the need to overcome the obstacles I met during the course of each therapy by using my empathic intuition in order to follow the patient's slightest reactions. This way of working can be compared to that proposed by other authors in the psychotherapy of autistic children. In her therapeutic work with autistic states in children, Tustin (1986) distinguishes three successive phases: the first aims to modify the autistic barriers in order to allow the relationship to develop, the second aims to treat the damaged parts, and the third adopts the traditional analytic technique. Bion's notion of containment refers to a dynamic situation that tends to maintain an equilibrium between two different tensions (1962a, 1965). Alvarez (1992) develops Bion's concept of containment by distinguishing the analytic process in autistic children in four consecutive phases: (1) a receptive phase of containment; (2) a phase in which the analyst has to transform within himself the messages received; (3) a phase in which the analyst attempts to furnish an interpretation by giving back or not to the patient his projections; (4) a phase in which the analyst considers the resulting effects that the interpretation produces and verifies whether these effects coincide with the ones analyst desired.

During the first of the three phases in my system of working, I simply had to listen and wait rather than understand the material offered. It was a state of suspended animation in which I made no attempt to work out the material but just collected the emotional, cognitive, verbal, and bodily elements that came from the patient and my personal countertransference. During the second phase, I reflected on the material collected and worked it out. Finally when the relationship was more firmly established, I was able to carry out the work of interpretation.

The first phase of containment and attempt to approach the world of the patient at an appropriate distance is the necessary premise to the subsequent phase. In the first phase, it was necessary to build and encourage trust in the relationship and to help the patient understand the objective of the therapy. As the autistic part is recognized and analysed, it is possible to reach a greater integration of the self, and the analyst can thus proceed in the analytic work.

It was initially important to create an analytic space that was conducive to recognizing the anxieties experienced and the emergence of psychic functions that had hitherto remained confused and frozen in an embryonic state. This space can be considered as a common, auxiliary mental space where the patient's psychic elements, and those of the analyst that derive from his work with the patient, can come together. In this way, a place is created where the process of symbolization can occur.

The analyst will have to defend this space actively, in the sense that she will have to maintain the setting and protect it from the patient's tendency to attack it by interruptions and by actings-out. There is the constant menace that the patient will actually flee and that the therapy will fail because of the patient's desire to withdraw into his autistic island and thus protect himself against the relationship, refusing to maintain a long-lasting relationship or trying to break the emotional bond. It is evident that initially analytic attention will be mainly directed at the patients' fear of remaining in the relationship, while interpretation of the destructive part will be put aside until later.

This function of the defence of analytic relationship and of the setting against the patient's attacks has a paternal connotation, since it represents a strong, decisive presence against the destructive forces. It must be accompanied by sensitive attention, which has a more maternal connotation and which Alvarez refers to as "caring attention" (1992).

Houzel (2001) points out that analyst must carry out a paternal role that gives a structure to the analytic relationship and sets limits between the internal and external worlds, between the child's mind and that of the other, between mental and bodily space. In analytic work, it is desirable for the child to be able to experience both the maternal containment and the paternal resilience and solidity that can withstand his destructive attacks.

The analogy with the maternal function does not mean that the analytic relationship has to mirror the mother–child relationship, but that the model of maternal care can represent a model for the analytic relationship, especially when faced with pathological situations that date back to very primitive stages of life. How and when to handle these countertransference functions will depend on the analyst's particular attitude. In this connection, I would like to point out that the analyst must not try to replace the real mother or give back what the patient lacked in his original experience, but must only provide new ways of identification for the patient in order to retrieve his sense of self.

We can think of those moments of wonder, amazement, and uncertainty that a mother experiences when for the first time she sees her new-born baby, who belongs to her but whom she still does not know, whom she imagines as being full of potential to develop but does not know what his real destiny is. She feels ready to alleviate all his suffering and hardships but cannot imagine what problems he will have in the course of his life; she is faced with a natural and atavistic task that is unknown in the immediate present. We therefore imagine that, as analysts, we are in an analogous situation when dealing with regressive patients, who expect us to fix certain primitive states of being or to understand painful experiences, even without knowingly asking us to do so. This situation requires the analyst to be very patient while waiting for the therapeutic treatment to develop.

However, experience teaches us that even by making available the same therapeutic attitude towards patients, we are not always fortunate enough to reach the end of the therapy in a positive way. There are many factors interacting at both the conscious and the unconscious level which can determine a premature interruption.

The patients described manifested symptoms that replaced psychic activities with overt behaviour such as obsessive rituals, somatic disorders, or addictive behaviour including addiction to sex. Since these symptoms replaced psychic elaboration, during certain phases of the therapy I had to tolerate the ambiguity of a situation in which I merely had to wait and remain with unanswered questions, without any certainties as to the results that were expected from me. I realized that sometimes theories were useless and that I had to rely mainly on the transference–countertransference exchanges. What can be of invaluable help is our hope in the effectiveness of analytic work and our desire to continue our own self-analysis.

Searles (1965, 1986) regards the analyst's identity as an instrument that can be used in the therapeutic process. Resnik (1972) thinks of analytic work as the search for something unknown and unexpected that makes it possible to tolerate what one does not know or understand at a particular moment and that makes the analyst favourably disposed towards the patient. Certainly, in autistic states, characterized by a lack of emotional responses in the transference, the impossibility of establishing a therapeutic alliance—a seemingly chronic situation caused by obstacles and the patient's own vision of eternity—heightens the dismay felt in countertransference. However, despite all this, it is necessary to work tirelessly day by day and to continue hoping that we shall be capable of rediscovering the patient's dormant potential and new openings in perspective within ourselves. We must also accept the fact that we shall feel discouraged and sad and, at times, even unable to understand. In this way, the experiences of integration that we feel during the course of the analysis will be transmitted to the patient so that he can use them.

The main thread running through these therapies is the awareness that we are in the presence of autistic defences. For this reason, I would like to make some observations regarding the maternal function in the psychological development of the newborn and the pathogenetic hypotheses of autism.

Winnicott (1965b) defined the mother as the newborn's total environment, in that she senses his needs, alleviates his discomfort, and creates a space for communication. According to Winnicott, the world of the newborn is initially made up of simple phenomena related to bodily sensations. His physical needs are related to sensations and represent the first question he asks an external object, even one he does not know; they represent the beginning of a subjective wish. The mother puts herself in the child's place in order to understand what his needs and anxieties are, and she expresses her love in terms of physical care. Winnicott speaks of a "good-enough mother", by which he means a mother who can satisfy the child's needs and dedicate herself to him in such a way that the child will be able to experience briefly a sense of omnipotence when he emerges from the unity of the couple. Thanks to the mother's support, the child gradually experiences contact with subjective objects and also "not-me" objects.

Bollas (1987) extends this concept of the mother as the transformational object and identifies her more as a process than as an object. In the process of integration, he attributes more importance to the rhythm of the relationship than to the quality of the object. According to him:

> A transformational object is experientially identified by the infant with processes that alter self experience. It is an identification that emerges from symbiotic relating, where the first object is "known" not so much by putting it into an object representation, but as a recurrent experience of being—a more existential as opposed to representational knowing. As the mother helps to integrate the infant's being (instinctual, cognitive, affective, environmental), the rhythm of this process—from unintegration(s) to integration(s)—informs the nature of this "object" relation rather than the qualities of the object as object.
>
> Not yet fully identified as another, the mother is experienced as a process of transformation, and this feature of early existence lives on in certain forms of object-seeking in adult life, when the object is sought for its function as a signifier of transformation. . . . [Bollas, 1987, p. 14]

The subjective experience of being emerges from a symbiotic relationship in which the other is still not recognized as an external representation but occurs as "a recurrent experience of being". The mother is still not identified but is "experienced as a process of transformation". Only subsequently will she be recognized as a separate object.

The development of the first psychic organization will depend on the facilitating function of the mother, who initially helps the child in his illusion of fusion with the mother by trying to maintain, in a certain sense, the condition of dependence of prenatal life. Subsequently, as the physiological functions develop and the child begins to possess his own instruments and experiences his own subjectivity, the mother herself will have to help him break away from her. The mother will help him overcome the disappointment of separateness and help him gradually achieve his own individuation.

If, at this stage, there are some problems that prevent the mother from helping the newborn overcome his anguish, or if his suffering is too intense because of his weakness, he will be unprepared to bear the weight of his being-in-the-world, because separateness has taken place far too early. If the child is constitutionally weak or has some serious health problems (e.g., malformations or brain damage), the mother may find the facilitating function particularly difficult. In this case, the infant may not have an object whom he feels can act as a mediator, bear his suffering, and sustain him. He may therefore withdraw into the auto-sensuous world that is the only one he knows. This might mark the beginning of the autistic organization.

Once he has left the protective environment of the uterus, the child experiences a situation in which the mother takes care of his bodily needs. The object, which is still not recognized, is identified with sensations of physical contact. Subsequently, the different sensations will be recognized as being different and thus differentiated and integrated. The transition from the auto-sensory experience to the relationship with the object occurs because the mother takes care of the child and transmits emotions. If this transition does not occur, the child will remain attached to his auto-sensuous world and will be unable to abandon it, since he is afraid of sinking into an unknown world that has no boundaries or meaning. Various authors have described this situation in different ways, referring to it as catastrophic anguish (Bion, 1962a), psychotic depression (Winnicott, 1965a, 1965c), and falling into a black hole (Tustin, 1972, 1981b, 1986). If the degree and duration of these situations of anguish are excessive for the child, autistic defences become hypertrophic and can lead to infantile autism or leave greater or lesser traces of autism in the psychic organization of the subject.

In order for the child to develop, the mother must be flexible enough to satisfy the needs of the newborn. In fact, the mother continues to modify the child's internal and external environment according to his needs before he himself can modify them as the emerging physiological and psychological functions develop. This development depends both on the external environment of care and the infant's capacity to experience that care. Looking at the course of a child's development, it becomes apparent how important it is, when treating adult patients, to retrace the phases of symbiosis and then promote the patient's gradual differentiation, which allows his autistic part to turn into a symbolic area.

I shall now briefly illustrate these functions analogous to maternal care by giving some examples taken from the cases described in greater detail in part II.

Establishing a human presence

Establishing a human presence might seem an obvious or incomprehensible formulation if one fails to take into consideration the autistic child's attempt to blot out the presence of the other. The therapist's impression of not being seen or taken into consideration when treating children in therapy also occurs with adults, though in a less evident way. Faced with a situation in which I am not recognized as being a human being, I repeatedly asked myself how it was possible to become important or significant in the patient's emotional world.

> For years, Elisa (chapter 7) always arrived late, because in her eyes I did not exist as a separate person who was waiting for her and could experience feelings of irritation or disappointment by the long wait. I might have been considered just like the walls of my room, which were always there and never changed. It was useless to point out the repetitiveness of her actions, attempt to find the meaning of the symptom, or suggest changing the appointments to make it easier for her to come to the sessions. The persistence of such behaviour might make one intervene in order to underline the repetition, although this might increase the persecutory thoughts. I could have said to her that she wanted to change the world by imposing her vision of time and cancel the time we established together for our session, but during that particular phase of the therapy it would have been counterproductive. In the end, I realized that the patient needed to experience a real relationship in which a person desires her, waits for her, and keeps her in her mind.

> At that time, I felt that the role of victim and neglected person that Elisa forced on me was a necessary phase to make it possible for the transference to develop. She finally stopped being late when she was able to recognize our emotional relationship and turn the therapy into a precious moment.

In such a case, interpreting the aggressive behaviour might be appropriate in the case of neurotic patients but might put us on the wrong track in the case of autistic subjects, increasing the patient's impression of being misunderstood and more distant from the therapist. The approach to adopt in these cases is to act like a living person who has feelings and a mind that observes, understands, and gives meaning to experience. Only later can the aggressive aspect of the behaviour be pointed out.

It must be borne in mind that, because of the absence of total or partial differentiation from the object, in autistic organization the object is not separately perceived or can be mistaken for a part of the self. Making one's presence felt means preventing the kind of manipulation that tends to make the analyst passive, by refusing to let the patient remain in a condition of passivity or immersed in his obsessions. The analyst must express her own will in defending the setting.

Studies by child development researchers (Alvarez, 1992; Miller, Rustin, & Shuttleworth, 1989) have pointed out that the interactional contact between mother and child is rhythmic and cyclic. Normally, mothers respect their child's moments of isolation or withdrawal and alternate other moments of stimulation, arousing their interest. An important function of the mother with the newborn is to help him look at her and to catch his attention. This is a decisive factor in the central cohesive organizing function of the psyche. Stern (1977) pointed out that the gaze of the mother and the changes in her facial expressions have a great impact in catching and keeping the child's attention. Other authors compare the parts of the mother's body (face or breast) to a magnet that attracts objects: the child's experiences of being attracted are internalized, so that he, in turn, is driven to try to make a human contact.

A steadfast presence

The setting should ensure the framework of the meeting, but it is not always respected by the patient. This can accentuate the analyst's own experiences of feeling useless and ineffectual and may even make her want to give up. On the other hand, it can make the analyst act with too many interpretations because she feels irritated. It is necessary to fight against this inclination by countering the patient's discontinuity with the analyst's belief in the continuity of the therapeutic project, even when it seems at the point of coming to an end.

A steadfast presence introduces the idea that the relationship is solid with regard to the existence of the object, thus helping it to develop. Even if the patient attempts to interrupt the therapy, it is for the therapist to counter this by demonstrating her desire to continue. Since we must bear in mind that the continuous maternal presence contributes to the idea of the continuity of existence, it is important to stress our presence.

Transmitting vitality

The function of transmitting vitality corresponds to Alvarez's concept of "reclamation" (1992). Very regressive or autistic patients "might lack the will or the sensation of being alive and have the perception of being near death" (p. 56). As in any emergency situation, even in these cases the seriousness of the situation must be faced before trying to understand the causes that brought it about.

One of the functions of the analyst is to bring some life into the relationship with these patients. Alvarez (1992) underlines the importance of one maternal function that consists "in arousing the newborn's interest in new objects by means of the mother's visual expressions, the sound of her voice and use of the breast" (p. 61). In the same way, when adult patients withdraw into their apparently meaningless repetitions, I think it is important to discourage them from remaining alone with their rituals, since this prevents them from changing.

Tustin (1986) suggested intervening directly in the psychotherapy to set precise limits to repetitive autistic activities so that a conflict would emerge. In situations in which autistic children avoid contact, Tustin suggested creating a situation of contact. Barrows (2001, 2002) adopts a technique that is different from the traditional one and consists in giving the child indications as to how to play a particular game. This makes it possible to introduce a symbolic element or a play with a reciprocal exchange that can interrupt the obsessive behaviour; this is a technique that I, too, have used.

The therapist may need actively to intervene in order to help the autistic child stop repeating his rituals and the autistic adult stop talking about the same thing. According to the specific situation and her own sensitivity, the analyst will have to evaluate how and when to intervene actively. As an example, I shall briefly describe the case of a boy of about 10 years of age whom I treated several years ago (Tremelloni, 1988).

An autistic child (I call him Guido) who was particularly passive and isolated in his obsessive rituals and echolalia made the sessions especially boring and monotonous. In addition to his isolation, there was his evident desire to exercise an omnipotent control over me, and this prevented any kind of exchange in the relationship. His early interpersonal exchanges had been devoid of any feelings, and the relationship with his parents had been characterized by obsessive behaviour.

In the countertransference, I felt bored and irritated due to my sensation of impotence and the communication vacuum. I therefore tried to find a way to make the psychotherapeutic work possible and more pleasant. I felt the need to create an area in which the infantile part of me, which liked games, could express itself by playing some enjoyable games and thus establish some contact with the boy. I began by introducing some indoor games like dominoes or bingo or memory games. I explained the rules of the game and refused to allow him to remain obsessively attached to any particular one. After a certain period of time, Guido began to accept changes, actively participated in the games, and really enjoyed himself. He began to express feelings that had never emerged during his obsessive rituals and a certain intellectual capacity that had never been demonstrated at school. In the relationship, he recognized the active presence, which was not rejecting, of the not-me.

I also introduced games such as tag, which required him to move around and shook him out of his static passivity. We took turns playing the role of the wolf and the sheep. In this game he always wanted to be the sheep and never the wolf, because if he was the sheep he could continue to remain passive but also felt chased, seized, and desired by me. At this stage of the game, he would gleefully cry out, laugh with enjoyment, and ask me directly to play the game again. An infantile relationship had been established between us in which feelings that were usually blotted out emerged. When I decided to change roles, he briefly accepted to play the wolf but then, laughing, rebelled since in this way he refused to accept my decision and could openly demonstrate his rebellion. His smiling was meant to attenuate his open rebellion. At this point, what emerged in the relationship could be pointed out and interpreted. This could occur because my spontaneous infantile part introduced a childhood game that I would enjoy playing again and that would express my interest in "living" with the patient in a climate that was not boring ("live company") during the session.

Some analysts might object that in this way the analyst loses her professional role and presents herself to the patient as a playmate, thus preventing the patient from accepting his position of dependence. Others might also object that the game of wolf and sheep might unduly influence the child's mind or might stimulate his senses and therefore cannot be considered an acceptable analytic tool. However, in the light of my experiences with my patients, these attempts can serve to make them interrupt their obsessive rituals and obsessive need for omnipotent control. This is an exercise to encourage the patients to abandon the pleasure in exercising control. These direct interventions can be used as exceptional instruments during moments of impasse and are not meant to substitute for the traditional analytic approach (Tremelloni, 1987). According to Resnik (1999b), the cycle of empathy develops in a certain atmosphere that is created by both participants. When the patient has no intention of creating such an atmosphere, it will be up to the analyst to do so. The analyst needs to be especially interested in the therapeutic relationship in such cases, in order to help the patient be interested in the analysis!

When working with adult patients, the analyst is faced with the repetitive organization of the session. The patient begins with the same unchanging obsessive accounts. At this point, the analyst can interrupt the patient's communication by asking some questions. She might ask the patient about his neglected dreams, or ask him to answer questions he avoided or refused to answer during the previous session, or take the opportunity to express her own associations and thus stimulate his associative capacity. In this way, thought patterns are modified. Although patients themselves may realize that such obsessive rituals and thoughts lead to boredom, they find it difficult to abandon them.

Understanding the significance of non-symbolic communications

The different levels that come into play in communication need to be carefully studied by the analyst. By means of the countertransference, she will be able to differentiate between them. Let us take, for example, silence, which in neurotic patients can represent a resistance and must be interpreted. In patients with autism, it might be a manifestation of an emotional and ideational vacuum or an experience of psychic death. It can dramatize a situation in which there is an absence of holding and a lack of confidence that the other is listening. At that point, the analyst can attempt to take up the dialogue again, so that the patient will not isolate himself and withdraw into a desolate place.

> When he was a child Renzo (chapter 10) used to try to stop me physically from opening the door and letting him out after the session was over. These rituals could have irritated me if I only considered them as aggressive behaviour towards me. But if I imagined that they were rooted in archaic anguish caused by separation and the fear of falling into an emotional vacuum once the session was over, I would respond differently and be more in tune with his state of mind. If I had only responded to the

aggressive, sensory side of the message, I would have acted just like him without understanding the unconscious meaning of his behaviour, and I would also have pushed him away from the relationship.

Adapting to variations in the symptoms, being aware of their intensity, providing flexible responses

The request for, for example, extra sessions at times of acute anguish due to crises of depersonalization or serious depression represents a change to the usual setting. As I mentioned earlier, the analyst can decide to move outside the usual setting when there is an emergency situation, but this does not mean that she is no longer capable of interpretation and symbolization. However, the analyst must be sensitive enough to discriminate, above all, between the levels of communication the patient offers at a given moment. As Money-Kyrle (1956) points out, in receiving the projections it is necessary to distinguish between aggressive and destructive significance and that of despair. It is similar to the distinction we made between the baby who cries during a sudden temper tantrum and the one who cries because he experiences serious physical pain. We must not forget that at certain times during the therapy, the regressive, autistic, or psychotic patient needs support to prevent fragmentation and dispersion.

The obsessive symptoms need to be tolerated since they represent a way of defending against the past and are a part of the patient that exists in the present and from which he cannot separate. At the same time, it is useful to give signals that there are new possibilities of expressing the self.

Discriminating and recognizing sensations and transmitting emotions

The difficulty of recognizing one's own states of mind and relating them to thought is a characteristic of psychosomatic patients and those with autistic capsules.

Elisa's persistent crying (chapter 7) during many of the sessions indicated an emotional state that words cannot express. Interpretations can only be formulated after the transference relationship has been established.

In the same way, the analyst has to tolerate persistent somatic symptoms for a long time before they can be interpreted in a significant way.

In the case of a pathology related to preverbal states, when communication only regards the body, the analyst can provide help by expressing some of her immediate feelings perceived in the countertransference. In this way, she offers her own way of feeling as a new emotional experience for the patient, which might awaken a capacity that had become frozen and was preventing the experience of emotions.

The therapist will have to use her own voice as an instrument of communication and will have to modulate it in order to transmit her emotions. In interpreting or expressing the emotional significance of the messages, it is also important to give them a name so that the patient can recognize them. The following example is taken from the case of Irene (chapter 8) and relates to certain symptoms that caused her particular anguish:

Irene had a serious crisis of anguish when she was unable to tell the difference between the mannequins displayed in shop windows and people walking on the street. On this occasion, it was a question of her visual perceptions that were not sufficiently integrated with her emotions. The perceptions were not integrated with the sense of really existing in this world and were associated to a sensation of death.

Whenever Irene was faced with some psychic problem, she reacted with somatic disorders so that the effects of interpersonal relationships short-circuited and were transformed into bodily sensations, which could not undergo any mental elaboration.

When she attended a funeral of a supposed friend of hers, she wondered in amazement about the emotions others felt that made them cry. She was unable to understand or experience similar emotions.

In the obsessive repetition of rituals, the connection with emotions seems to have disappeared. In interpreting or expressing the emotional meaning of the messages, it is also important to give them a name so that the patient can qualify and recognize them within himself.

When Renzo (chapter 10) was a child, he did not realize that during his rituals he moved in a mechanical fashion, and he was unable to relate these movements to his emotions or to my interpretations of what they might mean. When he became an adult, he felt that as a child he had suffered due to the absence of affection, and that his physical needs were met, but in a cold, unfeeling way. Therefore, the sensations produced by the care of the body could not be related to the emotions resulting from the relationship. As an adult, he felt compelled to seek out the same sensations of contact with others.

Giving importance to memories of sensations and attributing meaning to symptoms

The function of giving importance to memories of sensations and attributing meaning to symptoms can be understood in the sense of Bion's (1965) transformation and can be put into practice when the basic relationship has become more stable. The transformation of sensory experiences or generic impressions into symbolic material can be worked on by the analyst and then transferred to the patient to serve as a framework for his development.

The following example is enlightening with regard to memories of sensory experiences that have not been integrated:

One of the most significant childhood memories Elisa (chapter 7) continually spoke about regarded the time her mother threw a bucketful of water on the courtyard pavement one very hot day. Elisa was a child at the time and was playing with a friend of hers. Although her friend moved aside to avoid the water, Elisa remained glued to the spot and got wet. She gave the contact with the water the significance of a real contact with the mother regarding the water as a mother's caressing hand.

This episode illustrates how a search for cutaneous sensations expressed the need for emotional warmth and closeness.

Helping patients to remember and connect thoughts

A useful function in certain cases is to try to get patients to remember what was said during the previous session and to connect previous observations to the present communication. This prevents thoughts from being dispersed and adds to the material that can be subsequently elaborated.

Over the years, Renzo (chapter 10) gradually progressed from a refusal to talk, saying he had no thoughts in his mind, to a fragmented and irregular manner of speaking. Finally he reached a more accurate and even elaborate way of expressing himself. He could even begin to take up the thread of the thoughts he had left off during the previous session, and this made it possible for him to connect his thoughts to my interventions so that our communication could develop. However, for a long time I acted as an external memory and stimulated the connections between thoughts.

It was surprising to see in him the spontaneous reproduction of this attitude, because it led to the emergence of an intellectual capacity never used or even imagined before. These connected thoughts allowed him to create a woven pattern and associate ideas.

Interpretations

Interpretations regarding resistances and aggressiveness can be made only when it is clear that the patient can listen to them and use them.

During the first phase, it is advisable to intervene only in a way that makes clear that the analyst understands the patient's feelings and shows a rather similar sensibility. This means that the analyst is trying to understand the secret core of the patient's suffering and is willing to form a therapeutic alliance. The analyst has to approach the patient's world without being seductive or intrusive but has to understand his emotional needs. As Steiner (1993) suggests, if interpretations are given too early, they drive the patient away because they are considered inopportune and aggressive. If the timing of the interpretations is always wrong, the patient senses a lack of containment.

It must not be forgotten that the autistic position represents an area of development that has been damaged and therefore must be respected, bearing in mind that the patient continues to be fragile even after a long period of therapy. However, this does not mean that when the patient's ego reaches a greater integration, interpretations regarding resistance and aggressiveness cannot be made in relation to the specific degree of the therapy development and the analytic material.

Importance of the face-to-face position in the analyst's consulting-room

The face-to-face position, which represents a change in the classical analytic technique, has been widely discussed in connection with the differentiation between psychoanalysis and different kinds of psychotherapies. This position has been mainly used in cases of adolescents and borderline or psychotic adults. Whereas the traditional couch position favours the analysis of the intrapsychic representations because of the regression it determines, the face-to-face position seems the most suitable for treating the primary traumatic areas, by directly fostering the emergence of a human relationship.

Although the couch position can make the patient relive the mother's inability to receive his bodily signals (Brusset, 2002) and underlines the absence of the capacity of free association, the face-to-face position favours the beginning of the analytic process. In fact, this position reinforces the emotional participation and underlies the reciprocity and symmetry of the two participants of the analytic couple.

However, the face-to-face position can present some problems that the analyst must take into account. For example, the patient can express his need for advice or support through his gaze or body language, try to convince or seduce him, or try to introduce himself into the analyst's mind more easily than he would be able to lying down on a couch. At the same time, the analyst is driven to act or protect himself from being overly involved with the patient. He therefore has to accept these risks by constantly paying attention to sending out messages that are coherent as regards verbal, bodily, and facial languages. In this case, what comes into play is the analyst's personal training and analytic experience (Brusset, 2002).

It should also be pointed out that the face-to-face position stems from childhood and represents the first experience of interpersonal relationship, which is the starting point for the subsequent development of the person's individuality. When the patient observes the analyst, he can include within himself the analyst in her entirety, provide a support for his representations, and correct his projections.

Anzieu (1979) asserts that the patient needs to grasp an overall sensory image of the analyst through her facial expression, bodily position, and gestures, as if he could touch the body with his gaze. In this way, he satisfies his childhood need to be touched, warmed, and held by perceiving the smiles, stability, and solidity of the analyst, in addition to listening to her verbal messages.

Green (1990, 1997, 2002) recognizes the usefulness of the face-to-face position in the cases called "psychic desertification with apparent mental death", in which the sense of solitude and vulnerability might rule out a classic analysis on the couch. In these cases, the representations of a bad internal object result in a loss of representation and the absence of the association mechanism. The subsequent feeling of psychic void might therefore make it impossible to establish a fruitful analytic work.

Searles (1986) discusses the importance of the analyst's face in the therapy of borderline patients and describes cases in which the process of integration and differentiation improved once the patient acquired the capacity to focus on the analyst's face. My experience with adult patients was analogous. In this connection, I must admit that the passage of the patient from the position of lying down on the couch to a "face-to-face" position facilitated analytic work and accelerated the process of the integration of the ego.

With Irene (chapter 8), initially I felt the need to use the couch in order to be freer to collect the emerging communication and not to be disturbed in my state of suspension and confusion. Also, I did not want to influence the patient, who was already so confused and disoriented. Subsequently, when the analytic work had reached a phase of greater individualization of the patient, I decided to use the "face-to-face" position. This marked an important turning-point, since there was an improvement in our relationship and in the patient's capacity to develop.

At that point, it might have been my own personal development or a different phase of integration of the patient that made me feel freer with respect to my own feelings so that I did not have to protect myself from the meeting by maintaining a neutral expression on my face. Once we were really able to observe each other, our relationship became more real and the patient's idealization decreased.

Becoming aware of the patient's exhibitionist desires and the capacity to obtain complete attention combined with the concentration on the emotional significance of my face made it possible for the analytic process to develop more quickly.

This position allowed patients to take from my facial expressions elements that were more significant than words. The patients were therefore able to experience our relationship as more human and less idealized and were able to tell the difference between different feelings, and I came to have a more complete vision of the patient and our relationship.

The choice of the face-to-face position cannot be adopted in a systematic way but has to be decided according to the specific moment of the therapy and psychic features of the patient. The following example shows how the patient's position during the session depends not only on the specific pathology or the peculiar analytic moment but, especially, on the evaluation of the individual case.

From the very beginning of the therapy Ambra (chapter 9) used the couch. On the rare occasions when our gazes met, Ambra tried to seize my thoughts and feelings in order to adjust to my way of thinking and be like me. Her gaze was devoid of meaning but was intrusive, especially at the end of the session when she would have liked to know the effect of her communication on me. The only time her gaze was meaningful was when she gave vent to her violent rage. When she sometimes decided to sit in front of me and I could observe her at length, I realized that I was the one who was upset, considering the absence of meaning, inner coherence, and feelings, and even an apparent absence of psychic pain expressed in her face. All this disturbed my empathy and my capacity to think.

Non-analytic interventions

Non-analytic interventions were useful in particularly acute periods of anguish in order to make the patient feel that a human presence was close to him with no attempt to interpret or give advice. These types of intervention provided words or phrases that could express understanding and the sharing of difficult situations, or give meaning to what seemed incomprehensible, or provide an indirect response to questions related to concrete facts. Some scholars think that these non-analytic interventions belong to psychotherapy and not psychoanalysis, but in my experience they furthered the analytic treatment. They might be used alternately with the more analytic ones, depending on the patient's specific pathological level.

Perhaps when faced with moments of great anxiety or depression in patients, this approach was spontaneous for me because of my previous experience in medicine, where a word of encouragement or of sympathy was useful for therapeutic alliance, even if it didn't replace a diagnostic assessment or a therapeutic prescription. The level of suffering of such patients may be so intense and disintegrating that it calls for an immediate support from a human being who is at the moment a psychoanalyst.

Faced with the persistence of the obsessive and somatic symptoms, and after repeatedly trying in vain to clarify and discuss their meaning, I found some non-analytic but more pedagogical approaches that aimed to limit such repetitive behaviour.

I have already pointed out that one of the defences that makes it difficult to continue the analysis is represented by the obsessions and monotonous repetition of the somatic symptoms. Obsessive thoughts allow the patient to remain in an undefined, intermediate position, neither too far nor too close to the analyst, thus preventing separation and maintaining the situation chronic.

Elisa (chapter 7) used to perform a series of compulsory, mechanical movements, which had to be made in a precise way. These rituals had originated in her childhood. After having interpreted for years the various transference meanings (including, for example, opposition to the introjection of our therapeutic work, nothing changes) and, on the other hand, the persistence of a symptom in order to continue the analysis forever, to continue to feel damaged and ill, I suggested she try to exercise her will power and stop doing "so-called automatic activities". Exercising her will power, which in other areas was intransigent, represented a function of her adult ego and could function to place limits to the obsessive activities. The patient had to become aware of the fact that the function of the will in the service of the ego represented the adult part that had to be integrated with the elaboration provided by the analysis. This, however, meant separating oneself from childhood and giving up the eternally existing defences that emerged at an early age.

The patient subsequently accepted my advice and later recognized that this type of intervention helped her strengthen the healthy part in fighting against the omnipotence of the more regressive part. Although it took a long time for her to achieve this transformation, it was profound and definitive.

Although these interventions are sometimes not very important as regards the content, they demonstrate that the analyst shares the patient's situation of anxiety and uncertainty and is attentive to his emotional needs.

Irene (chapter 8) presented a serious cognitive impairment for a long time. At one point I accepted her desire to help her correct a job application form, since she was unable to do it herself. Subsequently, when she began to study and our relationship had become more solid, I helped her organize the chapters of her thesis before an examination. I did this since I believed that her long autistic closure had prevented her from learning to use logical thought patterns. The patient, emotionally deprived in her childhood, became more confident and subsequently acquired a greater capacity to use her intelligence and was able to write other examination papers by herself.

Conclusions

To sum up the main elements of the work, I would like to point out that it is necessary continually to monitor the patient's level of communication and adapt to the variations in the transference and the patient's changing needs in order to determine the internalization of a more symbolic thinking in harmony with emotions and feelings.

In all the cases of patients with autistic capsules, the most important therapeutic factors include a tolerance for non-symbolic communication, patience linked to the hope of reaching a possible expression of feelings, and the courage to face obstacles or disappointments. The resolution of the autistic defences, the integration of frozen feelings, may set the patient on the road to the depressive position. Improvements are heralded by the patient's initial capacity for self-analysis and by the attempt to become independent, even by criticizing the analyst in a more responsible way. Moreover, during the session, the analyst can experience less concern about the fragility of the patient and can adopt a more classic technique.

In the mind of the analyst, the hope that the patient will make progress must not be anchored to a model in her mind. It is helpful to keep in mind Bion's phrase about working "without memory or desire" (1965, 1970).

It is impossible to know how the patient can develop, or whether he cannot or does not want to change. The hope of the analyst is a hope with no definite model in mind as to how the patient's personality will develop. It might be related to the analyst's desire to try to fathom that part of the mystery that surrounds the origin of her own primitive experiences.

PART II

CASE STUDIES

CHAPTER SEVEN

Elisa

History

Elisa came to my attention when she was 24 years old and finishing medical school. She was a beautiful, fair-haired girl, dressed in an elegantly understated way, and interested in sports. A previous psychotherapy had ended in failure, so she started the therapy with serious misgivings about the therapist's ability to help her. Because of the high level of depression and anxiety as well as the failure of the previous therapy, Elisa's mother accompanied her to the first interview with me. Although Elisa would have to make a rather long journey each time she came to the three or four sessions a week, she agreed to begin psychotherapy.

Her evident symptoms included serious depression, ritual behaviour, obsessive thinking about perfection, and foreboding about the future, as well as her tendency to repeat actions and to being overwhelmed by parasitic thoughts. She suffered from crises of derealization, when she would be overcome by an uncontrollable psychotic anxiety. When walking down the street, the environment would appear unfamiliar, lifeless, and cold, devoid of any human presence, and filled with foreboding of imminent death. I discovered over the course of the therapy that all these symptoms were intensely felt and did not respond to medication. The experiences of derealization were even more acute in spring, when the sun and wind make the landscape shine, heralding the reawakening of nature. All this was in sharp contrast with Elisa's sadness; during the years of therapy, spring also came to signify that summer was approaching together with the inevitable long separation from me.

An especially troubling aspect concerned her inability to love. As her mother often said, if Elisa experienced feelings of love for someone, these feelings had to be total and all-encompassing. However, in the presence of the slightest mutual criticism or divergence of opinion, the feelings were doomed to disappear. Since she was prone to criticize others, every time she fell in love the relationship was destined to end.

In her everyday life, Elisa was hyperactive: she got excellent grades at school, was committed to her work and active in sports, and had close links with old school friends. However, overwhelming passivity and anguish characterized her inner world.

She was the youngest of three children and felt that her mother reserved a special love for her brothers. She had grown up in a family that was particularly bent on improving its social and economic status. From a very early age, she demonstrated a strong physical attachment to her mother. When she was an adolescent, her father died suddenly in an accident. She was upset because she did not feel as bereaved as her novel reading led her to believe she should, and she felt responsible since she had not loved him enough.

The mother had begun to suffer from depression, phobias, and obsessions after the birth of her second child, although she did not realize she had personal problems. She felt depressed, though for no identifiable reason, and decided that a new pregnancy would make her feel better again. After the birth of Elisa, her mother felt she had no more psychic disorders, and she devoted all her energies to the family and the work.

It seemed possible that in Elisa's mind, this maternal reverie was transformed into a hidden and deeply rooted feeling of responsibility for taking care of her mother's depression and providing the support that was not forthcoming from an uncommunicative and absent husband. At the same time, taking her mother as a model, she became certain that there was no psychic world made up of feelings, thoughts, contradictions, and motivations and that everything was based on action and real facts. She deduced that she could not share her feelings of anguish with the family, and this was how she always felt about herself. At the same time, she idealized her family, which seemed to her a close and exceptional group, socially prominent and with moral values. Her goal was to become as self-assured and perfect as her mother.

Elisa chose to study medicine even though she was not particularly interested in the field. On the one hand, she felt obliged to alleviate the suffering of others; on the other, she wanted to find a profession that would differentiate her from the family. Obtaining a university degree was a way of finding reassurance, since she was afraid of being of no value as a subject.

In the psychotherapeutic relationship a real plea for help did emerge even though Elisa was convinced it was hopeless, either because of her earlier experiences or because of the almost delirious belief that she had an incurable psychic disorder of genetic origin. There had been cases of serious depression on the paternal side of the family, and her mother suffered from both depression and obsessive disorders. Elisa's medical studies confirmed that heredity could be a factor, so she felt predestined to suffer from psychic illness. In this connection, her masochistic side dominated and she used rational thought to reject all possibility of improvement.

She imagined asking an ideal analyst for help. He was supposed to show great interest in her suffering and problems without being lured by her need for symbiosis. Elisa had always felt omnipotent in attracting others into her project of creating symbiotic couples who would share her depression, her only real characteristic. In this case, her partners were interchangeable as long as there was someone to form the couple. If an analyst identified too much with her, he lost his ability to differentiate himself from her and was regarded as weak and, in this way, lost his role as therapist.

Elisa insisted that she was unable to love, but she seemed to be talking about an ideal love with no specific object. She could never speak of aggressiveness but only of depression. She imagined that the therapeutic relationship would succeed when she fell in love with the analyst, in the sense of experiencing a feeling of complete adoration. Instead, the coldness and mechanical behaviour that had characterized her since childhood prevented the relationship from developing.

Feelings were replaced by attempts to keep everything under control, acting-out, and the obsessive organization of thoughts. Her thinking was dominated by compulsive, parasitic thoughts represented by long sequences of numbers and operations that obsessed her even when she studied or worked and which she obsessively justified in a rational way. Initially, she had few dreams or fantasies.

Some of her childhood memories seemed to me quite significant, especially as regards the possibility that an autistic part had been formed in order to escape from primitive terror. She remembered what her mother had told her about breast-feeding her at night, that she used to keep Elisa with her in bed but, as she was too tired to give her the breast, she would let the baby find it herself when she was hungry. Elisa thought that she was regarded not as a small child in need of attention but, rather, as a small animal. The thought of having been abandoned and left to her own devices when she was an infant filled Elisa with despair (without the support of a thinking mind). She later specialized in gynaecology.

Elisa said that during her childhood she felt terribly lonely and different from her peers because she tended to experience crises of moral conscience, strong guilt feelings, the fear of hell, and a chronic depression she never manifested and that nobody imagined existed, which was hidden behind the incessant numerical calculations she made and kept secret from everyone. She had never been a carefree child and did everything out of a sense of duty. Moreover, she felt she had no particular personality traits except for her tendency to be intro-spective.

As I previously mentioned, Elisa remembered playing with a friend of hers in the courtyard of her house on a hot day, and to cool things off, her mother threw a bucket of water over the cement pavement. Her friend instinctively jumped away so she wouldn't get wet, but Elisa remained rooted to the spot to benefit from the cool, refreshing sensa-tion her mother wanted to give her (see chapter 6)

During the first years of analysis, the problems that emerged in the therapeutic relationship coincided with the onset of a physical disease, ulcerative colitis. This fact almost pleased her, since everyone worried about her and she was cared for by doctors and nurses. The world of her psyche was no longer the main concern.

The psychotherapeutic treatment was very long and difficult. At the beginning there was no verbal exchange, and the only way she communicated her suffering was by crying. Subsequently, she started talking about her dreams or episodes from her daily life. She spoke in a high-pitched voice, without pauses or periods of silence. A mechani-cal, formal presence pervaded the room, never pausing.

After a few years, the symptoms of depression and the obsessive disorder diminished. She was subsequently hospitalized for ulcerative colitis; soon after this she became pregnant and unexpectedly decided to interrupt the therapy, though she did not discuss her decision with me. The birth and the fact of having to bring up the child were another reason for prolonging the interruption of the therapy and finally ending it. My participation in the therapeutic alliance was cancelled, with no second thoughts.

A few years later Elisa came back, complaining of serious bouts of anxiety due to emotional problems. I was then able to explain to her how serious her psychic condition was and that interrupting the therapy was a way of acting out. I suggested she resume the therapy, with four weekly sessions. The analytic therapy followed this regular schedule for several years, despite the long way she had to come and her career.

In addition to the contents of the sessions, the main problem I came up against was her ambivalence and the coldness of the relationship itself. This was the same coldness that Elisa had experienced as a child in her social relationships and that she considered at the root of her difficulty in experiencing emotions. The other element that prevented the analysis from developing was represented by her obsessive ideation. During much of the analysis she oscillated between a desire to take refuge in a protected place and a feeling of rebelliousness and wanting to flee from the relationship.

The course of the therapy

First phase: crying

The failure of the previous therapy was due to a mutual misunderstanding between Elisa and her first therapist. The reaction of that therapist to the patient's obsessive, stereotyped—though meaningful—question "How do I love someone because I have no feelings" was apparently to consider it the wrong way to start psychoanalytic treatment. Elisa said, in anguish, that the analyst had considered her request to undergo analysis as impossible because he thought she could not establish a relationship since she lacked feelings. His response had filled Elisa with despair and reinforced the idea that she was incurable. The failure of this therapeutic relationship was followed by a therapy with drugs but without clear improvements. If we consider the analyst's response as a technical error, we can hypothesize that he might not have recognized the autistic capsules that were hidden behind a mask of an obsessive organization of the personality.

At the beginning of the therapy, she used to cry a lot for no apparent reason. It seemed to be an expression of suffering experienced during a preverbal period when she lived in a body that did not receive sufficient attention or affection and therefore had no psychic life. This wordless drama could be the expression of a death wish or resignation at being unable to give her life meaning since there were, at that time, no particular situations in her life to cause such suffering.

Her crying, a kind of concrete, non-symbolic way of expressing herself, did not have a specific cause but expressed the need to be contained and given meaning as if she were an infant. One hypothesis was that the primitive desires to fuse with the mother had not been understood and satisfied since the mother might have been depressed or emotionally blocked, and this urge re-emerged during the first phase of the analysis. During the crises of derealization, she experienced feelings of terror and annihilation which up to that time had remained buried. In those moments, Elisa was terrorized because she completely lost her sense of vitality and had the sensation that there was no human presence around her.

These early, unsatisfied symbiotic desires might explain her need to remain physically close in order to find some emotional comfort and reassurance. In the same way, the analytic situation represented a shelter but, unfortunately, also a static position where neither real communication nor changes were expected. Only after many years of therapy and my own strong interest in her was it possible to speak of a relationship between two people who could exchange feelings and thoughts.

Second phase: obsessive ideation

Crying was gradually replaced with talking, which was dominated by the obsessive ideation that invaded every aspect of her life. Her crying and uninterrupted descriptions of daily activities were a kind of pseudo-communication. They represented a protective armour of words and tears which allowed her to avoid real interaction on an emotional level.

Elisa's obsession with numbers that she continually rearranged in a secret order according to fixed rules, and the significance she attributed to mathematical operations, represented a rigid support structure and a companion that was always available, like autistic objects. The belief in the continuity of these objects (perhaps a precursor of the obsessive symptoms) represented the continuity of her own existence and erased from her mind the trauma of separateness experienced as too painful and as a portent of death.

"Autistic objects and "autistic shapes" have been described by Tustin as a way of withdrawing from the painful world of emotions (a form of self-soothing activity: Tustin, 1984). This sort of self-hypnosis (Tustin, 1981a) was a kind of protection, but it also impeded the patient's cognitive and emotional development. Just like autistic objects, autistic shapes serve to prevent awareness of bodily separateness and represented a secret, protective shell that is always trustworthy, present, and reassuring.

The presence of numbers secretly reassured her but also heightened the importance attributed to the rational faculties shared by all human beings. She also attributed to numbers magical, almost superstitious powers. However, they prevented any kind of authentic and profound communication with other human beings.

It is interesting to note a memory of the perception of herself which Elisa remembered and placed in the early years of her childhood. At that time she imagined being a triangular-shaped plastic bag full of sand that blew away in the wind, and she compared this to her own disappearing from the world. This representation regarded a geometrically shaped container, but one that had no precise consistency of its own: a plastic bag. Inside the container the content was sand, which is undifferentiated and can be blown away by the wind. I compared this three-dimensional image to the representation of her own primitive evanescent self which could easily disappear, as subsequently occurred during her crises of depersonalization.

Human relationships were superficial and only served to give the patient the illusion of a fusion, not of an adult relationship with its implication of a certain space for communication between one person and another. The impenetrable defences she had developed were difficult to break down. The possibility of being helped was rebuffed because she feared acknowledging her enormous emotional needs.

For a long time the transference was represented, on the one hand, by the desire for physical closeness or fusion and, on the other, by her aggressive behaviour, expressed above all through acting-out or attacks against psychoanalytic thinking, and denigration of the analyst. If I mentioned small signs of a negative transference as an expression of her aggressiveness, these were rejected because of the family cliché of perfection and omnipotence and because she feared the opposite situation—that is, that she was a witch.

It was evident that the sadistic part of her personality attacked not only me but also the parts of her personality that suffered and needed to be understood and helped. At the same time, however, she stressed medical and scientific knowledge and the statistical research that was part of her study.

For her, I represented a dangerous enemy who gave importance to psychic activity and proposed a different world from that of her idealized family. Whenever she was overwhelmed with anxiety, I always had to be present, like a wet-nurse breast-feeding a newborn. When I did not take on this role, I represented a constraint from which she had to free herself. She seemed to think I was the one who wanted her to stay close, because she was very afraid of seeming to be emotionally attached to me. She could accept being partly dependent on me only if I was the physician and she was the patient with an organic disease, thereby denying any kind of psychological relationship between two human beings. In the same way, she could accept playing the role of a newborn and imagine I was her nurse.

During this period, Elisa complained of the mechanical nature of her obsessive thinking, beyond which there was an emotional vacuum with no fantasies. For a long time she denied she had dreams either because she thought they were fantastic, illogical elements or because she denigrated them since they had to do with popular beliefs.

Third phase: beginning the work of interpretation

The work of interpretation could only be effective much later, when Elisa recognized the existence of a real relationship in the analysis. The absence of fantasies and dreams, coupled with the fact that she belittled their importance as a banal production with no rational basis, limited the material for discussion. She had fewer dreams and fantasies compared to the subsequent periods when we started to develop a relationship. She always arrived at the session very late in order to avoid waiting and thinking about the thoughts, fears, and hopes remembered from the previous session and having to work them out. Only when communication and dreams began to increase was it possible to start to interpret the material and to allow the analysis to develop.

My determination to continue the relationship and put up with her coldness, aggressiveness, overwhelming narcissism, and ambivalence made it possible to continue the therapy and overcome many problems. As occurs with the newborn, constancy and a continuous relationship are indispensable in establishing a reassuring relationship with the patient.

The problem was in finding the right therapeutic approach. If I was too kind and permissive, she felt I was being seductive because I wanted to make her dependent on me for my own professional or financial reasons. If I was patient or felt sorry for her, it was because she was so unfortunate. If I was neutral, I became like her mother, who was cold and rejected her. If I got too close, freedom would be restricted or I would get sucked into her network of reasoning or obsessive thoughts. If I did not immediately find the solutions to her problems, I was worthless. At times she expressed her satisfaction at my perseverance, which had been stronger than her destructive impulses. This was a sign of the difference between us and the start of her own differentiation. Elisa could hope that there was a current of feeling between people that had nothing to do with fusion or symmetry.

What happened in our relationship was often denied and transferred to other outside relationships, so that feelings were seen in others and not within herself and so were not directed towards me. For a long time the transference feelings could only be expressed indirectly through the vicissitudes of a real relationship outside the analysis. A lateral transference was therefore created. The idealization of a highly narcissistic couple that had been created outside the analysis reinforced the fragile image she had of herself, but as soon as the relationship became too close, the idea of being part of a couple made her feel persecuted. Elisa was afraid she would no longer be free, and she wanted to run away. She was repeating what she had experienced in the relationship with the object, where her mother had apparently kept Elisa tied to her and considered her indispensable.

The projection of feelings onto other persons and other relationships initially allowed me to make interpretations indirectly, at a good distance from our relationship. She did not then feel they were too persecutory and close. This process of working indirectly allowed her secretly to work out my messages, which she was able to understand at one remove. She was not, therefore, obliged to recognize her dependence—something that during that period still frightened her.

When our relationship became more solid, I focused my interpretations on the feelings that were beginning to emerge in our relationship. Her primitive anxieties regarding the danger of not existing or disappearing into the void were shifted by Elisa onto her medical patients, who, she feared, would die because she did not care for them properly or because they were vulnerable and unable to react. She experienced a sense of great anxiety because of what she saw as her inadequate professional behaviour.

Dream material

Elisa's dreams were very important for the development of the analytic work, given the quasi-absence of emotional communication and fantasies in the previous phases, and show the emergence of the autistic parts of her personality. The first dreams bear witness to Elisa's profound anguish and reveal her feelings projected onto me.

> *"You and I were together and I was consoling you because you were crying. You were sad because you thought I wouldn't make any progress. I tried to cheer you up."*

In the transference, this dream reproduced what she had experienced with her mother. She was born in order to help her mother get over her depression, and Elisa was unable to find meaning in her own life outside a therapeutic relationship. In this dream, Elisa could come into contact with me only by recognizing the depressed parts of her personality projected onto me and by taking on the role of the therapist.

Elisa might have imagined that she had been used as an antidepressant and that she had never lived just for herself. She had therefore created a false self by deciphering what the mother wanted from her. She could not accept being dependent and created an armour of strength to show she did not need anybody. She always felt that her role was complementary to the other person, whether in her relationships with friends or in those with colleagues at work. Originally the symbiotic relationship with her mother was imagined as being indispensable to the survival of both. However, since this prevented Elisa from differentiating herself from her mother, it prompted feelings of aggression, which Elisa, however, denied. She only admitted experiencing fear and weakness.

Another dream indicated that, for her, the analyst's studio represented a refuge with respect to the outside world but became a prison if the relationship between two persons continued:

> *"A man is holding my hands firmly in his, and I have to struggle to free myself from his powerful grip. I finally manage to free myself, but this is a form of aggression towards him and I'm afraid this will ruin our relationship."*

She found herself on the horns of a dilemma: on the one hand, she was afraid of entering into a relationship since she was sure she would be disappointed; on the other, she had the need to be helped. What appeared in the transference was her indifference and the fact that she did not listen. However, on a more profound level, this corresponded to her retreat into a protected, secret area where she could avoid coming into contact with me, a place where she could live with her repetitive thoughts and prevent feelings from emerging. Communication was expressed only by her need to determine reality and be in total control so that she could feel certain she would be not be neglected or rejected.

Her obsessive ideation allowed her to remain in a state of permanent paralysis, in a position that was half-way between being too close to the object and too far away from it. In this way, she did not have to admit that she was responsible for her own emotional and real actions. She imagined she was passive and was afraid of being imprisoned or abandoned.

The idealized image of herself, which mirrored that of the mother, prevented her from admitting that she had an aggressive side. This side only came out in the way she acted or the gestures she made, and she refused to admit that this feeling existed within her. Her tone of voice, the way she signed or made out a cheque, the way she greeted me or entered a room, her sudden decisions to go on holiday or to a conference, her habitual lateness and frequent requests to change our appointments all showed her need to be in total control of the situation and wanting to deny that I existed.

There was never any show of emotion during the sessions. Her authoritarian attitude, the speed and haste with which she unleashed a torrent of words in a high-pitched voice without ever pausing, showed the need to be always on the alert. This was what her depressed mother had apparently expected of Elisa, since she, the mother, had never received any support from her absent husband. The fact that Elisa had became precociously independent in order to protect herself against relationships and avoid suffering from the lack of relationships re-emerged in the analysis

The idealization of the self, the mother, and the family hindered a dynamic vision of the self. Elisa felt she was condemned to be depressed, just like her mother, and had no hope of finding her own identity.

The next dream shows how she felt persecuted in the relationship with the internal object and in the transference:

"I am in a very big house with walls covered in fabric. I am very frightened. As in a horror film, I expect something terrible to happen or to be

sexually assaulted. Someone might leap out and hurt me or make me feel guilty and so I go looking for him. I see my mother who is holding me tightly but I realize it is the devil or my mother who has turned into a devil. I am terrorized and wake up."

She associates her childhood fear when she was separated from her mother with the fear of finding that she has changed or is unrecognizable. Another association concerns the true story of a raped child. She wonders whether this can lead to mental disorder when the child becomes an adult. This goes back to the topic of violence experienced in childhood and the fear of going mad if a connection is found between early experiences and psychic disorder.

In his work on the fear of psychic collapse, Winnicott (1974) speaks of the fear of death or the void experienced by some patients and says that these are caused by very primitive experiences that date back to a time when the persons were not mature enough to recognize them. The void, which can be easily attributed to past trauma, can, however, represent the lack of something positive and good that did not take place.

This dream seems to emphasize the patient's unconscious attempt to find a precise, traumatic event of a violent nature in her past, such as sexual assault, to provide a logical explanation of her primitive suffering and the related persecutory fantasies. In fact, primitive suffering generally occurs at a time when it is still impossible to recognize experiences and remember them in autobiographical memory (Fonagy, 2001; Sandler & Joffe, 1969).

Her violent and destructive fantasies were not recognized as belonging to her but were magically transformed into her identity as a witch, so that her wickedness was mysterious and unchangeable. When her father died in a road accident, it confirmed that she was a witch since she had forecast his death through her fantasies and her fears regarding the death of her parents. This event proved once more that she wielded omnipotent power over the course of events: through her destructiveness, she felt as if she were an omnipotent child.

She had many dreams about her father. Elisa always desperately sought him out in her mind, even though she had rejected him when he was alive because of her need of a symbiotic relationship with the mother. A memory of her real relationship with her father did not seem to exist, except for his tendency to criticize her. The aggressive fantasies directed against her father, who had also been emotionally distant, made her feel extremely guilty for her imagined crime and this worsened at the time of his death.

"I'm sitting in front of a computer as if I were in a control tower. I'm trying to see if can manage to find the whereabouts of my father, who was lost on an unknown island. There was a fascist dictatorship, and no one could tell me what had happened to him. I wondered why he didn't let me know where he was. I then see my mother who is holding my brother tightly in her arms—like a child holding a teddy-bear. I watch the scene from a distance and cry because I had never felt her hold me like that."

Although on the one hand she drew strength from her protective armour, on the other she acted like a passive infant and only wanted the support others could provide. At the same time, however, she feared that others would take advantage of her. Her passivity was also shown by her slight tendency to addiction, another element that clashed with the analytic work. She would sometimes drink too much wine in order to forget and to avoid thinking about her real problems.

The development of the analysis was hindered by one part of her inner world which seemed characterized by an atmosphere of coldness and rejection. The actions that took place were regulated by strict laws and ferocious criticism. What she kept protected were her emotions and feelings—as if they had been locked away in a strong-box and she had lost the key. The idea gradually came to me that there existed an area that was distinct from the rest of the psyche and contained memories of terrifying and unutterable experiences related to the fear of possible disintegration because a primitive support structure had been lacking. This would explain the co-existence in the transference of her diffidence and refusal to enter into a profound relationship as well as her pressing need for fusion.

Another element that belongs to this autistic core regards the relationship between feelings and the body. Elisa imagined that her body was always exposed to possible somatic diseases, and this was a constant source of concern. The body, which seemed to have been unaffected by the libido in her early years of life, was considered as something unimportant, foreign to her, functioning in a mechanical way. A bad case of constipation had not been taken seriously, and the cause was attributed to an imaginary intestinal impairment or defective peristalsis, as if the intestines had stopped functioning and were, therefore, completely dead. Heavy breathing was considered a sign of bronchial stenosis. Any painful symptom was regarded as a sign that she might have a tumour in one of her organs.

On a somatic level, at the beginning of the psychotherapy Elisa developed ulcerative colitis, which I thought represented her need to get rid of dangerous, toxic poisons without having to become aware on a psychic level of the violence of her aggressive feelings. The medical treatment she received and the attention others gave to her intestines had surprisingly attenuated her depression and anxiety attacks. Conversely, whenever problems in the transference relationship occurred, physical symptoms appeared and subsequently hypochondriac convictions arose, which were expressed in dreams in which Elisa suffered from a tumour and was destined to die imminently.

She used to mistake destiny with unalterable, inexorable fatality to which she had to submit. She refused every opportunity to reflect on her inner world and determine her own destiny: her depression and isolation had to be chronic. Her conviction that she was incurable and had a genetic disease that was responsible for her psychic state was of the delirious type. She had innumerable dreams in which she was supposed to die of cancer of the lungs or intestines—organs whose function was ingestion or expulsion—or dreams of the uterus, which is the centre of fertility. Other repetitive dreams concerned very primitive periods of life: newborns or children with serious, incurable diseases or birth defects. The central topics concerned, above all, solitude and death, always in situations where it was impossible to make amends.

> *"I am an observer in the emergency-room of the hospital and am watching a doctor operate on a young woman who is suffering from bronchitis. He is using the aspirator without anaesthesia and the woman is terrorized but can't say a word since the aspirator is down her throat. I talk to the doctor about giving patients anaesthesia in order to alleviate their pain but a voice from outside says: 'No'."*

In the associations of this dream, Elisa speaks of the need to anaesthetize intubated newborns, who are not supposed to feel pain, and this again suggests a sadistic model of primitive relationship.

> *"I'm expecting a baby and I go to the hospital to give birth, but it is still too early. I go away but then return, and the obstetricians ask me if I am a doctor and why I wasn't examined before. In fact, the baby is not well: he is very small, ugly, and sick. I answer that I didn't feel like taking care of myself, as if I didn't want him. I feel guilty for being so negligent."*

She associates her continual sadness by imagining that in her infancy she had not been loved or felt wanted and remembers what her mother had told her about being breast-fed: that she had to find the breast by herself. In the dream, the desire to take care of herself and her concern about the child were absent, and this apparently implies a lack of vitality in her primitive relationships.

The following dream seems to demonstrate that subsequently the function of support and care had became stronger:

> "I am in the hospital where there is a newborn with serious problems. I think he has a cerebral haemorrhage, and I am very worried. A nurse makes an incision in his head, and blood streams out. I think that the baby is suffering from having lost so much blood and that it is necessary to stimulate his blood circulation. My colleagues do not agree, but I attach a drip to nourish and hydrate him. I try to find the veins, but I'm alone and in a hurry so I break two of them and am unable to insert the needle. I'm terrified that I can't help the baby and am afraid he will die, but in the end his colour comes back and he is out of danger."

Here we can see the primitive state of terror, experienced for such a long time, between life and psychic death. The associations concern the vital weakness of the baby and Elisa's inner world, which is marked by fear, guilt feelings, and obsessions. She realizes that she has filled her life with practical things without having cultivated her emotional side, even if in the dream she does attempt to save the child's life. In the dream, where she has to stimulate the newborn's blood circulation in order to keep him alive, Elisa seems to represent the function of the analyst which she herself needs (what Alvarez, 1992, refers to as "reclamation").

Another dream:

> "I go to take a public written examination in medicine. In order to help me, my boss gives me a little book to copy from, but a colleague who has just taken the exam says the topic is about tigers."

In the associations she said that she was amazed and thought that even though she couldn't take the book with her since copying was forbidden, she felt well prepared on the subject of foetuses, though less on children up to the age of 3 years. Here there seems to be an allusion to a happier prenatal period with respect to the period following birth. The subject of the tiger seems to represent the recognition of one's own aggressiveness as something to reflect upon.

In the dreams there are often situations of danger or imminent death, and what emerges from the stories or associations is a sense of desperation comparable to the one hypothesized as the origin of autistic withdrawal. These dreams would seem to bear witness to the presence of unconceptualized experiences that are very primitive and relate to life-threatening situations or imminent death. These memories, which are not recognizable in conscious memory, are seemingly buried until they are recognized during the analytic treatment.

As the analysis developed, feelings such as greed, violence, contempt, and arrogance—all of which she had earlier denied and projected onto others—re-emerged in her dreams, but it was difficult for Elisa to regard them as part of herself. She was disconcerted by the subjects of her dreams, and although she rejected them, in the end she saw her need for emotional contact emerge as well as all her feelings. Despite her conviction that she was unable to love, she gradually came to accept the idea of a therapeutic relationship.

> "I am in an empty unfurnished two-room flat. I'm having problems with my crooked teeth, and the dentist says he can't do much to straighten them. It would be necessary to put in a bridge, but I didn't want a foreign object in my mouth. In the end, I convince myself that the treatment might improve things. I go back to a house with no floor— just a dirt floor and not even a toilet."

In the dream she admits that some parts of her are weak, imperfect, and need help, and in the end she accepts having a bridge put in her mouth—that is, she accepts the idea of communicating with others.

With the realization that there existed a hidden core that contained her potential emotions, there were other dreams in which there appeared cysts, in the mouth or hidden in the body, that had to be removed.

> "There is a woman who has been buried alive in the earth near a road. I see the earth move, and a tall, thin woman gets up and starts walking. I think that traditional medicine has made this woman, as well as many other people, suffer and is responsible for making many wrong diagnoses."

> "I am in an operating-room where there is a blond surgeon with the face of an angel decapitating a newborn with an axe. But before killing him completely he takes out a cuttlefish bone from his body, which I imagine is the newborn's soul. This pains me, and I start crying. The surgeon proceeds but tries to console me. I tell him to strike swiftly to lessen the

newborn's suffering. I continue crying, and my patients ask me why the child has died."

From the associations it is deduced that the cuttlefish bone represented the hard autistic core that had protected her from primitive suffering and had withstood destructive attacks.

"I go see an old school friend who is affectionate, and I'm happy. Then I am holding a baby who is not well. I examine his mouth and find some knives and forks in his throat. That is why he can't breathe or move and is so rigid. I start removing the objects and bring him back to life again."

The introjection of rigid, sharp objects seems to be responsible for the rigidity of the psychic suffering that was shifted onto the body.

Final phase of the therapy

As our relationship started to take on the characteristics of an adult human communication, Elisa was able to listen to my words and get in touch with her emotions, which before had been frozen. A reflective silence replaced her fragmentary and interrupted utterances, and careful attention to her emotional experiences replaced her earlier coldness. This led to the disappearance of the initial symptoms and to a considerable change in the way she lived and perceived the world.

In connection with her desire to consider herself perfect, there was the following dream:

"I'm on the divan in your studio, but you were younger than me, with long, blond hair. I don't remember what you were saying, but I had to admit that what you told me was true—that is, that I'm not perfect, just a normal person with average intelligence. I then cry out in pain, thinking how difficult it is to accept that. Just as I'm crying out, I'm happy to experience a new sensation of joy: the fact that I can accept the words and affection of another person. I decide to remain lying down on the divan to reflect and hold on to this feeling."

She associates this dream with the time I was absent and the authentic feeling of missing a person who cannot be replaced with another, as in the past when one person was as good as another as long as she was not left alone. She is happy to experience a new sensation of pleasure and attachment to another person.

Discovering and recognizing the existence of hidden, encapsulated emotions beneath the organization of her personality was a long and difficult task because the attempt to escape from the relationship and the danger of depression prevented her from becoming aware of it. When Elisa finally realized that she could experience emotions and affection and the desire to be close to another person, we were both moved. This confirmed the awareness that the separation had taken place, that the need for fusion and symmetry had been overcome, and that there was a space between two persons that was full of feelings.

In addition to indescribable primitive fears, the autistic capsules also contained potential feelings that had remained frozen, unused, and unknown.

Just as, in the child, weaning and the beginning of independence can occur after the bond with the mother has provided a reassuring experience of dependence, so too, in the case of Elisa's analysis, the journey towards her own identity could begin only after a long period of fusion with me. Although she recognized that the early symptoms of depression—her intense anxiety, persistent obsessive ideation, hypochondriac fears, and mechanical movements and thoughts—had all disappeared, Elisa found it difficult to abandon the idea of being perfect and remaining in an endless therapeutic relationship. She therefore could not imagine being separated from me and not expressing the feelings that emerged from our relationship.

Her desire for perfection no longer meant reaching a top-level position at work but establishing human relationships that were supposed to be completely satisfactory but were, however, never perfect. As we approached the end of the therapy, our bond, which she had initially regarded as a prison, seemed to become too inconsistent and not protective, so she felt that I wanted to expel her from the relationship. The idea of eternity masked her difficulty in accepting the separation, experiencing the pain of mourning, and having to abandon her narcissistic ideals.

As in other patients with autistic cores, it was difficult for Elisa to accept the idea of separation and approaching the depressive position, because the thought of loss makes fears emerge that bring back to mind analogies with the primitive "catastrophic depression". In the outside world, these patients are unable to find an emotional relationship to replace the primitive attachment they experienced in analysis. They are afraid of being unable to overcome the solitude that follows the end of the long therapeutic relationship. Moreover, avoiding the thought of the separation prevents them from introjecting the loving bond with the analyst and moving towards psychic autonomy.

In these therapies, establishing a specific time when the therapy will end makes the patient abandon his illusions of an endless relationship as well as his childhood fantasies. Similarly, in the countertransference, the analyst realizes that these problems are difficult to solve because they evoke analogous feelings of mourning in her, as well as fears that the patient's internalized bonds are not strong enough to allow him to stand on his own. For the patient, considering the word "end" of the analytic relationship as something real and admitting the existence of one's separateness requires additional work in order to prevent old fears from re-emerging.

Discussion and vicissitudes of countertransference

In case presented in this chapter we can find the presence of elements that Sidney Klein (1980) considers significant due to the presence of autistic capsules. These elements include attachment to the therapy and "tenacious clinging to the analyst as a source of life", obsessional rigidity, non-communicative language, flatness of feelings, inability to maintain confidence, and extreme slowness to change. There is also a hypochondriac nucleus, which David Rosenfeld (1992, 1997) considers autistic.

As already described in chapter 1, the absence of direct verbal communication and the negation of the importance of the therapeutic relationship, by both autistic and adult patients, makes the analyst modify her approach.

I was aware of Elisa's acute psychic suffering for a long time, but I was unable to alleviate it because in her plea for help there was an implicit refusal of the interpersonal relationship. In particular, the idea that she was exploited and trapped in the therapeutic relationship and that her suffering had an organic or genetic cause, coupled with the rigidity and repetitiveness of her obsessive thoughts for a long time, all prevented the therapeutic relationship from developing.

For many long months I followed my "maternal reverie" rather than attempting to offer interpretations. I gave her my utmost attention and even provided immediate "first aid" whenever she needed to see me in addition to her usual scheduled sessions. For many months at the beginning of the therapy, she used to cry without being able to say a word, and I felt powerless to help her. She regarded this as proof of the fact that it was impossible for me to develop a therapeutic project based on verbal communication. Moreover, she thought that I had accepted the psychotherapeutic work in order to entrap her because of my own theoretical convictions or personal gain.

What might confuse the analyst is the big difference between one part of the personality, which appears strong and determined in carrying out logical tasks, as in the case of Elisa, and another part, which seems near psychic death and loss/deprivation of vitality. This second part coincides with the autistic core and expresses the absence of communication with inner vital objects. What characterizes this type of pathology is the gap between an active aspect that solves day-to-day problems and the underlying sense of emptiness and weakness of the self.

If we admit that the autistic retreat dates back to a preverbal period, we can realize how difficult it is to put such profound experiences into words. We will first have to wait and see whether the experience of containment of the patient's anxieties during the first phase of the therapy will allow him to experience the existence of a bond, even before he becomes aware of his own separateness and feelings. Only in a second phase will he be able to express his experiences through direct verbal communication.

Traumatic events experienced in a pre-symbolic period are unthinkable and cannot be expressed. Since they cannot be identified by others, they therefore create a barrier of non-comprehension and make these patients seem odd. In the treatment of autistic children, we are faced with the same repetitive, apparently meaningless behaviour. Only if we try to understand and interpret such behaviour through our intellect and emotions will such behaviour become comprehensible.

The fits of crying during Elisa's first year of therapy were the nonverbal re-evocation of this dramatic encapsulated event. It was related to the dramatic situation of an interpersonal relationship destined to be significant and, because of this, all the more frightening and painful. Elisa's frightening sense of depersonalization and derealization evoked a terror of total annihilation and re-emerged even when there was no real external threat. The dreadful feeling associated with symptoms of derealization and depersonalization seems rather archaic and can represent something experienced during a very early period of life even before the development of thought. If we consider the hypothesis that in the early years of life an autistic capsule was formed as a means of protecting the self from falling into an unknown abyss, we can realize why such patients arouse such a strong interest in the analyst.

A long phase of containment was necessary during which I used the sessions to observe and work out which analytic material had emerged. This phase can be considered as preparatory to enable the patient to recognize the object.

In the analytic treatment of neurotic or borderline patients, it is essential to realize the existence of these autistic capsules so as to overcome the impasse that these situations represent. It is, however, difficult to uncover these autistic capsules since they are protected and hidden beneath a personality that seems to function normally. The analyst can recognize the existence of these capsules through the transference and her own countertransference. By repeating the primitive relationships of dependence in the analytic relationship, the underlying anxieties—which attribute every problem to the absence of the analyst's facilitating function—emerge.

Just as the mother must try to establish the right distance between herself and the newborn so that he can come to know her and she can learn to understand and satisfy his needs and make herself known to him, so, too, in the patient–analyst situation the analyst must be very sensitive and flexible in order to create a situation where constructive exchanges can take place. For these reasons, I initially responded to Elisa's pleas for help when she had serious anxiety attacks, even though I realized it was important to maintain our scheduled sessions.

Alvarez (1992) describes the urgency of reclamation that she felt necessary during certain phases of her patient Robbie's therapy because she felt he was approaching psychic death. In the same way, I felt the urgency of establishing a human contact with Elisa in an analogous situation of psychic danger by making her feel protected and close to me.

As time passed, however, Elisa tried to avoid coming to the scheduled sessions and sometimes gave rational excuses saying she had to come a long way or had job commitments. The main reason, however, was that she wanted to be the one who decided the date of the sessions and holiday periods. My determination to make her come to the scheduled four sessions a week made us both quite aggressive. The patient could not tolerate a permanent relationship in which certain rules had to be obeyed, and I realized that there was the danger that the therapy could suddenly be interrupted and end in failure. This was the only expression of feelings during the early phases of the analytic relationship. Elisa fought against my attempts to help her continue the analysis and observe the rules of the setting. She thus transformed the situation into a rigid and hostile environment instead of a protective one. I often felt Elisa would abandon me without acknowledging in the least the efforts I had made to help her.

For a long time during the therapy I was overwhelmed by a sense of utter impotence, since the patient vented her enormous anxiety and depression on me. Her rigid thought patterns, her aggressiveness, the fact she was cold and unresponsive and continually attempted to denigrate my role prevented me from helping her in a constructive way.

Although her request for help was contradictory because she both needed and rejected it, her request was so urgent and alarming that it stimulated my interest and moved me. Elisa's anguish marshalled my feelings, although I was well aware that she utilized clever techniques to escape from the analytic relationship and attempted to obliterate my presence. Elisa got rid of her feelings of rejection, coldness, and deprecation and projected them into me, being careful to notice how I was able to contain them or reacted to them.

In repeating the original situation of dependence, represented by the analytic relationship, the underlying situations of anguish emerge that attribute all problems to the therapist's lack of support and understanding. In order for this to happen in an effective way, it is necessary for the analyst to possess a specific tolerance and sensitivity regarding the difficulty of expressing in words the hidden world of affective states. If the patient has a destructive attitude and feels that his attempts to communicate through projective identification are misunderstood and he receives no adequate response, this signifies that his primitive experience of a relationship with the surrounding environment was a disappointment and a failure.

Both during the first phase of Elisa's therapy when she would cry in desperation and during that where her hypochondriac fears dominated, in the countertransference I felt the intensity of the sense of imminent psychic death and the absence of hope which at that stage could in no way be transformed through psychic elaboration. The tendency towards addictive behaviour and her excessive obsession with numbers or somatic symptoms represented mechanisms to avoid thinking and psychic suffering. I hypothesized that an initial disorder in her emotional experiences had caused, on the one hand, her obsessive defences and, on the other, the psychosomatic solution.

Alvarez (1992, 1998) points out that in autistic children there is a deficit in the sense of self and object, and she attributes the absence of social interaction to the lack of living contacts with their own inner objects: the autistic child seems to lack internal objects that are interested in the subject and that interest the subject himself.

In the case of Elisa, the internal parents seemed very strong in their desire to affirm themselves in social circles, whereas on the emotional plane they were very weak. For years, Elisa continued to underline the fact that she was unable to love, and this conviction might be related to her not having an inner model of vitality and good emotional relationships between her internal objects.

The possibility of continuing the analytic relationship with Elisa was due to the fact that I identified with her profound experiences of feeling fragile and in need of help and always on the brink of non-existence. I always considered that her acting-out did not mean that she was attacking the bond, but that she wanted to look for it and experiment with it in order to satisfy her emotional needs. It was essential to understand and tolerate the rage of a small, exasperated child without overly reacting with interpretations that underlined, for example, that actings-out were a non-symbolic form of communication.

The initial emergence from the chronic state of depression occurred through behaviour of a slightly manic nature. Although this behaviour could be seen as a triumph over me or as a denial of the bond between us, it represented the emergence of a self that was no longer imprisoned in a paralysing depression. For example, her sudden decision to skip one session and go on a brief holiday was not to be considered only as a resistance to the analysis, but also as an attempt to feel that she was a subject who was strong enough to act independently. Elisa motivated her decision as a sign of improvement because she was finally able to do something pleasant and emerge from her obsessive behaviour. Interpreting her denigration of our work and attacking the setting would have weakened our bond and might have been counterproductive and castrating. It was important for our relationship for me to stress the emergence of her new vitality with respect to her previous obsessive presence in the sessions and differentiate the sessions she missed from the ones she had missed in the past.

The function of containment also concerns the attention the analyst must pay to the relationship between the type of interpretation she makes and the degree of development of the patient's capacity to introject them. For example, with respect to Elisa's frequent late arrivals, it was important sometimes to make her aware of this in order to introduce the concept of my real presence, my waiting for her, and the time limit. However, it was also important to point this out to her at the right time and not too frequently, so that my intervention would not be felt as overly persecutory. If my interpretations had been overly rigid and repetitive, this would have reinforced her defensive armour, which was already hard, as in a play of reflections in two facing mirrors. I therefore had to adapt myself to the successive phases of her development until she was able to listen to, accept, and introject my interpretations.

The transition from the couch to the face-to-face position made this introjective identification process possible, since Elisa could observe my facial expressions in addition to hearing my words. She could thus become aware of my presence, which was flexible and sensitive to her emotional states and represented a caring and attentive gaze. When she protested that she was not making any progress in experiencing feelings, I wondered whether it was Elisa who could not get in touch with her emotional needs, or whether I was the one who could not offer the warm, emotional support that might help her to change. Was I more interested in the intellectual exercise of trying to understand and analyse her because her emotional closure triggered my defence mechanisms?

Faced with these doubts, the advice of a supervisor was essential for the therapeutic relationship to develop. This allowed me to differentiate myself from the patient and to work out the material. In order for the analytic work to develop when dealing with autism, the analyst must carefully observe the emotional field of the analytic situation. However, she must also be aware of the existence of her own rigidity and of the part that does not listen to others. Moreover, she must recognize her difficulty in expressing her own emotional experiences, even though these have already been worked out during her own analysis and along the way of her personalization.

Conclusion

The result of our joint effort was that Elisa abandoned her obsessive symptoms, her acute or chronic underlying depression, and her hypochondriac fears. Her professional capacity was reinforced, and the integration of her personality allowed her to assume a more responsible professional role and to feel more creative and independent. Elisa always said that she did not have any feelings and therefore was unable to love. However, by working together, we were able to discover that her feelings were really frozen and detached and could gradually emerge. This new inner richness thus replaced the long-suffering aridity that she thought would never leave her.

CHAPTER EIGHT

Irene

History

I first met this girl, whom I shall call Irene, when she was 17 years old. She had been brought by her mother to the children's neuropsychiatric outpatient clinic because of a serious crisis characterized by fainting spells and uncontrollable anxiety due to episodes of derealization. Once it was ascertained that there was no physical damage (temporal epilepsy), she was put under diagnostic observation, and psychotherapy was suggested. The main psychic symptoms were the following: crises of derealization and depersonalization; and a phobia of public places, especially crowded department stores, where she would become paralysed with fear due to her inability to distinguish between the living people around her and the mannequins in the window displays. She could not tell which bodies were real and alive and which were fake or "dead". She did not understand whether she lived in the real world or in some other kind of world.

She had her first anxiety attack when she was an adolescent, during a party given by some friends. It was held in the basement of a house, and the confusion, the music, the smoke, and the voices gave her the impression of being in hell. Irene ran out of the building, utterly terrified, not knowing where she was and feeling as if she no longer existed. Subsequently, she would experience analogous sensations, though with less intensity, when she wanted to escape from difficult situations.

Irene was of a normal build and had brown hair, regular features, and large azure eyes that had an inexpressive, fixed gaze like her father's. She was always slovenly dressed, her hair was unkempt, and she spoke in a childish fashion. She had a childish voice, like her mother. Irene always spoke in the same sing-song and monotonous way, irrespective of the subject she was talking about: the end result was hypnotic and all-enveloping. She made grammatical and lexical mistakes because she either transformed the dialect spoken at home or used neologisms. She drew out her words, and her sentences seemed endless, suspended in space. She sometimes repeated the question she was asked as if she suffered from echolalia; she sometimes appeared to be daydreaming and not listening; she paid no heed to schedules, was unable to keep track of the sessions or pay for them, and also forgot appointments. Of note was the way she greeted me, in that she never looked me in the eye, and at the end of the session she would quickly leave, avoiding shaking hands.

When she spoke to other people, she often had the impression that there was a glass wall that prevented any real communication, and the voices she heard seemed far removed from her in space and time. She could not tell whether there was any real contact, and she concentrated her attention only on the single words that expressed either rejection or acceptance. All this created an unreal world that frightened her.

I remember an initial event that I now find particularly significant. Before the psychotherapy began, I accidentally met Irene's mother, who begged me to accept her daughter for psychotherapy. Her insistent plea for help seemed rather strange at the time, since she did not know very much about me. However, I subsequently realized how, during the initial interview, my listening to her had already represented a form of support for both the mother and Irene. It was as if up to that time no one had ever listened to the childhood experiences of both mother and daughter or attached any importance to their emotions. In her request for help, the mother demonstrated how completely lacking she was in any kind of internal or external support that would allow her to help her daughter cope with her psychotic anxiety.

Bion (1962a) hypothesizes that the newborn has innate preconceptions that expect confirmation through contact with a mother who is open to fulfil his requests and will therefore enable him to develop his mental apparatus. Perhaps the request of Irene's mother was an attempt to have this experience on behalf of her daughter—that is, to ask and receive help.

What struck me most about Irene was how important the sessions were for her, even though during the session itself her psychic presence seemed totally absent: she appeared inattentive and emotionally uninvolved and had nothing particularly significant to say. Her only need was to be in a place where someone would listen to her and magically alleviate her fears.

She was the only child of unskilled, working-class parents who were poor and were emotionally deprived. I had some interviews with her parents before the beginning of the therapy, and I realized that they had not had a close and warm relationship with their own parents.

Irene was described as always being hungry as a newborn, and she was nursed by her mother for just a few months. When she was little, her paternal grandmother took care of her since her mother had to work during the day. Her grandmother was an active, practical, and aggressive woman who was almost completely deaf. The mother and grandmother hated each other so much that they even attacked each other physically. In this family atmosphere, the father remained detached and never intervened, so that the child grew up in an unstable atmosphere full of hate and aggression, with two different women taking care of her. The feminine models oscillated between two opposite poles: the weak, slow, and depressed mother and the strong, active grandmother. The figure of the father, isolated and absent, was a mere shadow.

According to Irene's parents, she had had a normal childhood. However, during the therapy, as Irene became increasingly aware of herself as a person, she spoke of how isolated she had felt as a child, unable to express herself or interact with others. No one imagined she had any problems.

During her adolescence, Irene started becoming very aggressive towards the family, and this made life very difficult at home. She would not listen to advice, would pick a quarrel for the slightest reason, expected to be waited on hand and foot, and behaved in a provocative way. Such behaviour was a way of standing up to her mother, who wanted to control and disparage her. Despite all this, she never thought of leaving the family, and she continued her childish dependence, taking advantage of the benefits of living at home. In this way she showed that she wanted to be close to her parents in spite of the tense atmosphere, the continual clashes, and the unconscious

desire to steal things from her mother because of feelings of deprivation. Once she finished her training as a nursery-school teacher, she
had sundry jobs that never lasted very long.

Given the family's working-class status and deprived background,
family life was almost non-existent and was reduced to satisfying the
most elementary needs. They all had to work hard in order to live, and
there was no room for either feelings or the expression of feelings, nor
the desire to learn and improve their position. Irene worked on and off
as a hospital attendant and as an assistant baby-nurse in day nurseries,
but she often had to change jobs due to incompatibility with her supe-
riors and colleagues. All her relationships were negatively affected by
a delusional idea of persecution and by her refusal to acknowledge her
limits and defects; the failed relationships left her feeling rejected,
misunderstood, and helpless.

The psychic symptoms were intermingled with somatic ones: migraines and uncontrollable fits of vomiting in all social situations resulted from her problems in relationships. Irene would take to her bed
for two or three days, full of pain-killers, and no subsequent attempt to
interpret the situation brought about any change. The migraines represented concrete opposition to the psychotherapy, which was difficult
to carry out since she fully blocked the mental participation it required.
After crises of migraines and vomiting, she had periods of hypersom-
nia (she slept for two whole days). On the opposite side, for a long time
she complained of insomnia related to the fact that at night she would
get up to eat in secret: she still stole things from her "refrigerator-
mother" without being caught. Therefore, the food she gulped down
cold, instead of representing a pleasant "introjection", caused her great
physical discomfort.

A recurrent symptom was a sense of fatigue that was alleviated
only by consuming great quantities of food or drink such as coffee.
There was no sign of psychic depression, but the body expressed it
through tiredness. She put so much effort into physical exercises and
sports activities that she became thoroughly exhausted and went from
feeling omnipotent when she strenuously exercised to feeling totally
impotent, completely unable to move. In this way, she mirrored the
opposite behaviour of her grandmother and mother.

Others symptoms included constipation, amenorrhoea, acne, and
an eating disorder. In connection with eating, Irene had alternating
periods of bulimia and anorexia: weight loss and amenorrhoea expressed her refusal to accept a feminine identity. It was difficult to find
the correct diet, ideal weight, and physical form. She could not tolerate

the round shape of her stomach, which she considered enormous. Her illusion that she was omnipotent and could change her body by exercising or dieting was proportional to the intensity of her feelings of being persecuted.

After stuffing herself with food, she would vomit. However, Irene often tasted and chewed her food in order to savour it and experience the pleasure it gave her and then would spit it out. This eating disorder was similar to the way she acted with people: she exploited them, then ignored them, and finally drove them away. This is also the way she treated her partners.

The eating disorder was linked to the unending search for a physiological equilibrium and a physical appearance that she found difficult to achieve. Her strenuous physical activity was in marked contrast to her extreme psychic passivity. She was unable to think, reflect, or remember the things said to her or reach conclusions intuitively. Her sexual life was limited to sexual acts devoid of the emotional connotations of an adult relationship. In fact, her relationships with her partners were limited to a kind of addiction.

The course of the therapy

Irene agreed eagerly to begin psychotherapy with three sessions weekly. The constancy she demonstrated in coming to the sessions was in marked contrast with the fact that she did not listen to me and seemed to be present only as a body and not as a complete individual.

Although it was impossible to establish a meaningful relationship, she came to the sessions assiduously, thereby demonstrating her need for a fixed reference point that could "contain" her and make her feel safe. She would always seek my advice on everything—what to eat or how to behave at work—but seemed unable to learn from her experiences or those of others.

The sessions followed the same pattern, and for years I had the unpleasant sensation that the situation did not modify and that she was unable to work things out in her mind. My attempts to intervene in the material she brought to the sessions were ignored or were interpreted as persecutory. For a long time, I kept all the thoughts and conflict about her to myself. Initially, she would talk about her body in an obsessive and repetitive way: it was the only language in which she could express herself since it was easy and required precise answers. During the sessions it seemed to me that an infant was present but not an adolescent.

It was difficult to get Irene really to listen. She entered and slipped away from my studio without leaving any trace; it was all impersonal. Even my words left no trace, and it was impossible to determine if she was interested or irritated. In the absence of any meaningful verbal communication, I thought that the important signs were those related to her body. She looked scruffy and unkempt, wore no jewellery or make-up, and went around carrying huge bags. She gave the impression of being a vagrant, someone left to her own devices, a prey to destructive impulses. Her model seemed to be her mother. Her fixed stare and deliberate avoidance of the other's gaze indicated lack of interest in the other person and an attempt to remain absent and detached from the relationship. In this case, the model seemed to be her father.

For long time, the sessions were taken up with her physical symptoms, sometimes accompanied by serious states of anxiety. During a certain period of time, one of the most worrying symptoms was face acne, which Irene regarded as a visible element that ruined her physical looks. In order to make the scars less visible, she underwent some special beauty treatment, which caused a general erythema. In the subsequent days, Irene was overwhelmed by a psychotic anxiety since she was afraid of being transformed, losing the limits of the self, and dissipating in the world.

Since it was impossible to talk about mental representations related to emotional experiences, the sessions were boring and difficult. It was impossible to interpret the few dreams she did mention because there were no associations or because they expressed dreaded primitive terrors. These dreams expressed a very primitive terror, like the first one:

> "I was at the foot of my grandmother's bed and I found two eyeballs which had been torn out of their sockets and thrown on the bed. It was a terrifying scene of violence: I was terrified."

I thought, therefore, that it was better not to underline this terror, because I was afraid of worsening her suffering in re-experiencing it once again (or was I the one who was afraid of remaining in such emotional terror?).

Although she came from a culturally deprived environment and continued to live there, at a certain point she began to want to study and improve her cultural background. Her parents opposed her attempts to study because they did not understand what studying signified or might have feared that her studies represented the possibility of separation and differentiation from them. They thought that studying was only a waste of time and money. Her interest in studying might have marked the beginning of an identification with me, a new female model. She would always bring to the session a bag full of books, as if it were an autistic object.

Irene began to attend many different schools, training programmes, and social support groups. Her excessive preoccupation with filling her free time represented a manic aspect and an exaggerated idealization of both herself and me. I was aware of the danger that she might be disappointed and frustrated when she came into contact with other people, since her intellectual capacities were blocked. However, I also saw in this new activity the hope of her overcoming the inner emptiness and the self-denigration. My hope, however, was not born out of a rational evaluation of Irene's ability and behaviour, but was the expression of my need to reinforce her sense of being alive compared to her underlying deadness. In this situation it was important not to interpret this hyperactivity as a manic defence, but to consider it as her need to triumph over her past depression and sense of death.

During this period she felt the need to obtain a higher level of education which would open new avenues in the future. However, she found it extremely difficult to prepare for her examinations, because she had trouble concentrating and understanding concepts. She had to learn everything by heart since she was unable to relate one concept to another: she did not know how to solve the problems she was presented with or to organize her thoughts and write a composition. She knew many things, but she mixed them all up so that in the end her ideas were extremely muddled. Irene realized that it was difficult for her to learn and understand, but at the same time she found it almost impossible to take her teachers' advice.

After much effort, she managed to pass the school-leaving examinations and obtained her diploma. She then signed up for a number of evening courses, which took up all her free time: foreign languages, drawing, gymnastics, dance, sports coach, music, and horse-riding. She also joined a social club to meet people but quickly fled when she became too involved in the relationships. She used to ask her partners, much to their amazement, exactly what they wanted from her. She was unable to give a meaning to human relationships, with the exception of emergency or danger situations.

All the activities that took up her free time were supposed to give her practical experience, and she hoped that in this way she could improve her ability to think. Her approach to reality was unusual:

Irene tried out new experiences without really knowing what she was doing. Experiencing the real world attracted her because she thought that in this way she would fill the lack of mental activity.

For example, she became a member of a group of volunteers that helped mental patients, though she did not know who they were or what their problems were. She only thought that she would learn something new from this experience, without knowing exactly how to help them. She was curious about the superficial or concrete aspects of this group: for example, the name of this association and its location. She participated in a nonverbal way and was only interested in trying to understand what it meant to be mentally disturbed or to discover how it was possible to communicate verbally. At the beginning, she was amazed at seeing such strange verbal communications and the related pathological manifestations of these people and, for the first time, was able to compare them to her own pathological fantasies and behaviour. By coming into direct contact with this world, she became for the first time aware of her own inner world and her capacity to think.

I could not imagine what she really did with these groups, but I answered her questions regarding the situations she experienced in that context and agreed to interpret only her observations regarding the people she worked with. In this way, instead of being persecutory, my remarks became acceptable because they referred to other people and not directly to her. After having experimented coming in contact with reality in all these attempts, Irene's thinking was able to develop in the analytic relationship because she was certain of benefiting from my presence as a mediator who could work out her experiences. All of these experiences were discussed and analysed during the sessions, so that the amazement she had felt by coming into contact with these patients was transformed into a sequence of thoughts and verbal exchanges, mediated by my mental activity. Starting from analysis of actual facts, a psychic network was shaping up to include feelings.

She experienced great difficulty in using language to express her thoughts. Above all, communication was completely blocked because she was afraid of not being considered as a person or of being criticized inside and outside the analytic relationship. The contents of her talk were scanty, the formal elements of language and the way they were connected through grammar and syntax were often incorrect, and the terms were distorted or invented so that what she said seemed elementary, childish, and inexpressive. The container—the voice—was singsong, childish, monotonous, and questioning as if she could only wait for answers or else mechanically repeat what others said, so that language became echolalic.

The problem of communication was of fundamental importance for Irene, even though she was not consciously aware of it. The fact that she became interested in working as a volunteer at a centre for deaf-mutes made her realize that there was another way of communicating with others—through sign language and gestures. She realized that deaf-mutes also had a profound and unknown psychic world of their own, and she tried to find a way to get close to them. She felt she was like them since she, too, found it impossible to express herself through words.

In order to communicate with deaf-mutes, she learned sign language. This experience made her realize how limited sign language was in expressing the thoughts that these people were unable to express in words. She wondered whether the deaf-mutes could only communicate concrete acts and not feelings. She thus developed a greater ability to observe others, and this heightened her self-esteem since she was willing and ready to help them.

Often acting-out took the place of verbal communication and thus became a significant means of expression. She mistook our appointments, forgot payments, and broke off our sessions on the pretext of an unbearable migraine. The transference was split into two parts: a positive part characterized by her constant presence in the sessions, which did not, however, signify emotional attachment but, rather, the need to cling; and a negative part, represented by her indifference and by the way she denied my very existence and continually tried to destroy the setting.

Face-to-face phase

In the sessions so far, Irene always would lie on the couch. This allowed her to regress but probably made her feel she was physically ill and chronically entrenched in the analytic situation. When she began experiencing her own inner space, I suggested continuing our sessions on a face-to-face basis so that we could look at each other and see each other's facial expressions. This new position led to a change in our relationship and enriched our exchanges. Our sessions changed and something new was added to the way we communicated. In fact, this eye contact was much more important than words, which were meaningless for her.

The reason why I changed away from the couch was in order to make our relationship more real. Looking at me face to face meant recognizing my real presence, the situation of dependence, and her responsibility for participating in the relationship. In this way, we were able to analyse and face together the fears of persecution. Only then were we able to begin really working on her feelings of being persecuted. Our analysis focused on her habit of avoiding any kind of interpersonal relationship, her lack of confidence, the impossibility of recognizing a situation of dependency, and her contempt for others. I realized that the couch had increased her sensation of non-existence of both of us and the emergence of fantasies.

The problems she constantly experienced were due to the overlapping of her persecutory anxieties with the real experience of being rejected and criticized by the others. Becoming aware of her own aggressiveness and her childish omnipotence was essential in order further to modify her behaviour. These problems gradually gave way to manifestations of affection, a desire for closeness, and feelings of gratitude. At the beginning of this phase of the analysis, our conversation regarding these changes was characterized by extreme caution, for fear that the relationship might become too involved and binding. Her face also changed, in that now it was more mobile and expressive; she smiled in response to specific situations, and our meetings became more meaningful.

She also tried to learn horseback riding as another way of becoming more real. For the first time, she experienced a close relationship with a living creature, an animal, the horse. In such a situation, her feeling of being persecuted was related to only one thing: the fact that she might be thrown off by the horse. However, on this occasion she was taught that the horse understands the signals the rider gives it and that in order to ride with confidence the rider must be at one with the animal. Relying on the horse means trusting it—that is, establishing an emotional bond. She managed to listen to the instructors, and, as a relationship based on trust and collaboration was established, her initial fears of persecution diminished. This learning experience brought her great satisfaction, starting from the physical and psychic sensation of being in a harmonious relationship, as if she were part of a couple, with no need for language. She said with great satisfaction:

"Finally I have understood what it means to get along with someone!"

She began to tackle two problems: putting together a correct sentence that would clearly express her thoughts, and eliminating her sing-song intonation that so annoyed those talking to her. After initially rejecting the criticism of her interlocutors, Irene began becoming aware of her faults and was sorry she was incapable of communicating clearly.

During the sessions, I suggested she first concentrate on the idea she wanted to express and mentally formulate it in words before say-ing it. This allowed Irene to speak in public and make herself under-stood. Previously, she used to expect the other person to understand her thoughts without expressing them in words. Now she began to become more responsible for what she said, and some kind of identity appeared.

It was possible to start the real work of analysis only after years of accepting, containing, and listening to Irene. Being superficial had allowed her to survive, since understanding was too painful and un-bearable. She tended towards autistic withdrawal and lying as a way of escaping from understanding.

Changing jobs and developing mental activity

The different phases of Irene's working life reflect the corresponding psychological development that occurred during the psychotherapy.

Initially, her job at the day-nursery working with small babies served to calm her, at least when the babies were little and she could treat them like dolls. She was particularly careful to satisfy their physi-cal needs, but when they began crying she didn't exactly know what to do, whether to feed them or put them to bed. When the babies fell asleep, she used to lie down herself in order to sleep. Although she was duly reprimanded by her colleagues, she seemed to feel she had the same rights as the babies. She was generally criticized for such behav-iour, which underlined how inefficient, unreliable, and rather strange she was. Apart from that, she was well accepted by her colleagues because she was a good worker and always willing to help out.

There were some children she particularly liked because they showed they liked her, and she especially preferred infants since she could exert more control over them. However, she felt hostile towards the children's parents and most of her colleagues. In particular, meet-ing the children's real parents reminded her of her own conflict with her own parents, which she had internalized. Fortunately, Irene's work was done together with a team of nurses and supervisors, who checked how she took care of the children and therefore could verify and make sure that she carried out her duties in a non-detrimental way for the children.

Although she was apparently patient and helpful with the infants, her fantasies and dreams during this period were characterized by aggression and violence towards children and by the fear of being cruelly punished by the surrounding world. She was very upset at becoming aware of her aggressive fantasies and could not link them with her own feelings or conscious thoughts. Her dreams and fantasies about attacking children occurred in her mind out of the blue, but in her opinion they confirmed the fact that she was dangerous and that others would reject her. These thoughts made it difficult for her to work at the day-nursery. I was not really worried that she would act out her aggressive fantasies in real life, although I realized that she might lack maternal intuition towards the children she took care of.

> *"I am not able to understand why the children cry after I have satisfied their basic needs, like feeding and cleaning them. I am very attentive to their bodily needs and work very hard—even much more than my colleagues—but feel lost if the children remained dissatisfied and cry despite my efforts. I am afraid that their parents accuse me of not taking care well."*

Since many of her colleagues rightly criticized her stunned look and the slow way she talked, this diminished her self-esteem and increased her persecutory feelings.

After her murderous dreams she was terrified and asked me:

> *"Am I really dangerous as a person? Could others read in my mind these thoughts and discover my fantasies?"*

In my countertransference I wanted to make her feel that I trusted and supported her and that I accepted her feelings of aggression, but this did not mean that I encouraged them. I thought that my trusting her could make her keep at bay her desire for revenge. I pointed out that she should not let the freedom of experiencing within herself feelings and thoughts lead her to failing to accept the responsibility of acting. I thought that she needed most of all to feel accepted and encouraged, because she had been emotionally deprived and neglected. What I wanted to do was to add to this encouragement some advice that would make her reflect on the consequences of her actions, containing within myself my fears of her possible actings-out. I also recognized in her a great dedication to work.

After taking care of infants for a long time, she started working with older children but had trouble organizing them into groups and assuming a position of responsibility and authority. Following many years of working at the day-nurseries, she asked to be transferred to work in school administration, where the need for order, formal rules, and respect for the space–time coordinates required a greater integration of the ego. The reason she gave for wanting to change jobs was that she was looking for something less tiring. The real reason, I believe, however, was that she had become less interested in the neonatal period, which had been at the centre of our attention and had been so important because of her need to regress and identify herself with the newborn.

From feeling like a frightened infant herself in need of protection, she became a little girl with a minimum of autonomy, and went on to become the secretary of a school where she held a position of authority. She had to focus her attention on the real world, which did not allow her to behave in a confused or careless way. This change required an enormous effort on her part since it meant she had to come face to face with reality.

I was worried that she might lose her job, since she had to support herself and needed to maintain social relationships. Fortunately, since she worked for the public administration she was guaranteed job security, despite the fact that she was so unstable and quarrelsome. By changing her working environment, she came into contact with many different people. However, in her eyes, they were all the same, and she went from one to another without being able to form any lasting friendships since she considered people as being interchangeable.

As she began to realize the existence of deep-rooted problems, which gradually emerged during the analysis, she once again decided to change her job. She left her post in the public administration, which she found too impersonal, and attended a training course for teachers of disabled people and another one for event organizers. The study programme included courses in psychology and group psychoanalysis and opened up new avenues of interest and learning. She was able to participate in the study groups and accept the rules of the game without any fear of the past.

She accepted a job as an educator in a centre for people with physical and mental disabilities where, besides developing her relationships with the patients, she also succeeded in improving relationships with the staff by trying to be more cooperative instead of continually causing trouble as she had in the past. She finally found the courage to speak out and suggest new teaching ideas without fear of being rejected. She had to make quite an effort to find the right balance between the great difficulty she had in expressing herself and the desire to impose her ideas as the absolute truth.

As the person in charge of organizing social activities, she also worked with elderly people and discovered the problems that depressed patients had. She realized they were alone, often abandoned by their families, and dependent on the institute for psychiatric assistance. She began to experience empathy with others. She made further progress when she worked as a social events organizer at a retirement home. The situation reminded her of her relationship with her grandfather who had died when she was a child, and for the first time in many years she was moved to tears. Hearing the elderly people call her by name and seek her help made her feel like a real person and not a child dressed like an adult, and she understood just how abandoned and helpless the elderly people felt. This coincided with the beginning of a period of depression and an awareness of how she felt about the issues of separation and death.

She had once been asked to create an emotionally pleasant situation that would help a group of elderly people living in a retirement home to re-live feelings they had once had. She told me:

"I had them sit in a circle, and I placed in the centre a basin of water and some smooth stones I had collected in the mountains. I put on some classical music that brought to mind the sound of flowing water. I wanted to transmit how fascinated I had been by the beauty of nature and, in particular, by the shape of the stones, which, over the years, had become smooth as the river flowed over them."

She associated walking in the woods with pressing her feet on a cradle made of stones. She had felt supported and fascinated by the shapes and colours of the stones.

The situation Irene imagined, which I compared to a fantasy or dream, represented something new, because the significant element was a feeling of well-being or pleasure that she herself had experienced and now wanted to share with the elderly persons. The stones were meant to represent the natural environment but also the support provided by our relationship, in which Irene had begun to walk with greater confidence. She gave importance to the aesthetic aspect of the shapes and colours without referring to the hardness of the material that she had experienced in her early life. I thought that the material she had chosen was related to her early difficult relational experiences. Indeed, considering the real appearance of these ordinary stones, which she even brought to the session in very heavy bag, I was unable to see their beauty; however, despite the hardness and grey appearance of these stones, I was able to appreciate their round shape and smoothness, and I thought that Irene had made a symbolic transformation and had discovered an aesthetic aspect of significance beyond the ordinary appearance of the stones.

During this last period, it was moving to see how sensitive she was towards these elderly patients, how she had the courage to report staff members who treated the patients in rough manner, and how she could express her opinions. All the things she was now able to understand filled her with amazement as if she had suddenly discovered the psychic mechanism involved.

Irene's emotional development was considerably influenced by participating in a theatre group directed by a musicologist-psychotherapist who staged theatrical arrangements of operas in which psychiatric patients acted. The patients contributed to preparing the script and the staging by listening to the musical excerpts (usually popular operas) and expressing in words what the music made them feel. In this way, the script was modified as different mental associations were made—sometimes with comic or surrealistic effects—and then they would stage a comic version of the opera.

Irene's performance met with particular success, especially her dancing. She felt extremely gratified since the newspapers and television spoke highly of the theatrical group. On stage, in the midst of many people, Irene was able to express her feelings without any fear by singing and dancing and thus taking on an identity. Her great love of dancing, both as a form of physical expression and as a way to learn dance therapy, can be seen as a concrete attempt to bring her depressed parts to life.

Only after many years of analysis did she realize that she was a real person and could reflect on her past life and admit her pain, instead of acting aggressively. Irene's voice has by now changed, in the sense that it has lost much of its sing-song quality, and she herself realized that at work she expressed herself in a much firmer voice without drawing out her words as she used to.

In the past, she had been deliriously certain that her vision of reality was the right one and never questioned it. This defensive belief protected her from disintegration. Understanding her own pathology made her stop projecting it on others, lessened her feelings of being persecuted, and enabled her to consider different points of view. Coming in contact with the outside world of reality was one of the major benefits of her analysis because she could finally begin to become aware of the existence of her own inner world. Neither of us expected to reach this objective, and, although she came to understand better her personal history, it also resulted in a narcissistic depression (Resnik, 1999b). For the first time, Irene experienced feelings of sadness.

Resnik (1972) claims that one of the analyst's tasks is to encourage the patient to make the painful comparisons between his internal world and the external world and to find a coincidence in the space–time registers, between conscious and unconscious language, and between the narcissistic attitude and the willingness to socialize.

Discussion

This is an interesting case not only because, as the patient's symptoms disappeared, her personality developed, but also because it was possible to observe the changing interests and activities which mirrored the different phases of our analytic work over a span of thirty years. During this period the therapeutic relationship was, at times, interrupted for different reasons, but it was always resumed by the patient.

If we consider the story of this child, born into a culturally and emotionally deprived background, we can hypothesize that the human presence was represented by two alternating figures: the grandmother, who was active, and the mother, who was more passive and less clearly defined. These two women struggled to take possession and control of the child, who from an early age experienced an atmosphere where opposing forces existed side by side: aggression, apathy, and depression. Although the father was physically present, he was emotionally absent and of no consequence to the family. No one paid attention to her emotional needs, and the two significant female figures were more interested in their ability to control and dominate Irene rather than to create a protective environment for her.

Unlike most autistic children, Irene was able to establish formal relationships and express herself simply and adequately, so she gave the impression that she was, to a certain degree, "normal" or a "high-functioning Asperger". As the interpersonal relationship developed in greater depth, there emerged the absence of emotional experiences or any awareness that they existed, the impossibility of understanding the feelings of others, and the absence of symbolic thought, accompanied by a serious intellectual deficit.

Before the psychotherapy, Irene's life had been very superficial and seemed only to be made up of concrete actions. She had managed to learn the rudiments of schooling so that she was able to finish her compulsory education and start working. Her life, which was apparently normal, was reduced to the minimum due to her inadequate integration between body and psyche. It was not only a question of intellectual deficit but the lack of a psychic life. As regards her mental functioning, there was no creative relationship between the things she had learned and her own subjectivity, and no intuition. When she managed to understand the thoughts of others, she used all her energy to oppose them. For example, when she trained as a nurse, she learned some principles of sanitary measures and then deliberately did just the opposite to challenge the teachers. When she talked about these details, she expressed only slight guilt feelings about her behaviour.

Irene's principal characteristic was that she lacked a mind and was utterly passive. She was unable to think, remember, or study: she could only mechanically repeat what others said. She believed everything she was told without being able to distinguish between what was true and what was false. She herself told lies without being able to tell the difference from the truth. She was always suspicious, ready to attack, and refused to accept the opinions of others. I thought that her only relationship was with a hated breast from which she knew that nothing good would emerge. She was like autistic children, who do not reach the stage of possessing their subject identity and are unable to think. The longer they remain in an autistic state with no psychotherapeutic assistance, the less they are able to have vital experiences and occasions to learn and the poorer their emotional state becomes.

The autistic type of organization had created, in addition to an inability to recognize emotions, an intellectual deficit that was so serious that it made the patient appear to be stupid. When she was attending school, Irene managed to get along with others, but, later, people realized that she was unable to understand the significance of normal human behaviour or emotional interaction between persons. This led Irene to appear strange and unreliable.

As with Irene's intellectual deficit, we can hypothesize that in addition to the primitive defence mechanism of an autistic nature, there was also failure of the oedipal triangular space. This was due to the insufficient consistency of the paternal presence, which, in turn, prompted confusion with the maternal figure and the persistence of a pre-symbolic world.

When she spoke, she made many grammatical and syntactical errors and never found the right words to express her thoughts. This corresponded to the fact that she was unable to perceive the existence of a harmonious inner world, as was evident in her outward behaviour.

Today the deficit of the self in psychotic children is considered the result of an emotional and cognitive deficit. If in the mother–child relationship there is a deficit in transforming the child's preconceptions into thoughts by means of a positive coming together with the mother (Bion, 1962a), the child might develop a psychological deficit unrelated to his constitutional factors. If the child's mind fails to develop during the early phase of development, this deficit can become chronic and result in cognitive impairment, as in the case of Irene.

Alvarez (1992) underlines the importance of not mistaking the states of non-integration in autistic children with those of disintegration in psychotic children, In the latter case, "It may be necessary to conceive of a mental condition where thoughts remain not dismantled but unmantled, not projected but as yet never introjected, not dissociated but as yet unassociated; not split defensively but as yet not integrated; and where thoughts remain unlinked not because the link has been attacked but because the link has never been forged in the first place" (Alvarez, 1992, p. 95).

Alvarez (1992) agrees with Tustin (1981a) and Meltzer (Meltzer et al., 1975) regarding the problems autistic children have with notions of time and space due to an inadequate development in their inner world of a relationship between their infantile self and their maternal and paternal object. "An adequate sense of space, time or causality involves the notion of at least two fixed points of reference and these two seem to arise from those two great organising principles" (Alvarez, 1992, p. 98).

Irene lived in a world of bodily sensations. All the medical treatment she received proved unsuccessful, and the migraine attacks and fits of vomiting would often force her stay in bed for days on end and interrupt all activity. These symptoms were overt manifestations of her refusal to exist in the world and of a primary depression, which became chronic: the body represented a bothersome reality that could not be changed. There seemed to exist a primary confusion between being a body and having a mind that could think.

At the beginning she told me that when she shook someone's hand, she was afraid it might be the hand of a lifeless body (the living dead?). The first of Irene's associations was a memory of scratches on her mother's skin resulting from the fights her mother and grandmother used to have. So I thought that, to her, hands became "alive" only when they were used in an aggressive way. Many years later, Irene asked her mother some memories regarding the circumstances of her birth. The mother told her that during the pregnancy she was terrified of the delivery and was convinced that the child was dead because she did not feel it move. At that point, Irene realized that there was a connection between her mother's fantasies and her own confusion between dead or living bodies or parts of the body (this was one of the first symptoms she experienced in department stores).

The repetitiveness of her physical symptoms was reminiscent of the obsessive, unchangeable rituals of autism. It seemed as if the circular and closed nature of autistic thinking (Resnik, 1986) was applied to the organs of her body—for example, to the digestive system, which has the function of introducing and expelling food and could be seen to have links with the mechanisms of introjection and projection.

McDougall (1982a, 1989) regards psychosomatic states as manifestations of archaic conflicts intertwined in the psychic organization. The psychic vicissitudes that occurred at a time when they could not be represented in the psyche leave a dead space as a trace, and then the psychic pain is easily eliminated through actings-out that replace the psychic work. The painful experience is not a matter of cathexis or repression but is removed from consciousness.

These ways of discharging emotions through actings-out or bodily symptoms are different from hysterical symptoms, because there is no symbolic meaning. It is more a question of a disorder of the economy of feelings rather than an unconscious conflict. The life of these patients was built around preverbal connections between body and psyche, and the psychosomatic states represent a regression to a level of pre-symbolic functioning. Bodily functions such as smell and touch take on the utmost importance, as we can see with Irene.

Even though the somatic symptoms had been present in Irene for a long time, the first symptom to appear before the beginning of the psychotherapy was of a psychic nature—namely, an uncontrollable anxiety due to the experiences of derealization and depersonalization. Irene had a sense of impending doom, as though her conscious awareness had being totally destroyed. These initial psychic disorders indicated the lack of a sense of identity. The contacts with the real world triggered paranoid anxiety, which became so intolerable that it led to the sudden outbreak of psychosomatic symptoms.

In the transference, it was evident that she had reproduced a mechanism of emotional deafness similar to the real deafness of her grandmother, who had looked after Irene in her first weeks of life, and to the emotional deafness of her parents. Irene paid no heed to my code of signals and wanted to be the one who made the decisions by fixing appointments when they suited her. Her later work with deaf adults may have re-stimulated latent thoughts about this experience.

The only fond memories of her childhood were those of her paternal grandfather who was paralysed and lived in a retirement home. Irene told me that she could smell "the smell of old age" when she was near him: this confirmed my impression that she was living in a world of sensations rather than feelings. Again, her choice of working with the elderly to retrieve their earlier senses of "alive-ness" could be connected to this early phase in her life.

From the time we adopted the face-to face position, she slowly developed the ability to recognize and work out her fantasies of persecution, and this allowed her to participate more in the analysis and therefore to listen and think things out for herself. As the analysis proceeded, her ability to understand coincided with her growing capacity to understand other people better.

At the beginning of the therapy, the glass wall that she felt existed between herself and others and prevented any communication could be considered no longer as a concrete object, but as an inner defence mechanism against any sort of relationship. Irene realized that she was the one who isolated herself and blotted out reality. The glass wall represented an autistic defence. With the wall, she became as deaf as her grandmother to messages coming from the outside world (as well as her inner world). It was interesting to note that the defensive barrier that she had built was not a real wall but one made of glass, which allowed her to see the real world but kept the sounds out.

Irene's voice has by now changed in the sense that it has lost much of its sing-song quality, and she herself realizes that at work she expresses herself in a much firmer voice and without drawing out her words as she used to. Compared to the past, she realizes that different situations and persons require her to behave accordingly. It was possible to see how becoming aware of one's own intrapsychic processes meant making them subject to the control of the ego, and thus attenuating the destructive impulses.

In the beginning, Irene's facial expression had been static, she did not gesticulate, and she tried to avoid eye contact, as if she were autistic. In the transference, she reproduced what she had experienced in her early childhood: no loving gestures, but rejection or contempt, a bodily presence that was not mentally present, a request for immediate, concrete help. We can hypothesize that the inability to obtain suitable responses from the important figures in her early childhood made her imagine that she was excluded. This rendered the transference relationship impracticable and, instead, gave rise to a desire for intrusion and possession of the other.

The recurrent, psychosomatic symptoms and obsessive rituals continued unabated and were a reaction to any kind of change. They were accompanied by a tendency to become addicted to drugs and food. In this sense, Irene was similar to the patients McDougall (1972) describes as "anti-analysands in analysis" who are addicted to their analytic sessions but unable to communicate their feelings. They attempt to get rid of psychic tension through acting-out or all types of addictive behaviour.

We see how part of Irene's own emotions became lost, as did her emotional ties with the surrounding world, so that in the end these emotions became unrecognizable. This resulted in a split between the outer and inner worlds of emotions and made it impossible to establish social relationships. Once the intolerable feelings were eliminated, the only thing left was the biological threat; in order to protect herself, the patient had to resort to addictive elements such as medicine, food, or coffee.

The real analytic work was possible only later, when communication had reached an emotional level. The analysis was gradually able to give a meaning to the reality that the patient encountered. I had to wait a long time before being able to utilize the interpretations in the context of a real relationship in order to initiate a process of introjections and projections.

As Lechevalier-Haim (2001) points out, in long-term treatment of autistic children the analyst must be receptive and ready to accept the unknown, non-familiar elements that the patient brings to the session, including those related to bodily perceptions, even when archaic anxieties concern death. In addition to this receptivity, the analyst must also offer libidinal forces full of energy. Since I interpreted events that happened to other people in an indirect way, Irene was free to transfer these interpretations from the others to herself and secretly to decide whether to accept them or not. A direct interpretation at that moment would have been premature, rejected, or felt as an intrusion.

This way of proceeding made it possible gradually to establish a therapeutic alliance and an emotional bond that formed the basis to start analytic and interpretative work despite the inconsistency of the initial relationship, the scant progress, and my frustration at the stalemate situation. Sometimes I experienced the need to give some "non-analytic" advice, when, for example, during the session, I suggested she formulate a thought in her mind before expressing it in words. In the past, she expected other people to understand precisely what was in her mind without the need for her to express it clearly in words.

Vicissitudes of countertransference

Despite the apparent immobility of the analytic process, my countertransference worked incessantly to understand and adapt to Irene's communications and experienced continual swings between hope, doubt, and preoccupation.

Irene's initial request for help was very dramatic due to her fears of derealization. This aroused my intense interest in her case and direct emotional participation in her state of psychotic anxieties.

As I have already said, the only way to get close to autistic or psychosomatic patients and understand them is through the analyst's countertransference reactions, which act as a compass. But Irene's actings-out and some physical manifestations led me to fantasies of rejection. All these elements ended by paralysing my hope and empathy in the countertransference. Moreover, as the relationship developed, I became increasingly amazed by her bizarre and unpredictable behaviour which I was required to accept beyond any possible intellectual understanding.

The work that occurred in my countertransference could be made thanks to the sharing of emotions that Irene found difficult to recognize in her inner world and that had not been shared by her primitive environment. I sometimes felt afraid or worried, sometimes amused, sometimes amazed due to the bizarre content of her thoughts. I therefore actively participated in her emotional swings and tried to find a possible adjustment between her object relationships and my inner experiences. By sharing this continual work of my inner transformation, Irene was able to experience being close to another human being, unlike her primitive relationships. At the same time, her assiduousness in coming to the sessions and her investment in the psychotherapeutic relationship contributed to deepening my bond with her.

Although I understood the intensity of her aggressive feelings, I always saw the enormous effort (though not conceptualized and finalized) she made to modify the quality of her life and her attachment to the therapy. I thought that her determination to continue her work with the children represented an attempt to be a "good mother" and, at the same time, to feel like a small child who was grateful and satisfied by being taken care of. At this point, my hope that the analysis would stimulate changes in her representations coincided with a hope she herself nourished but was unable to formulate.

I identified myself both with the parental figure and with the deprived child. For example, at one point she told me that, after completely satisfying the day-nursery children's needs and putting them to bed, she also went to sleep since she felt she had the same rights and was subsequently amazed that such behaviour was criticized by her colleagues. I identified myself with her infantile part, which felt victimized and protested, and in my countertransference I justified her being tired like a newborn who had to act as a mother with many children. At the same time, although I recognized her effort to be as a good mother as possible, I also identified with the needs of the children she took care of and pointed out that she had to take on the responsibility of her adult role.

Although the aggressive and destructive fantasies that Irene manifested during the analysis were full of violence towards the outside world, I did not feel they were directed towards me. Instead, it seemed to me that she was trying not to recognize me as a real person, keeping me at a distance like a shadow or, perhaps, like an idealized object.

As regards the fact that she changed her appointments, and her continual questions about practical problems, I had to consider this repetitive behaviour as the rituals in autistic children. I could only present myself as a real person who was always present and available, neither frightened by her nor destroyed by her projections. Only when Irene's real behaviour represented a danger for her or for her job did I assume a paternal role, pointing out to her the real consequences that this could have on her work environment and what she should do in order to protect herself and keep her job. I consented to her telephoning me if she experienced an unbearable anxiety attack, since it was enough for her to hear my voice to calm down and face her problems, even though what I said merely aimed to give her some support. It was very important for Irene to experience the presence of a person who was attentive and willing to listen to her before considering the specific messages I could transmit to her. Nevertheless, even if the diligence with which she continued her psychotherapy could also be considered a kind of addiction, and not the expression of a real relationship, a form of transitional space did emerge in our relationship in which emotional exchanges occurred, and very slowly she created a space in her mind.

For a long time I myself wondered exactly what kind of analytic relationship existed with a patient who could neither dream nor work out her thoughts or my comments but, instead, acted immediately and repeatedly to get rid of emotional tension, someone who consoled herself by becoming addicted to medicine or food or who withdrew into her body and manifested psychosomatic symptoms that did not respond to medical treatment. How was it possible to continue the analysis and hope to find a way to understand the patient better, despite the apparent absence of a mental space? I often wondered how the bond between us was formed and became so intense and long-lasting despite the many problems we both had.

In such an atmosphere, what made it possible for me to build empathy and be reasonably optimistic? What worked in our relationship to make the patient change and grow? How could I believe in Irene's capacity to regain her intellectual capacities, which had apparently been lost? Did the point where we met and understood each other coincide with an area in our unconscious?

I think that a therapeutic bond is particularly facilitated when the analyst's interest in the patient's unconscious problems coincides with her own particular sensibility. In such a situation, the analyst can find in herself the traces of primitive experiences related to the development of her own self and which can be traced back to what the patient presents in the psychotherapy at a macroscopic level.

These observations seem to coincide with the theories of Alvarez (1995), who asserts that the analyst's subjectivity is inevitably involved in the patient's process of transformation and that there are some unconscious processes in the countertransference that are unknown to the analyst despite her continual attempt to understand and elaborate the inner and outer material.

Conclusion

Over the years, this case oscillated between psychotic and psychosomatic symptoms. The psychic symptoms were related to a delusional ideation of persecution attributed to the outside world. When the psychotic anxiety became intolerable and the psychic activity was unable to work out a protective strategy to cope with painful emotions, psychosomatic symptoms emerged or the tension found relief in acting out. This situation prevented Irene from developing her sense of identity and contributed to creating a serious impediment to her intellectual faculties.

After many difficult vicissitudes in the transference and countertransference, our relationship—which, for a long time, Irene had refused to acknowledge or had denied in order to protect it from her aggressive attacks—was finally accepted and enhanced by feelings of gratitude and affection. The somatic symptoms disappeared and gave space to a mental activity.

I would like to end by mentioning one episode Irene described during the last phase of the therapy. While she was attending a course to train as a social activities organizer, she had been asked to select the pictures she liked from a magazine. During one session she explained to me how she selected them. One was the photograph of a polar region and had the following caption: "The outermost territories". She said:

"I lived too in an outermost, glacial area, a cold land no one visits. Analysis had allowed me to find some good things in this inhospitable, freezing land without movement or light."

Her face expressed the emotion of having discovered something she had never realized even existed.

CHAPTER NINE

Ambra

History

I first met Ambra when she was 20 years old: she was a tall, stout girl with a mass of long, golden hair. She had a pale, rather strange face, with a questioning look and expressionless eyes. She looked as if she came from Mars. Both the tone and inflection of her voice, the way she moved, and what she said all expressed violence and were intimidating. Her questions required immediate responses. Her body wanted to impose itself on others in spite of her neglected and scruffy appearance. Her arrogance and desire to prevail over others were constant.

At that time, Ambra was prey to an acute dissociative crisis with erotomaniac delirium and ideas of being influenced and persecuted or envied by others. The acute phase, during which psychotic symptoms prevailed (delusional ideation, and a dissociative state) lasted several months and was accompanied by impulsive behaviour that was difficult to avoid, complications in her social relations, and the tendency wilfully to put herself in dangerous situations. The psychotic crisis exploded during her university studies.

During the phase in therapy of the dismantling of her personality, I felt overwhelmed by the confused and contradictory accounts she gave of her life and as though I were in the midst of chaos. This prevented me from evaluating the entire situation and entering my own reverie (Bion, 1962b). Apart from her verbal violence, I was unable to understand and sense her mood: no shade of feelings was projected into me (apart from her open aggression), and I could not feel a moment of empathy, which is an indispensable condition when initiating psychotherapy. I could not find in her any human qualities that I could appreciate. Nevertheless, I was interested in continuing our relationship because of her request for help.

She told me about her childhood spent in an Asian country, with a mother who was always psychically ill and who had been removed from her social environment of origin, so that Ambra was taken care of by different nannies indigenous to the country. Ambra was the oldest of three children and came from a bourgeois family. Her childhood was marked by a number of traumatic events. Her mother suffered from a psychosis; her father was often absent for reasons of work and thus was unable to give mother and daughter any support during that difficult time; and, moreover, there was no extended family that could represent an alternative to the relationship between mother and daughter. The nannies who took care of her spoke a different language. All these factors, together with the fact that the family had to move abroad, increased the isolation of the parental couple and made the relationship between the child and the mother even more exclusive. When Ambra was 23 years old, her mother died.

The persistence of traumatic events at a very young age might have been what led Ambra to assume an autistic position and to feel persecuted. Her early relationships were marked by episodes of destructive violence alternating with others of total indifference—an atmosphere that was reproduced in the transference. When the mother was prey to her psychic problems, she would oscillate between different states of mind and was completely preoccupied with her personal anguish. After the father's prolonged absences, which the child found inexplicable, he would suddenly reappear only to disappear again almost immediately.

During Ambra's pre-adolescence, her mother once told her—following a dissociative crisis—about her own delirious fantasies. The girl shared her mother's suffering and became frightened, but after a few days the mother would retract everything and say that the stories were the fruit of her sick imagination. The child would remain disorientated since she did not know what the truth was or what the words meant. For a long time, the real relationship with the mother oscillated between Ambra's inability to separate and detach herself from her and violent outbursts of aggression directed towards her.

When Ambra was at elementary school, it was reported that she had some psychic disorders, but the parents did not take the matter seriously. During her adolescence, Ambra was anorexic for a brief period. She continued her studies, with mediocre results, and enrolled at university. However, after the first few years she had to interrupt her studies suddenly because her thought disorder worsened following a psychotic crisis. Attempts to resume her studies and take examinations proved unsuccessful.

The course of the therapy

This case presents some complex problems of a patient with alternating psychotic and hysterical symptoms. Over a period of thirteen years she underwent uninterrupted treatment. Psychoanalytic psychotherapy (four sessions a week) was accompanied by psycholeptic drug treatment that changed according to the variations in the symptoms and was administered by a psychiatrist who also maintained contact with the family.

The first phase of Ambra's therapy included symptoms of dissociation and delusional ideation of persecution. The second phase included bodily symptoms of a hysterical nature. The third phase marked the emergence of the autistic core.

According to Ambra, the spark that set off her psychotic crisis occurred when she was preparing a psychology examination at university, where her studies clarified and confirmed what she had suffered as a child.

At that point, her early experiences re-emerged and she was afraid of being completely annihilated as a woman by her peers because she felt they wanted to persecute her. Believing herself to be exceptionally beautiful, strong, and clever, she felt that the girls who formed a group of friends envied her powers of seduction and intelligence and slandered her to the men of the group.

At first, psychotherapy was characterized by the need to contain, tolerate, and accept her, to listen to her, and to come to terms with the fact that I could not understand her and had to abstain from any sort of interpretation. It was difficult to continue hoping that the therapy would develop in a positive way and that a therapeutic relationship might emerge. But Ambra was very assiduous, always arriving punctually. She agreed not to smoke during the sessions, although she was addicted to smoking. Instead of a relationship of dependence, she asked for precise answers to her questions: she did not want to learn from me, but just to rob me of something.

This first dissociative phase was followed by one mainly characterized by recurrent childhood memories and embellished by her lively imagination so that it was impossible to distinguish real events from fantasy. To overcome her enormous solitude and emotional confusion in her childhood, Ambra found relief in playing by herself or with her brothers. She used to invent play scenes in which they wandered around the world and imagined their parents were dead. This game allowed her to imagine that she could transform the environment in which she lived into some remote land. Outside her imaginary world, she had to put on the mask of "an adult child" because she felt she had to be the one to take care of her mother and that she could never leave her alone.

The stories she told me represented elements I could neither remember nor talk about because they were so evanescent: these elements could not be communicated, even though they weighed heavily on the sessions. For a long time the sessions signified meeting in an unknown "neutral territory". Referring to transitional phenomena, Winnicott (1951) says there is a neutral area in which the unintegrated patient can experiment with the fact of existing and being discovered by the analyst and can thus hypothesize the existence of a self. But at this time I did not feel that Ambra could use our meetings in this way.

At first, I was more interested in understanding the logical sequence of what she was telling me, grasping her hidden feelings, and understanding the general meaning of her words rather than staying near my feelings. My continual attempt to give a rational meaning to Ambra's communications or understand her symptoms on the basis of theoretical knowledge might have represented my defence against the danger of madness. I had to protect myself from another danger—that is, succumbing to frozen feelings or falling forever in the void.

At the same time, through my countertransference, I was beginning to distinguish what was real and what was invented or completely false, but without mentioning this to Ambra since I feared this might reinforce her persecutory fears and thus distance her from me. In my attempts to get close to her, I would offer encouragement, understanding, and suggestions, but these attempts were doomed to fail miserably and were scornfully rejected.

The second phase was characterized by bodily symptoms that had also been symptomatic of her mother. The hysterical symptoms, which might have appeared during childhood when she was having trouble walking and had been misdiagnosed, represented a way of communicating by means of the body as if this were the only way people would listen to her. Soon all the symptoms of hysteria appeared, including asthenia, insomnia, intestinal and muscle pain, eye problems such as transitory double vision, lack of voice, lack of appetite or bulimia, some fainting spells, and so forth.

Unlike at the beginning of the therapy when she would come shabbily dressed, she later began to focus her attention on her body and disguise it by dressing elegantly in a provocative way, putting on heavy make-up, and continually changing the colour of her hair or her hairdo. She thus transformed herself into a seductive vamp who could conquer any man—indeed, metamorphosis was her passion. I thought that Ambra's body was invested with love primarily on the surface, and for this reason she became mainly interested in her mother's hair, skin, clothes, or physical beauty. In the countertransference, I felt invaded by the chaos of the patient's identity because, for her, clothes were more important than the person who wore them.

During those years, she would pass the time smoking, listening to records, and imagining erotic encounters. When she experienced a crisis, she would threaten suicide, destroy objects, and create scenes in front of her parents. Thus, ever since Ambra's first psychotic crisis, her father became her guardian angel. This triggered an oedipal relationship of an incestuous type (Racamier, 1995). Given Ambra's regression, the attention lavished on her by her relatives was more suited to a child than to a young woman.

In this period the issue of eroticism began gradually to emerge and with it, the consequences of acting out her impulses. What emerged was an instinctive and compulsive sexual drive, devoid of any feelings, which proved to be a vital attempt to dominate her old fear of death and annihilation.

Her interest in sex gave herself and others the impression that she was "a normal woman" and in touch with reality. But she was merely imitating popular social models: being a showgirl or disco dancer, exposing her body, and offering it to men were her greatest desires. In this way, she could act out her erotic scenario, but this was also her downfall because it made her re-experience situations in which she felt emotionally isolated and exploited.

She sought out imaginary relationships with men to replace the primitive relationship with her parents that was supposed to provide protection, security, and continuity. She could have found all this in a loving relationship had she been able to experience feelings of love towards her partner. However, as she based her choice only on superficial elements such as clothes or a car, relationships ended in failure and thus confirmed her inability to love. Unfortunately, love was something she only imagined and did not feel. The word "love", and the situations related to this word, were used without a mental representation of an actual emotional experience.

Her encounters with young men were supposed to be a source of pleasure but ended up being erotic games in which she aroused the desire of the other person. She herself, however, did not experience any real desire and would immediately start thinking of ways to get rid of her partner. Men found her behaviour incomprehensible and disappeared from the scene feeling bewildered and with a sense of failure. The dreams she had at night or during the day always had to do with being possessed or raped and were imagined accounts of sexual abuse. In this way, even her dreams tried to preserve her own narcissistic image. In any case, in her dreams she was the object of desire but her body experienced emotions as mere bodily sensations.

Emotional feelings were projected into others:

"I am in front of the window and I am undressing. In the opposite house there is a young man undressing, too. He is bare-chested, and I think he is provoking me for sex. On the contrary, he tells me that he was shooting a film, and he comes into my room in order to take away my furniture for the set. At the end, I also give him a T-shirt and a pair of trousers from my adolescence."

Another dream:

"I organize a very elegant party with important and handsome guests, but there is always something wrong: the food is not ready, my dress is torn, and so on. In the second part of the dream I see you sitting in a very high throne as a queen, and you tell me that we have to finish psychotherapy. So I touch my skull under my hair in order to find a point that represents the place where the analysis finishes."

She associated her hair with strength, and she asked me what "the end of analysis" meant: she could only think of death.

For a long time her sexual behaviour was obsessively the same: she would always choose men of a questionable nature, perhaps to try to dissipate her inner violence.

Emergence of the autistic capsule

After having realized that her eroticism was a defence mechanism, it slowly and gradually disappeared, and Ambra found herself empty and alone, unable to imagine a loving relationship. Only in this way could she stay alive without suffering. Although she always came to the sessions, Ambra remained silent, showed no feelings, and had very little to talk about, beyond physical ailments.

She would ask me:

"What are we supposed to do together? Think? Before, I never used to imagine that other people could think. Whenever I wanted something I tried to imagine how I could get it. How can I communicate my feelings— I don't have any. I never considered other people as persons, not even you. When the session is over and I leave, I have no imagination and I cannot imagine a conversation with you outside this room. Before, I only imagined things and could only communicate with my body—for example, by dancing or making love."

She experienced her isolation as a condemnation, since it was pervaded by a feeling of deadness. But it was also a retreat from the uncertainty of human relationships and the danger of emotional exchanges.

When I came into contact with the autistic capsule that had been buried under the other psychic defences, I felt annihilated by the intensity of the depression, which transmitted the sensation of psychic death. Her emptiness and inner icy core overwhelmed even me and seemed unbearable. Just like her, I also felt frozen and completely impotent. Both Ambra and her relatives regarded this loss of vitality, which seemed to be present during the manic or hysterical phases, as a form of mourning and as a sign that she was getting worse. In their opinion, psychotherapy was turning out to be detrimental.

It was necessary to have great patience (Rhode, 2001) and wait for some change until she emerged from the catastrophic depression characterized by the absence of any vital force. It was during this period that I tried to give meaning to this apathy and depression by introducing the topic of the suffering she had experienced as a child and which represented the most genuine part of her experience, which was often denied.

Although the absence of any emotional involvement had existed in our relationship from the beginning, it was sometimes masked by hysterical and psychotic symptoms. They represented a more vital reaction compared to the psychic death of the autistic condition. Coming into contact through the psychotherapy with these suffering and depressed parts, with "nameless dread" (Bion, 1962a), and giving up her psychotic and hysterical defences, was something too difficult for Ambra to deal with.

From time to time, she would emerge from her isolation, only to retreat once again as soon as her previous symptoms reappeared. However, there were rapid oscillations between approaching and moving away from the relationship, and my countertransference feelings were the litmus test of when she would enter or leave the autistic, paranoid–schizoid, or hysterical area. Her fear of being emotionally dependent on someone undid the progress she had made and caused her to withdraw.

When our relationship became warmer several things emerged: greater trust in the transference, the acceptance of being dependent, the introjection of my words, and the use of her cognitive capacities which seemed to have disappeared during the periods of intense isolation. All this made it possible for her to improve her social interaction, take examinations, start working, stop frequenting disreputable circles, and abandon her previous life style.

Unfortunately, the periods of activity and hope for change were easily replaced by periods of passivity and fragility in which the pathological organization of Ambra's personality was predominant.

Discussion

The biggest difficult within the therapeutic relationship was represented by the oscillations of the psychic framework, which made me directly experience contradictory countertransference experiences. The atmosphere of the transference communication was generally dominated by violence, and the signs of the presence of suffering autistic parts were minimal. The result of all this was that I felt confused and powerless.

In her interaction with me, Ambra was not interested in discovering new things. She merely wanted to repeat the experience of her previous emotional relationship and at the same time feel the safety of having someone who would listen to and look at her. In this sense, she regressed to a primitive stage of existence, dominated by physical sensations. Emotions were experienced as bodily sensations, which were not subsequently processed in her mind. The great attention paid to the body detached from the psyche represented a way of imitating the mother's external features. Ambra tried first to demonstrate that there was a good relationship between us by dyeing her hair the colour of mine. This was an attempt to imitate me and represents a preliminary stage of identification, but one that only concerns the surface of the body and not me as a person with feelings. In a subject who does not seem to have any inner space, the process of introjection cannot occur due to the absence of depth, which makes containment impossible as well as the exchange of conscious and unconscious fantasies.

Imitation, which belongs to a very early stage of normal development, is connected to sensory perception (Fenichel, 1945; Gaddini, 1969; Schafer, 1968). Like a newborn, Ambra used the process of imitation, which is linked to sense perception rather than to the process of projective identification. Imitation is also a way for the newborn to reach a certain degree of cohesiveness of self and serves as an important form of object relatedness (Ogden, 1989). In fact, in autism, tactile sensory experiences seem to be blocked at a primitive stage and are not integrated with the senses of sight, smell, and hearing. Because of her autistic experience of living on the surface, Ambra tried to imitate me according to what she saw only with her own eyes.

In this connection, as I said previously, it is interesting to note that sometimes when she came to the sessions she put on a different perfume and expected me to recognize its name and its intensity so that I would be able to know her mood—for example, love, jealousy, rage (see also chapter 4). Ambra used perfume since she hoped that through this primitive sensation I would recognize her as a particular subject with her own feelings and as belonging to my emotional world.

Her needs had to be gratified as if she were a newborn. Any kind of identification was only possible in a situation of imitation and equality. In this connection, in order to express her gratitude Ambra gave me a mirror and a lipstick as a present. However, in adults, the search for symmetry, in the sense of being the exact copy of the other person, represents the "anti-thought" and prevents any kind of introjection and the development of individual thought.

With Ambra, relationships experienced with others were only linked to the sensory experiences such relations produced. For example, if she momentarily got close to someone, it was not because she liked the person but because she liked the person's perfume or colour of hair or the material of the person's clothes.

The early, terrifying phantoms made it difficult for her to develop a real identity, and, moreover, the conflict with her mother prevented her from developing her feminine identity. Ambra incorporated her mother's anxiety of being a fragile victim and clung to her, imagining she was the mother's psychic lifeline. This hindered her from separating from her mother but also gave her a role to play. In order to feel she was an adult, she identified with the superficial, aesthetic aspect as a visible sign of her physical development (hair, clothes, make-up).

Moreover, on the subject of identification, Ambra's supposed triumph over men, by means of her overt and provocative sexuality, mimicked her father's authoritarian and self-assured manner. The father's social power represented a way of asserting himself in the world, and this was much more concrete than the vagaries of the mother's imagination. In the analytic relationship, Ambra went from being an innocent, lost child to being a forceful, authoritarian, and seductive woman.

Her vital drives were represented only by her physical needs. Her attention was concentrated on bodily sensations—sensations of heat, tension, pain, and what she referred to as sexual drives. Her dreams and fantasies centred only on masturbation and intercourse and were not based on a real loving relationship that could have given her something meaningful. There was no connection between pleasure and love nor any real adult sexual pleasure, only the desire for physical contact. But the symptom she complained about was not that she was frigid, but that she felt persecuted.

For Ambra, the whole world revolved around eroticism, and this idea was reinforced by regularly going to the only places that really attracted her—namely, discotheques. She felt that the only way she could triumph was to make the most of her body so that she could use it as an instrument of sexual attraction. Her successful role models were the stars of porn movies. Nothing else interested her or could bring her fulfilment. She actively and compulsively sought out sexual encounters and immediately imagined she was in love. These encounters, however, ended almost as quickly as they began, and she was left feeling disappointed and completely frustrated.

However, the absence of any emotional involvement made these experiences degrading or left her feeling persecuted. It was impossible to intervene and show how destructive this kind behaviour could be for her, since her persecutory fears tended to reject any interpretation, and the compulsive search for erotic relationships represented the only vital drive related to the underlying sense of deadness. She poured all her energies into making herself beautiful or changing her "disguise" by adopting different kinds of hairdos or make-up. Despite the investment of time and effort in making her body beautiful, she was not at all fascinating.

I did not feel anything apart from being annoyed by her continual transformations, which were supposed to confound me and which obliged me to adapt to her different disguises. To my mind, at that time empathy was impossible. In the transference, the experience of very frequent change and emotional void in the maternal relationship was repeated, and all my attempts to make the relationship more human were thwarted.

Her compulsion to imagined erotic scenarios and her sexual behaviour could be interpreted as addictive sexuality, as McDougall (1996) has pointed out. Sexuality represented an addiction like smoking, and in this way Ambra dispelled her feelings of anger or depression.

The sexual relations she so compulsively sought out aimed to preserve her narcissistic image and express her need to be loved. She dreamt:

"I was condemned to death and was in front of the soldiers, who asked what my last will was. I replied that I wanted to make love. I then went to a nun (perhaps you), a very feminine nun, who told me that she would rescue me from a death sentence since it was a shame to die so young."

She associated to this her need for protection and a warm memory of the time when I helped her call a taxi because she was so confused that she was unable to get home.

Once she recognized the projection of her violent feelings, the paranoid ideation gradually diminished and we were finally able to discuss the significance of her sexuality. Then she realized that her sexuality was compulsive, that it did not express the search for a real, adult, loving relationship but merely aimed to provide the emotional reassurance she had not experienced in the earliest years of life.

The confusion was between sensuality and adult sexuality; what was lacking was the language of tenderness. Racamier (1995) points out that tenderness is a delicate emotion that the mother transmits to the child during his early years. This vital experience forms the basis of the sexual impulse that subsequently develops. The characteristics of tenderness are the following: it is devoid of sexuality although full of sensuality, it is continuous but never reaches an acme, it does not express envy or aggression, it envelops but does not penetrate. One of its virtues is solicitude, and one of its derivatives is tact. It seemed to me that Ambra had never experienced any of this in a coherent and continuous way.

Her purely sexual relationships were more a way of protecting the narcissistic image from disintegration rather than an expression of her own sexual identity; they were protecting a vague subjective identity that was very primitive. The deflation of the narcissistic, omnipotent image that had protected her from feelings that were too painful to experience was followed by a long period of apathy and the emergence of an autistic core characterized by the absence of emotions, desires, and feelings (Tremelloni, 1999).

For a long time, manic defences alternated with paranoid–schizoid ones and seemed to ward off the experience of non-existence of the self as a subject. They prevented the depressive phase from emerging. According to Ogden (1989), early human experience is the product of the dialectical interplay of three different modes of generating experience: the autistic–contiguous mode, the paranoid–schizoid mode, and the depressive mode. They are connected and interdependent. The psychopathology emerges when the dialectical structure collapses and, as a result, one of the modes of the structure prevails. The failure in Ambra to integrate these different positions in her psychic organization led to the alternation of different symptoms. These oscillations required me to adapt my analytic technique to the particular structure that the phase presented.

When the previous symptoms disappeared the autistic capsule emerged in all its gravity, bearing witness to Ambra's lack of emotional support. Her passivity and the absence of any desires or feelings required an enormous effort on my part to try to bring life and movement to her inert body ("reclamation": Alvarez, 1992). However, my attempts were often thwarted.

In the transference, the indifference, the sense of solitude, and the feeling that she did not really exist—as well as the absence of any kind of thought or manifest interest—represented the same kind of relationship that one finds in autistic children. My countertransference made me aware that I was not considered as a human being either. Remaining in the autistic position obliged her to remain in a world of sensations, with no possibility of symbolization. The intensity and duration of autistic elements such as absence of emotional contact, rigid behaviour, and absence of symbolic thinking are intermingled with other defensive organizations.

In addition to the absence of feeling in Ambra, there was another similarity with autistic children—namely, the repetition of certain kinds of behaviour and speech patterns (rituals or stereotypes). The interminable stories she told or the dreams she made up on the spot represented, in my opinion, a sort of autistic cloud to withdraw into. It was impossible to communicate through it since it could not be shared with others. In a similar way her addiction to smoking served to create a protective shield around her, kept her in an imaginative cloud in which she could isolate herself and which allowed her to extend the limits of her body since she could penetrate wherever she wanted.

When the autistic defence prevailed, the transference represented a space devoid of all emotion, transmitting a sensation of not existing on the part of the patient and the negation of my presence. Ambra appeared to be empty and emotionally inaccessible: her face was expressionless and had a petrified look. I saw in her a lack of identity as a subject. She seemed to be unconsciously striving to deaden her emotional life in order to survive. The prevalence of elements that were portents of death meant an assault on her thoughts and emotional life. Consequently, the words she uttered were unreliable because devoid of all emotion and often related to events that were only imaginary. Although Ambra had an apparently normal social life and a fully developed language, she did not use language to communicate.

In the analytic relationship, she re-lived the experience of her early childhood. Even in this particular situation she was unable to experience a stable and protective relationship that could "contain" her; on the contrary, she fought against this possibility. Whenever any sign of affection appeared or she felt she was becoming dependent, her old fears would emerge—namely, the fear of being disappointed and the denial of any new feeling—so that the improvements she made were followed by periods of regression. In the transference, for a long time Ambra pretended that I did not exist.

In this undifferentiated climate, Ambra nevertheless behaved in a more sensitive way when I had had a fall and had to use a cane. On that occasion, seeing me so weak, she expressed her empathy and was quite attentive. She even tried to help me walk in order to alleviate my evident physical pain. In this way, she assimilated me into the image of the sick mother of her childhood.

Only after many years of steadfast determination on the part of both of us to continue our sessions, interspersed with frequent acting-out (in the transference, there were always aggressive manifestations), did a fragile relationship finally emerge. During a period in which the analytic situation and clinical picture improved, Ambra started having tactile hallucinations that she recognized as the result of her own imagination. She experienced sensations of being touched, fondled, aroused, or pinched on the surface of her skin by tiresome little phantoms who repeated my suggestions but prevented her from sleeping. These sensations bothered her by their constant presence but provided loyal companionship. So the skin contact began to raise an emotional meaning and represented a relationship.

The only time there was any real human contact was when Ambra alluded to her past suffering during her childhood. Compared to the confusion and inventions of the past, her dreams gradually became more significant and real so that it was possible to try to interpret them. During this period she dreamt that:

"My parents and all of humanity died of a catastrophic epidemic of AIDS. I went off alone and bereft, but found an anti-virus which brought them back to life. In the end, I was not satisfied with what I had done and wondered if it was worth it. It was not clear who was saved and who was not."

The question that came to her mind in this dream was whether relationships could offer love or were a source of fear. Taking into consideration the experience with her sick mother, the associations concerned her sensitivity to the suffering of others.

In another dream of this period:

"I was with some friends in a car speeding down the road. I wanted them to stop because they had run over a dog and I wanted to take care of it. Instead, however, I found the broken skeletons of some dead children. I wanted to collect them, but since they were crushed, I had a difficult time assembling the pieces before I could recompose them in their shape."

These were not "fabricated dreams" but dreams in which, for the first time, she was able to express her feelings and a desire to make reparation.

I think different traumatic elements might have been involved in producing the autistic and psychotic symptoms in Ambra: the continuous modification of the emotional and ideational state of her mother, which oscillated between violence and indifference; the absence of a father, whose function was to protect the child's psyche; and the great number of Ambra's nannies. These elements might have combined with a constitutional fragility.

The studies mentioned by Alvarez and Reid (1999) concerning the connection between one sub-type of autism and trauma include, among the pathogenic traumas of infantile autism, the influence of the parents' psychic disorders on the child's first years of life. Speaking of trauma in this sense, I am referring not to a specific event that affects the newborn at a precise moment, but to a set of factors that represent the absence of adequate support for his needs at a given developmental phase.

Although in dissociative states there is a disengagement from stimuli in the external world, in autism they are replaced by an "all-engaging preoccupation with self-induced body stimulation" (Alvarez & Reid, 1999; see also Alvarez, 1992; Frith, 1989; Meltzer et al., 1975; Tustin, 1981a, 1986, 1990). When trauma has occurred in infancy before a process of adequate differentiation of self from other and before the development of the capacity to symbolize, the child is unable to build daydreams and fantasies and remains concentrated on his body.

Ambra's development was skewed partially in the direction of pathological autism with withdrawal into her body, and partially to-wards the paranoid–schizoid mode of psychological organization. She took refuge in her confused fantasies. Her phantasmagorical life—what Winnicott calls a transitional space (1951)—was blown up out of all proportion in order to deny the existence of the real world, and she had cut herself off from it. She was therefore able, in part, to create imaginary scenarios to overcome the emotional impact of the trauma and, in part, to withdraw into a world of bodily sensations whose intensity, frequency, duration, and location she could control. In this way she was able to introduce a minimum quantity of personal will and potential in her self. These initially defensive mechanisms subse-quently become addictive and repetitive, as in the case of autistic children (Alvarez & Reid, 1999).

During periods of latency, when her life was dominated by disap-pointments and frustrations, fantasy replaced the real experiences of relationships, which were felt as persecutory. Ambra admitted having lived most of her life in an imaginary isolated world where she had withdrawn from reality. She described herself as an "autistic girl". However, this might not be the case, since she managed to attend school, though with modest results. Until the psychotic crisis ex-ploded, she seemed to have lived only on the surface of things. During her adolescence she was confronted with another world, separate from the world of her mother, and at this point the absence of a real identity as a person brought to the surface earlier, unresolved problems.

When her autistic defences collapsed and gave way to the first signs of feelings, there were periods when it was possible to communicate on an emotional level, and in the countertransference I felt a way of bringing new life to the relationship. However, when the first warning signs of separation and loss appeared on the horizon with the danger of disintegration, the autistic defences would reappear or she would have a crisis of dissociation. In the first case, every feeling was frozen; in the second, the paranoid aspect emerged, when she felt the entire world was persecuting her.

Gradually the assumption of time and space coordinates intro- duced the hypothesis of a real separation. Faced with a broken object, autistic children feel they themselves are broken; in the same way, faced with possible separation from the analyst, Ambra had a new crisis of dissociation. The isolation she complained of was steeped in feelings of death, but it also represented a shelter compared to the uncertainty of a human relationship.

The vicissitudes of countertransference

When I first met Ambra, I was struck by the disquieting expression on her face, which was unsmiling, expressionless, and quite enigmatic. The enigma of her face represented Ambra's early experiences with a mother who was enigmatic, incomprehensible, and unpredictable. It seemed that the development of a normal, primary relationship with her mother had been impossible due to the mother's instability and psychic impenetrability. The mother had been very ambivalent to- wards Ambra since her early years.

Resnik (1999b) points out that the body is a "living memory": it bears the traces of its story, and through body language we can trace backwards the development of autistic or psychotic patients. In this case, Ambra's face bore the signs of great confusion and of the non- development of her identity through the process of projective identifi- cation. There were only attempts to imitate the superficial image of her mother: what she had been able to see and verify with her eyes— namely, her skin, hair, and clothes. She lacked the third dimension— namely, the experience of remaining in contact with her own feelings.

What struck me was that, apart from trying to understand her symptoms and wanting to understand her, I was not emotionally involved in the relationship, unlike other cases of psychotic patients. I was certain of only one thing: the violence with which she wanted to impose her thoughts on others. I could only suppose that beneath this there was great despair.

Although Ambra did not seem to have any feelings or express the desire to be taken care of, I continued to be amazed by how assiduously and punctually she would come to the sessions. She agreed not to smoke, although she was addicted to smoking, but showed how painful it was for her to be there, as if the relationship itself was something she found painful and exhausting. It was a relationship in which I was partly idealized and partly considered a real presence, but someone without any qualities or feelings.

During the sessions she talked about her dreams or fantasies, which she would constantly change and give variable endings to. All this represented a kind of cloud around herself and which corresponded to a private area of psychic retreat. Despite the inconsistency of her protective shield, Ambra was obviously in a position of strength. Her psychic retreat was an area in which her imagination and sense of omnipotence could exist with no regard for me. In the countertransference, I felt isolated, confused, and without hope of making any contact with the patient.

During the early phases of the psychotherapy, I had intense and conflicting feelings towards her that arose simultaneously, and my greatest difficulty was that I was unable to form an integrated image of her between the suffering part and the domineering part, between the deprived girl and the violent woman.

Ambra subsequently became quite curious about my private life and the size of the clothes I wore, as well as my age, my skin, and my hair. She criticized or imitated the colour of my hair, then scrutinized my face to see whether I liked her hairdos or was envious. The sessions often seemed to me like hand-to-hand combat, in the sense that Ambra's attention and aggression were directly focused on my body, and the content of the sessions at times concerned only my physical characteristics. In addition to seeking a generic identity, the patient was also seeking a sexual identity, so the comparison she made with my femininity was at the centre of our communication. I often felt overwhelmed in my countertransference.

Resnik (1999b) introduces the concept of induction and distinguishes it from that of projection to indicate that, in the analytic context, the bodily presence of the patient reawakens in the analyst a willingness to introject what the body of the patient expresses, and vice versa. According to him, induction is a phenomenon linked to the physical presence of the other, whereas projection and introjection belong to the sphere of the imagination. Both patient and analyst incorporate the intended projections of the other by means of body induction. The patient might use this mechanism of manipulation by means of his body to make the analyst play the role that the patient wants him to play.

I found all the questions related to me intrusive and annoying, but it made me realize that she hungered for a real relationship. Perhaps she had not experienced any primitive contact with a loving, careful, and happy mother but, instead, had one who had been deceiving and dreadful because of her psychic condition. Balint (1968) points out that in patients with serious forms of regression, the analyst must be prepared to answer some questions truthfully since these patients cannot bear to hear anything but the absolute truth and are especially sensitive as regards this matter. But faced with Ambra's questions I was doubtful about this because of her use of my answers.

For Ambra, distinguishing between truth and lies did not seem to exist, due to her early confusing experiences, and her questions about me were an attempt to discover a new version of reality. She used to ask me some questions that seemed innocent, such as, for example, if I liked her new hairstyle more than the one she had the previous day. She seemed to accept my answers as real and comforting, but she remembered them and compared them to others I subsequently gave her. On the one hand, she hoped for my sincere comments, but, immediately after, she transformed them into a contradictory communication that was meant to show that my first comments were false.

I realized that while these questions represented the synthesis of her early relational experiences, they also indicated some element of hope in a new relationship based on shared truth. However, I also felt that her desire to know me would lead to a process of imitation or of adhesive identification. I realized that answering her questions with great precision would not help her process of integration.

I have to admit that for a long time I was unable to empathize with her depression, because it was hidden by hysterical and psychotic symptoms. I could only recognize this depression through her expressionless and lifeless eyes, dissociated from the rest of her facial expression, and I remained confused by her torrent of words. I did not perceive her feelings beyond her evident verbal and motor aggressiveness and her attempts to steal my thoughts and feelings. This emotional situation, combined with her attempts to manipulate me and make me respond, made the relationship very unpleasant and created a defensive barrier in the countertransference. This represented another obstacle to the analytic work.

All these countertransference feelings imprisoned me, so that I felt the need to emerge from this situation. In certain situations I would respond to her questions or behaviour by acting spontaneously and immediately, and this could be considered the opposite of analytic neutrality. It seemed to me more constructive not to reproduce the enigmatic mother or incomprehensible nannies, but to demonstrate that my feelings and words were not lies or defensive answers. This more spontaneous communication made Ambra realize that she was dealing with a person who was alive and attentive and who responded emotionally. This led to the beginning of a process of emotional closeness.

When Ambra's psychotic symptoms became somewhat attenuated, she began insisting that she wanted to resume her studies as she wanted to train as an analyst. However, her real attempts to study failed. In the light of this, her attempted identification with me was a kind of imagined reparation, although she was unable to realize that she was not really interested in her studies and could not recognize her fragile psychic situation. This also meant that it was difficult for her to accept her position as patient, since she wanted to pursue her grandiose idea of taking possession of the analyst's position. And in any case, it was a more significant attempt to imitate me than by simply dying her hair the same colour as mine. But at the same time, it was not easy to show her that she was attempting a projective identification on a large scale to avoid embarking on her own personal quest for identity, because she felt belittled when confronted with her own envy and greed. On the other hand, I had to be careful not to hurt her, not to minimize her efforts to get close to me and her efforts to change from her passive position to a project for the future. I wondered if her desire to become an analyst represented a projective identification in which she took possession of the object that she admired or whether by putting on the analyst's mask she disguised herself.

When our relationship was invaded by aggressive feelings, Ambra would begin by complaining that my room was too cold. She did not accept my hypothetical interpretations or the connection between her feelings and the possible meanings, between her psychic coldness and that of my room, or between her feeling cold and the unconscious attempt to lower her excessively high degree of emotional heat. Since it was impossible to speak of psychological meanings, I thought that the best thing to do was to turn on the heat. In this way, I thought it was better to offer a concrete model of the "facilitating mother" (Bollas, 1987) rather than the model of an intellectual analyst who wanted to impose an interpretation that the patient was unable to receive at that moment.

On the emotional plane, I felt she was provoking me in a subtle way, and she even accused me of not being sufficiently protective in providing her with a comfortable room for the session. This irritated me and made me feel guilty. Immediately afterwards, I felt that I had to contain her destructiveness and not emphasize it, because even though conflict between us derived from a "here-and-now" relationship, it was the result of an early deprivation and I had to pay more attention to the cold that she felt than the anger that filled the room. I was the one who had to help the process of integration between her destructiveness and her suffering through my own inner elaboration and provide her with an answer that would help her to overcome her inner conflicting feelings. I realized that I had to answer by appealing to my maternal feelings.

My countertransference had previously oscillated between the hope of emotional contact and the disappointment due to her destructiveness and contempt. When faced with the autistic part, I experienced alternate states of emotional closeness, due to her desperation, and a strong sense of impotence and inability to intervene. The only thing that I could do during the sessions was to be present, motionless, attentive to any movement, and willing to listen to my inner world and hers, almost as if I were the custodian of a relationship that still did not exist.

Creating a sense of empathy when treating autistic children is not something that can be done immediately; it takes great determination and effort to achieve, since it is not something the patient solicits. Ambra's emotional experiences were, for the most part, devitalized. Her emotional life was characterized by her "addiction" to violence, which is an automatic defensive response to the fear of annihilation.

During an autistic phase of the therapy, where the atmosphere was characterized by a deep depression and inertia, an unexpected dream of mine helped melt the frozen state of feelings in which we both found ourselves:

"Ambra and I were standing on a small rubber sailboat and had entered a port in the Mediterranean after a long journey. We were content, the sky was bright, the weather was sunny; we really felt on vacation and were

happy to be travelling together. I was busy figuring out how we could return to Italy (by train or ship) and had to decide."

The dream gave me the sensation of well-being and enjoyment; I felt satisfied with the trip and with the friendly atmosphere. The emotional climate of my dream contrasted with Ambra's long period of closure and apathy and with my frustration, but it signalled my unconscious alliance with the patient and some unconscious hope for future communication.

Benedetti (1980, 1992) referring to the psychotherapy of psychotic patients, underlines the importance of therapist's dreams about the patient. "Psychotherapists dream instead of their patients!" Therapist's dreams or fantasies might correspond to an identification with the patient resulting from the therapist's need to help him emerge from his pathological situation by giving new prospective or unforeseen hints. These dreams arise when they are necessary in a therapeutic way.

Only in the countertransference could I detect faint signs of emotional exchanges, and a more authentic communication began; I was then able to make more symbolic interpretations. When she started dressing more simply in jeans, stopped putting on makeup, and let her hair hang naturally, I felt a surge of hope that some progress was being made. At that point, her face was no longer disguised by her makeup, her gaze was direct, and eye contact was simple and immediate. At this time she had the following dream:

"You came to my house and approached my bed and told me it was time for our session. I woke up, but you told me that we could not meet in your studio as usual because you had to give a lecture at the university. I arrived in the lecture-hall, where there were many young people talking and making noise. You told them not to disturb you because you had to look after a little girl, who was me. I was sitting near you in a corner, and the students asked me how old I was. You then gave me money for a taxi to get home, but since I gave the taxi-driver the wrong address, he took me to the wrong place."

In the patient–analyst relationship a kind of work space is created in which not only emotional messages are sent and received through the mechanism of projection and introjection, but there are also unrecognized elements that belong to an area of influence unknown to both. For this reason, the parallel work of supervision must be carried out to uncover this blind area of communication that is unrecognized by the patient–analyst couple.

Conclusions

After a long period during which her symptoms improved and she was able to take some examinations and start working, a new crisis of dissociation was triggered in her by the thought that our relationship might end before she found a real loving relationship to replace the analytic one and provide her with support and hope. Moreover, if her life improved, our relationship would come to an end.

However, even though real events determined the painful end of the therapeutic relationship, from time to time Ambra managed to send me little notes expressing her affection and gratitude because I had given her so much attention during the therapy. This was enough to make me feel that the autistic part had been able to thaw and that she was able to recognize new feelings of affection that had emerged during the therapy. Our assiduous and tormented relationship had not been in vain.

CHAPTER TEN

Renzo

This case of a therapy started in childhood and continued into adulthood is included here to demonstrate how the emergence of the patient, Renzo, from autistic isolation was followed many years later by additional developments in his cognitive and emotional capacities after the therapy had resumed.

I was able to follow this patient for about twenty-five years, and this allowed me to make some interesting considerations regarding his autism. I shall not describe in detail the various phases of this therapy but only give an idea of Renzo's development by summing up the various phases and providing some significant fragments. The recognition of the autistic capsules made it possible to recover his vital energy that had been frozen and abandoned for a long time. Certain details and specific problems have been left out since they involved separate issues from those under discussion.

During the first phases of the therapy from 9 until 16 years of age, some changes took place in Renzo's relationship with me (Tremelloni, 1987b), supported by an improvement in his behaviour and learning capacity. Already this seemed to represent a good result compared to his previous autistic closure. However, many years later, when therapy resumed because of the appearance of behavioural disorders, another part of the personality, which up to that time had remained hidden, emerged. The thawing of this potential took place in the empathic setting of our sessions and made possible further development of his emotional and cognitive capacities.

If I had not met Renzo as a child, I would have considered him a borderline patient with autistic parts. The length of the therapy, the attention I gave to his initial enigmatic forms of communication, and my empathy allowed him to trust and listen to me. Further development of the analytic process was due to the fact that I became ever closer to his autistic part. For the first time in Renzo's life, he was able to experience a profound emotional exchange with another person. He succeeded in translating his feelings into words and discovered a mental activity that previously did not seem to exist.

I hope to be able to express what I learned from this experience—namely, that by creating an underlying trust and trying to overcome the obstacles represented by rigid defences, we can reach the patient's unknown psychic areas, which are full of an amazingly rich potential. His language development bears witness to his previous autistic isolation.

The diagnosis, made in childhood, was of infantile psychosis with autistic features (what we would now call Asperger syndrome). Renzo first came to my attention when he was 9 years old. He was very isolated both at home and at school and behaved aggressively towards everyone. He still had not learned to read or write. His pathology had gone unrecognized until he began nursery school, and much time had elapsed before a diagnosis of infantile psychosis with autistic features was made and psychotherapeutic treatment was begun. The initial period of psychotherapy with me included three sessions each week and lasted until he was 16 years old. During this period, his symptoms improved considerably and his learning abilities developed, so that he was able to finish primary and middle school with quite good results.

When Renzo was 25 years old, on the advice of a family member he asked me to resume psychotherapy since he behaved aggressively towards his relatives.

History

Renzo was the second-born child after a sister. Delivery was after-term; he was breast-fed and had some problems being weaned. From the time of his birth, he was looked after by a series of wet-nurses who took care of him when his mother was unable to do so.

When he was 3 years old, his parents separated. He first lived with his mother and sister, and then with his father; he always remained in contact with both parents. During the first part of his therapy, he would spend one week at his father's and one week at his mother's, and when he had to move from one place to the other he was accompanied by people outside the family, who were often changed because of Renzo's difficult behaviour.

Only his nursery-school teachers noticed his static expression and the strange behaviour of this child who was unable to participate in group activities or games. Although he was left-handed, he was taught to write with his right hand. A long period of time elapsed before a diagnosis was made, and an initial attempt at psychotherapy was interrupted because of a clash between the parents and the therapists.

Renzo's first years of life were characterized by continual change: people, home environments, schools, doctors, therapists. Renzo found all this incomprehensible, even though, in the end, he accepted it as his normal destiny.

He finished middle school and, because of the progress he had made, entered secondary school. However, he soon became very frustrated because he could neither meet the scholastic demands nor participate in the world of his adolescent peers. For a few years he remained inactive in the father's office, until he entered a vocational school when he was about 26.

The course of the therapy

The first meeting (age 9 years)

Renzo was a dark-haired boy, with dark blue eyes and a slightly effeminate face. His gaze expressed wonder and he seemed vaguely fearful. He kept his robust, chubby but not obese body bent forwards, and his head hung to his chest. In my studio, he walked in circles without stopping, taking long strides, his hands clasped behind his back. When he sat down, he collapsed in the chair, with his eyes shut and his thumb in his mouth. The only signs of his presence were the loud noises he made when he blew his nose or sneezed, the fits of coughing brought on deliberately, the kicks he gave my desk, and farts.

He often fell asleep during the sessions, and his return to reality was often painful because it signified the end of his isolation and the resumption of his difficult relationship with the babysitter of the moment. From the inertia of sleep, the expression of his face went from clown-like grimaces expressing wonder to forced laughter. The only time there was any real contact was when he started clowning around and imitated TV sketches.

His language was developed, but he sometimes used neologisms or used difficult words inappropriately, not knowing what they meant. He spoke slowly and found it difficult to express himself. As he continued to talk, what he said became increasingly incomprehensible and irrelevant. The result was that the listener became paralysed while trying to understand and remained rather confused. If an attempt was made to help him reorganize his thoughts, he got angry and stopped talking. It was possible to understand what he was trying to say by guessing from the words he said or the gestures he made.

The first phase (age 9–11 years)

The first phase of psychotherapy included the difficult initial period and corresponded to the period he attended elementary school.

The first months were marked by the inability to maintain a regular schedule because the baby-sitters often got it wrong. Appointments were often changed, and there were appeals for help from discouraged and irritated teachers. Renzo was always amazed by what happened and could never foresee anything except being punished or rejected.

The initial period was characterized by silences and withdrawal, alternating with fits of rage. Renzo began by observing everything that was in the room and the way I behaved. He alternated these attempts to understand with long periods when he remained locked up in himself, totally absent. He would close his eyes, suck his thumb, and stroke his chin. If I spoke to him and asked what he felt during those moments or why he felt so cut off from everything, he would lash out angrily, and his answers were full of hate and contempt. Perhaps he felt irritated because I referred to his hidden feelings and interrupted his fantasies in a situation he imagined as heavenly.

His language was well developed but was mainly reduced to a few unintegrated words. He spoke slowly and found it difficult to express himself, so what he said became increasingly incomprehensible. During those early sessions, his body language represented his ambivalence: with one hand, he kept alive the inner world of auto-sensuous activities by putting his thumb in his mouth or by stroking his face; with the other, he moved his toys around and made up imaginary situations.

He began to use the toys he found in the room and made up some incomprehensible games, talking softly so I could not understand what he was saying. Everything took place in a corner of the room, far from where I was sitting. What I understood was that he wanted to emphasize the "non-sense" of communication by means of sudden and unpredictable changes in the situations he created, or by magically transforming the characters. If I tried to participate by making a comment, he would shut me out and stop playing. In this way, he reproduced in me his experience of being excluded when he wanted to find a space to express himself.

It would have been impossible for me to describe the games he played, because to my mind it all seemed so incomprehensible and totally confused. The content of these games was not especially noteworthy; on the contrary, they represented an insurmountable barrier to any form of communication. Likewise, the speech of some adults serves to confuse the listener and what is said is far from the real emotional content. The intent, both unconscious and conscious, is to confuse others. He isolated me as he played in total silence far away from me. He made me feel useless, projecting his feeling of being isolated and rejected onto me.

Much more significant were the rituals he obsessively performed at the beginning and end of each session. When he came in, Renzo had to shut the door carefully and draw the curtain so that our words wouldn't be heard from outside. He would then decide whether to turn the lights on or off, speaking in an authoritarian voice. Halfway through the session, he would ask how much time was left and said he wanted to be informed ten minutes before the session was over. He could not stand being unable to control me. Later on, he himself kept track of the time on the two watches he wore and got ready to interrupt the contact with me when the time was up.

When the session was really over, he would suddenly get up, feeling stronger and less tired compared to his previous passivity. He would put on his coat and stand up next to me, physically preventing me from opening the door. In this position, he delayed his departure by making endless excuses. He would tie and untie his shoelaces, or button and unbutton his coat, so that the session would not come to an end. He then made me go out first, so that he would be the one to close the door. He was afraid of being thrown out by someone else.

During this first phase, only one part of Renzo showed he wanted to come into contact with me: his false self, the clown that had a talent for doing funny things and wanted to make me laugh and abandon my role as analyst. The other real part—the angry and desperate infant—was buried away in his autistic behaviour.

Later he started bringing comic books and enormous bags full of toys to play with during the session. Whenever I tried to break this habit and interpret it as a way of refusing to admit our separateness and denigrating what I had to offer, he would react angrily and the atmosphere would become even more tense. He continued to criticize my toys and replaced them with small, mechanical men that turned into spaceships when certain parts were moved. Since he did not trust anyone, it was too painful for him to ask for help, and my interpretations of why he wanted to shut me out apparently fell on deaf ears.

For a long period of time, sheets of paper were used to draw chaotic, incomprehensible shapes. This scribbling was always similar and repetitive in the special arrangement on the sheet and represented an internal "unthinkable situation". The scribbles expressed an internal world, indefinite, upsetting, and shapeless, full of destructiveness and confusion. Through his drawings he transmitted what he had experienced—that is, his inability to give meaning to what surrounded him.

In addition to trying to create a psychic dimension to the relationship, it was necessary to adapt to Renzo's particular way of communicating so that the relationship could develop. To this end, Tustin's theory of autistic shapes proved extremely useful in understanding Renzo's enigmatic way of communicating. According to Tustin (1984), these shapes might belong to a pre-image period, and no one can use them to communicate.

I thought that during his long period of emotional solitude, he had created and developed peculiar, idiosyncratic shapes in his nascent inner world. Because these shapes were secret and peculiar, they cannot be either reproduced or shared with others. They are only figments connected with bodily sensations and belong to a period before imagination develops. It was therefore difficult to create conditions in which sharing was possible, given the barrier he had built to isolate himself from others.

Owing to my attempts at interpretation of these signs through my associations, he later transformed the scribbling into drawings, which became increasingly more meaningful, and then into cartoons with a plot he invented. In this way, the concepts of time and space emerged. His verbal communication became more articulate and comprehensible, and this also led to him obtaining good results in middle school.

By carefully observing the material he brought to the sessions, his behaviour and my countertransference feelings made it possible to establish an emotional exchange that could provide the basis for some interpretations. About a year and a half after beginning therapy, Renzo's behaviour and cognitive capacities improved so that he was able to pass the fifth-grade examinations with good results.

When Renzo entered middle school, his behavioural disorder grew worse and his moods oscillated between aggression and apparent stupidity. He put on the mask of the clown in order to take part in group activities. In class, he was very isolated from his classmates and did not participate in games or apply himself to his studies. The collaboration of his teachers, a private tutor who helped him in his studies and stayed with him in Renzo's free time, and me made it possible to constitute a group of people who were interested in his problems and adopted a rather similar emotional approach. This contributed to creating an orderly and harmonious environment and allowed Renzo to acquire a basic education.

At the same time, during the sessions Renzo became increasingly silent. He spent many sessions stretched out on the floor without uttering a word, or would sit on the chair motionless, with his eyes closed. There were, however, some signs of life: he would make loud noises with his body, cover his ears with his hands, or sometimes repeatedly kick my desk. He did not accept any of the things I said, transforming them into messages of persecution followed by contemptuous comments.

In this gloomy, unchangeable atmosphere, there were some sessions that were full of exchanges and meaningful remarks, and this encouraged me to continue the therapy. A separation because of holidays or mutual absences made him withdraw even more and brought on fits of rage. My absence was transformed into a bad presence from which he had to protect himself (O'Shaughnessy, 1964).

During this period, Renzo began to use numbers at school, and in our relationship he recognized the significance of the number 2. At the same time, he began to recognize geometric figures and was able to stop using idiosyncratic shapes that were connected to his own autosensuous experience. The number 2 took on a particular significance since it represented the analytic couple.

Verbal communication developed sufficiently and became more comprehensible. He spontaneously began using the "*lei*" verb form, which in Italian corresponds to a more formal relationship and is a more adult way to address people compared to the more informal "*tu*" verb form used by young children. I thought this meant that he recognized the fact that there was a greater separation between us. He might have realized that there existed two different roles, the patient and the therapist, and therefore accepted his dependency and need.

By this time, Renzo had become a handsome young man, with a strong build but rather childish expression. He dressed very carefully and was extremely punctual. Although he was placed in a secondary school to keep him busy, he was unable keep up with the schoolwork because he was not as mature as his peers. He found it extremely difficult to make friends, and nobody tried to befriend him. He continued attending school for two years, even though it caused him to suffer because he could not fit in with the other pupils. Unfortunately, he remained inactive for many years, going to his father's office where he did some uninteresting menial tasks.

Once he emerged from his autistic isolation, his behaviour demonstrated some obsessive features both during the sessions and at home. These could not be questioned since they triggered violent reactions. Considering the general improvements he had made in his behaviour in the external world, we decided to end the therapy.

The second phase (age 25 years): development as a young adult

At the age of 25, Renzo returned for a period of psychotherapy following occasional periods of aggressive behaviour towards family members. During that time he lived permanently at home with his mother and sister and went to his father's office every day, where he was given minor duties to perform but, for the most part, was left with nothing to do.

Renzo had no social life. He only saw his private teacher, who had been with him since secondary school and had always stimulated his cultural interests by taking him to museums or, occasionally, to the theatre or on trips. He did not want to practise sports, and his life seemed dead even though his general cultural level had greatly improved. His use of language was adequate and was full of colourful expressions and metaphors.

For many months following an initial interview, Renzo reverted to his old patterns of withdrawal, provocative behaviour, actings-out, and childhood rituals. It took me a long time to discourage his repetitive behaviour, trying not to reproduce the intrusive and authoritarian family patterns. The sessions became monotonous, marked by long silences and the usual provocative responses on his part. When not attempting to annoy or play tricks on me, he pretended to be sleeping or kept silent so there was absolutely no interaction between us. He always waited for me to make some comments on the pretext that he felt empty inside. He really wanted to remain passive and hide his inner world. He tried to enter my mind, by scrutinizing my face and taking possession of my reactions.

Most of the sessions were characterized by the following rituals: he would stealthily enter the room without making any noise, so that I would be startled by his sudden appearance. With extreme precision he moved the chair as far away as possible from its original position, as though he wanted to defend himself by avoiding closeness. Then he would loudly and vigorously blow his nose many times, as though he were masturbating. If I pointed out this seemingly theatrical behaviour, he responded in a provocative way by saying I wanted to make him forget his family's rules of good behaviour such as cleaning his nose and behaving normally. Similarly, he sometimes coughed loudly to annoy me and make me feel resentful. He justified this behaviour by saying his cold made it impossible for him to communicate with me.

He would often pull his socks up and down many times, take off his glasses and put them back after cleaning them, and finally settle himself in his chair, closing his eyes with a dreamy look. He only opened them again to perform these rituals, but he sometimes managed to converse in a spontaneous and direct way when his eyes were closed.

As when he was a child, he checked the time at the beginning and end of every session, as though to emphasize that he was in control of the situation and to make sure I did not steal even a minute of his time. He projected his greed onto me. As in the past, on entering, he would check that the curtain I always draw after closing the door was in place so that everything he might say or do would remain in the room. On the threshold, when about to leave, he would turn back to check whether he had forgotten anything or whether some loose change might have dropped out of his pockets. He seemed bent on secretly catching every sound while not revealing anything.

During this phase, it also seemed clear that even though the rituals were a provocation, they represented a kind of protective mechanism against the anger he felt towards me as well as a practical way of making me experience the feelings of exclusion that he had felt as a child. In this way, he transformed the sessions into a waste of time for which I made him pay: it was a way of denying his need and projecting his thoughts onto me. For patients such as this, doing apparently useless, repetitive things is a way of challenging the outside world. We must not forget that rituals stem from deep defence mechanisms that have helped them grow and survive psychically and are, therefore, difficult to abandon.

Sometimes, instead of sitting opposite me, Renzo would lie down on the couch in order to astound me by indicating that he had suddenly become an adult and was adopting the standard analytic procedure. During such sessions, he remained totally passive, or even ended up falling asleep. I asked him to explain this behaviour, and after a number of plays on words and crazy associations to try to trick me, he admitted wanting to put a greater physical distance between us. This made him feel more protected and prevented me from seeing him more clearly and getting to know his inner thoughts; it also made him less likely to vent his aggression on me, as he did on his family. Even his habit of closing his eyes and avoiding direct eye contact represented his fear of the beginning of understanding, communication, and a resultant loss of control.

His passivity alternated with rare moments of excitement when he alluded to his problems, although in a vague way: he was unable to say clearly what he thought or felt or dreamed. When he managed to speak in an authentic way, he would open his eyes, but turn red. His gaze was direct and attentive, and the words came to him easily: on these occasions he would never want the session to end. I wondered if this represented a sort of sexual arousal in the transference relationship, or if the satisfaction of finally communicating through words and being understood represented a vital gain. I also wondered how I could respond to his plea for help if he could not describe in a comprehensible way the fantasies that lurked behind his autistic defences. My desire to understand and find answers came up against limits.

During the last three years of therapy, the rituals gradually began to disappear and he was able to express himself in an easier and more articulate way, thus making it possible to analyse the transference.

Some years after starting this part of the psychotherapy, Renzo was put in a special vocational school for people with disabilities, with the hope of a future job. This marked a turning-point and contributed to pulling Renzo out of his passivity. It allowed him to plan for the future and brought him into contact with classmates and specialized teachers. He found himself in a group of people of different ages and pathologies, and he had to interact with them. He began to study and obtained the best grades in the class: this helped increase his self-esteem.

He was finally able to play soccer, something he had always refused to do as it involved physical contact.

Attending the school coincided with an amazing development in his ability to think and express himself. During the sessions he had the chance to discuss the problems he had relating to his classmates and to understand the group dynamics. The active participation of special-ized teachers and the discussions of the group's behaviour with a psychologist helped him fit into the group and develop his thinking. After attending this school for two years, he was hired as a warehouse attendant in a large department store. Renzo became a good worker, used the computer, and maintained good relationships with his col-leagues.

Awareness of feelings
and development of verbal communication

For a long time, the absence of words and meaningful communication prevented Renzo from expressing his thoughts. I felt, on the one hand, the need to find a special way of indicating to him that I waited patiently for his thoughts. He could then experience the feeling of having a personal space to think and someone to listen to him. On the other hand, I thought of suggesting topics related to the analytic situa-tion or his problems that he would hint at from time to time. In this way, after I had made some suggestions or expressed my insights in words related to the few messages he sent me through his transference, Renzo was able to understand that thoughts and fantasies could be tried out and included in verbal language.

Given the situation of stalemate caused by the silence, actings-out, and rituals, I felt the need to directly express my associations, thoughts, and feelings in any given moment. I initially feared that introducing a precise topic even connected to the hints he gave could be too intrusive, but instead I saw that this triggered Renzo's capacity to express himself and consider his associations. Renzo was more willing to accept this more active and personal attitude of mine than my attempts to provide interpretations, and he participated in a situa-tion in which two persons shared thoughts and feelings. He no longer felt the need to hide his inner world. In this way, he demonstrated his need to have a model and imitated my freedom of expression. Moreover, before he emerged from his isolation he used to magnify his feelings so much that he felt they were dangerous and could not be shared with anyone. However, once he emerged from his withdrawal, a wealth of thoughts and associations came to light, thus making it possible to understand the unconscious process.

Renzo told me:

"I never existed as a child; nobody listened to me, they just told me to be quiet, to stop reciting and arguing. How can I manage with the problems I have?"

Renzo was gradually able to talk about himself and listen to my responses. This made it possible for him to invest in his thoughts so that he could daydream about his future and become aware of his own identity.

Thinking about his new way to talk about his inner world, he said:

"There is a kind of war in myself. . . . I don't know if it is safer to keep my thoughts to myself. I want and don't want to understand. I want to play and I want to be treated like an adult, but I don't know who I am, someone who always wants to be right, someone who gets angry. . . . I don't know if I'm wrong, why I become agitated. I don't know if I make a mistake so that people will think I'm stupid or because I don't think before I act; sometimes I feel strangely confused, I do things I don't want to do, or I don't understand or pretend I don't understand, it's not my fault, if I say so, you have to believe me, I'm not trying to trick you. . . ."

During this period it was vital to give importance to his communications and continually to discourage his tendency to provoke me and make a joke out of everything. If was necessary to maintain a firm position and show him that obsessively repeating the same useless actions or thoughts he complained about was an old defence mechanism of his. These thoughts prevented him from living, growing, and thinking. It was now up to him to abandon them and change his way of thinking.

What appeared evident was the scant differentiation between the different aspects of his personality, which were partly confused and partly projected into the other. It was necessary to discuss his identification with the suffering child of his childhood, who kept him a prisoner in a situation of passivity and chronic aggressiveness.

The dependence established when a child has psychic problems is difficult to transform after childhood by both parent and child. Passivity and fixed thoughts prevailed in Renzo's transference, thus preventing the development of new ideas.

Awareness of aggressiveness

During many sessions, the topics of violence and anger came up. He described situations in which he behaved aggressively and tended to utilize these situations as a form of self-criticism in a masochistic way, thus making me judge him negatively.

On the one hand, his identification was with the child, victim of a violent and disparaging environment; on the other, with the model of an arrogant and obsessive adult in the role of a father, not of a man. In the transference, the violence appeared to be an attempt to trick me, to make me say just the opposite of what I wanted, so that he made me sound ridiculous.

I managed to distinguish normal aggressiveness used as a protective defence from the aggressiveness used in the transference as a provocation. I also managed to talk about his tendency to transform our relationship into a war game so that he could control it without ever coming into real human contact. He succeeded in expressing the confused feelings he had, and finally I pointed out his tendency to project them into me in order to get rid of them. He remained frightened by how powerful and intense his impulses were and how violent his superego was.

I could speak of the impatience that made him act without recognizing his feelings and without thinking. Talking about them meant recognizing them and emerging from his confused state. We were able to talk about his desire to pour all his confusion or cruelty into me, imagining a symbiotic situation in which the differences and boundaries between two people disappeared. If he experienced rage, so must I. Differentiation means becoming an adult and becoming an individual.

He began to think that a relationship with another person separate from himself meant accepting that the external object was not something as fixed, immutable, and controllable as he imagined and that he was in part responsible for keeping up the relationship with the other person. The problem of passive states alternating with outbursts of violence came up again in everyday life as well as in the transference. After having a violent quarrel with his teacher-friend, he refused to contact her by phone. His passivity became a way to avoid facing the question of violence:

> "I don't want to phone her, but I'll answer if she calls. I am not autistic, but my fixed gaze might make people think I am. I really must decide what I am: being absent has to do with one's head. It is very easy to pretend

nothing is happening and stare into space; instead it is difficult to pay attention. I sometimes pretend I understand, but what's in my head? Have I been like this since birth, or have I made everything up?"

He expected the other person to act, to take the initiative; he attempted to eliminate his feelings of sadness, solitude, curiosity, and expectation and felt blocked. He therefore failed to recognize his fantasies and did not transform them into action: he thus adhered even closer to that mask of mystery he wore and felt even more powerful. We discussed the fact that his passivity is a way of hiding his aggressiveness.

Since he was frightened at the prospect of making decisions and being responsible for his choices, he tended to repeat the past situation of dependence. He said:

"As a child, my mind stopped thinking for a long time, and then, thanks to you, it started working again: why do I now have to be on my own without your help? . . . I can't manage on my own . . . at first you all insisted I get help, now I am the one who insists that you help me. Why do I now have to act on my own and you don't want to help me any more and give me advice? Now I am aware of who I am, but I can't talk about certain problems that assail me. . . . I feel more intelligent than before but also more diabolical!"

At this point Renzo was able to think, make associations, and communicate in a comprehensible way, as well as accept, discuss, and remember my interpretations.

The sessions alternated between periods in which there was intense communication and others characterized by resistance and withdrawal. Sometimes when I tried to interpret his behaviour, Renzo reacted by showing his irritation and acting in a provocative way, although, in the end, he managed to express his true feelings:

"You mustn't tell me that I am free to come here or not, to speak or not, to choose what to say. . . . I am obliged to come and it's much better for me to come here than to go around wasting my time. I have to come here because I decide to, and you have to help me talk, because if some topic comes out of your head, I can take it up and continue on my way."

I stressed the fact that, in part, he wanted to be helped but, in part, he wanted to paralyse me when he left me suspended or obliged me to take responsibility for his thoughts and decisions.

After a few sessions in complete silence, he said:

"You don't know how many doctors and psychologists I saw before com-ing to you. I feel comfortable with you and you've helped me a lot. If it weren't for you, I wouldn't know which way to turn!"

I told him that I saw him crying. He was amazed that he could talk about his feelings and said:

"I'm not a vegetable or a plant—I, too, have feelings. I'm sad when I think we won't see each other any more, I feel like crying when I think of what's going to happen to me when I'm alone!"

During the next sessions he lapsed into silence again. I asked him if he remembered anything about the previous session.

"I remember everything, as if it were engraved in my memory. Why don't you tell me why instead of crying I am unable to express myself in words?"

When Renzo could finally stop and reflect upon himself and accept new points of view with respect to his repetitive childhood thoughts, on the one hand he appeared satisfied, active, and full of hope and on the other he started feeling sad because of the possible loss of the object.

In some of the sessions held during this period, we were both moved when thinking of the long journey we had made together. Renzo became sad when he realized what his psychic condition had been and how much effort he had had to make to overcome it. Unlike the past, in which a relationship with another person meant anger or competition to see who was stronger, Renzo now experienced deep feelings about our relationship. His clown mask disappeared.

Conclusion

During this second phase of psychotherapy, Renzo was able to work out the problems regarding his persecutory fears, discuss his behav-iour, understand meanings, and considerably reduce his obsessive thoughts. He gave up transforming his aggressive thoughts into play-ful behaviour, irony, and jokes and accepted feelings of nostalgia and mourning.

In the analytic relationship, his expression of profound feelings in a sensitive way and the formulation of such articulate thoughts were beyond my expectations. Renzo continued to work at his job with dedication and conscientiousness, showing he was capable of adapting himself to the working environment. During the sessions, we were able to analyse the real situations at work and his emotional responses; this helped him adjust even better. However, there were still problems regarding his capacity to form new friends and increase his social contacts.

Renzo's fixed and obsessive thoughts were a response to the fact that his relatives were unable to imagine that he could change and develop his life or way of thinking in the future. For this reason, because he was living with the family his mind remained fixed on the past and on the bewilderment about the initial handicap. He was unable to think of the future and possible changes, which prevented him from developing.

Since the positions of identification were at the opposite ends—of suffering child and arrogant adult, people in a symbiotic relationship or always at war, intrusive or completely disinterested—Renzo was unable to understand the nuances of his feelings, to choose his own kind of being, and to become responsible for his behaviour. It was necessary continually to distinguish between the feelings expressed in the transference—that is, his sadistic feelings, masked by his playfulness and jokes—from the benign ones. There then gradually emerged the problem of his identity, and he could accept the feelings of mourning and nostalgia.

Concluding remarks

Recognition of autistic capsules

Although the cases described vary in their symptoms and overall problems, as a group they demonstrate the existence of more or less extensive autistic cores buried within the personality. Such cores are manifested primarily by the absence of emotional responses during analytic interaction and by the presence of psychological or psychosomatic symptoms. These nuclei of primitive experiences coexist with other, more developed parts, capable of symbolization, that can mask the existence of autistic nuclei and make the analyst mistakenly evaluate the entire organization of the personality.

As previously described, although these patients seemed to ask for therapeutic help, I felt from the beginning that in the countertransference there was no emotional contact. In the absence of a therapeutic alliance, it becomes very difficult to make any progress.

The need for therapy can initially be determined by neurotic, psychotic, or somatic symptoms, but progress can only be achieved by recognizing the existence of autistic capsules in the pathological organization of the personality. The recognition of autistic capsules prevents the analysis from becoming an endless, intellectual and sterile dialogue or from coming to a sudden end. Only a profound analysis of the two-person relationship can allow the autistic vestiges to be identified, because of the scarcity of authentic emotional exchanges and the presence of a profound underlying depression; the latter can become particularly evident during periods of great stress.

In the adult patients discussed, the recognition of autistic features in the psychic organization did not take place at first sight, as occurs in infantile autism. It only occurred during the course of the therapy, when, in the countertransference, I felt the absence of a therapeutic alliance and emotional responses and connected this to the primitive emotional experiences that the patient described.

Significant messages regarding the patients' sense of incomplete identity and emptiness of feelings together with a profound depression are picked up by the analyst in the countertransference. Since these are signs of early, preverbal suffering, they can be recognized more through empathy and insight than by intellectual understanding. As Joseph (1985) points out, the patient communicates most of his inner world through the feelings he arouses in the analyst before giving the autobiographic details of his past life. Therefore, we must listen to our feelings before using intellectual tools to understand these patients.

The extent of the patient's suffering indicates the underlying presence of delicate areas consisting of non-differentiation experiences, though these are hidden behind a rigid armour. The recognition and elaboration of these elements makes it possible for the autistic capsules to become integrated into the rest of the personality and for the sense of identity to become more consolidated. This helps to prevent the re-emergence of that kind of underlying depression that can lead to the sensation of non-existence. Follow-up inquiries in my treated cases, when possible, confirmed these improvements.

My clinical experience coincides with the work of Sidney Klein (1980). Following the studies of Tustin on autism (1972), Klein formulated the existence of these capsules in adult patients and compared this type of pathology to infantile autism. As he proceeded in the analysis of these patients, who were otherwise quite brilliant and intelligent, he realized that despite the normal course of the therapy, he was unable to come into contact with one part of the patient. Instead, he came up against a profound area that harboured intense fears of disintegration and death linked to the experience of separation. Klein also points out the importance of recognizing these capsules during analysis so that it will not end in failure or be followed by relapses.

According to Klein, even after making an effort to understand the material offered by the patient, the analyst finds herself faced with a cold, static world with no sign of emotion and therefore experiences a sense of solitude, uselessness, and closure, with no hope of making any progress.

In my opinion, patients with autistic capsules might be compared to the patients McDougall describes and calls "disaffected" (1972, 1978). These patients do not seem to lack feelings, as the analytic relationship shows, but seem to have kept these feelings at a distance at a very early stage of life, since they were unable to contain the excessive emotions they experienced.

McDougall (1972, 1978) describes a difficult transference–countertransference relationship in analyses of patients who "seemed unaware of the nature of their affective reactions". Their affective potential appeared to be dispersed in repetitive actions similar to addictive behaviour or in the creation of psychosomatic symptoms. What emerged in these patients was their inability to mentally represent an idea linked to emotional quality.

The process of recognizing the autistic capsules in my patients was followed by a delicate period characterized by the thawing of the emotional experiences contained in the capsules. These had then to be integrated into the rest of the personality. Since the origin of the pathology was rooted in an early pre-symbolic period in which sensory experiences and the non-recognition of the "me"–"not-me" differentiation prevailed, I had to modify my technique in order to create an interpersonal relationship that could provide the basis for the work of interpretation.

Technical issues

Without entering into the debate concerning the differences between psychoanalysis, psychoanalytic psychotherapy, and other psychotherapies, I would like to point out that when the pathology goes back to early traumas, it was useful to introduce technical changes such as "first-aid" interventions ("reclamation": Alvarez, 1992), non-analytic support interventions, and use of the face-to-face position so that a collaboration between patient and therapist could emerge.

These technical modifications were only adopted during specific phases of the therapy and proved to be complementary to the analytic work of interpretation (Goijman, 1984; Richard, 2002). The analyst can decide when to use them depending on the signals sent by the patients and on her countertransference feelings.

We know that the patient is continually fighting to demonstrate the absence or inadequacy of the object and that this autistic manoeuvre should be discouraged, but without presenting a too-intrusive transference object—for we must also keep in mind that primitive autistic reactions played an important role in helping the child survive, by warding off unbearable fears (Tustin, 1986).

Although classic analytic work consists in making unconscious processes conscious, in these cases the first step of the analyst will be to be receptive to the feelings of non-existence, emptiness, catastrophic fears of separation, and feelings of revenge, without immediately attributing to them a meaning of defence. In order to overcome fear and persecutory anxiety, containing the anxiety might make the patient feel more secure. The analyst's task should be first to stimulate empathy, which represents the starting point in order to facilitate the introjection of new messages and the development of the imagination.

In the case of Elisa (chapter 7), in order to create a new relational model it was indispensable to adopt an empathic way of communicating, making sure that she would not mistake my empathy as a seductive attempt to have some power over her. Since she was not used to a warmer relationship because of her early experience, she was afraid of being captured rather than accepted and liked. The rigidity of her obsessive organization protected her from emotional exchanges. The recognition of the analyst as a separate person and of an intermediate space through which feelings are exchanged takes place only after a long period of time as the patient's sense of identity becomes more defined. Elisa, who always used to arrive late, finally began arriving punctually when her identity became more firmly established and she began differentiating herself from me.

Unlike Elisa, in the case of Ambra (chapter 9) my biggest problem was to emerge from the confusion represented by the alternating psychotic and hysterical symptoms and to get close to her real emotional pain and thus form an empathic relationship that would make it possible to communicate. My first function was to contain her aggressive feelings, which were not always easy to bear: her intense and persistent sadistic attacks made it difficult for me to be empathic towards her. In the countertransference, this impossibility of sympathy/empathy represented a source of suffering that I experienced as my own lack of professional and human understanding. I therefore forced myself to maintain the setting rigorously. In fact, I think what helped Ambra at the beginning was my constant presence, the regularity of the sessions, and the rigour of my therapeutic role, since these elements—unlike her childhood environment, where everything was constantly changing and unpredictable—allowed her to formulate the concept of predict-ability.

In the case of Ambra, the therapeutic alliance was initially facili-tated more by the comprehension of the need for distance than by emotional closeness. Ambra needed to be considered as a separate individual and not confused with the other in the name of love. She had to experiment with a stable and definitive presence that was not intrusive.

When analysing the different features of the transference, we can-not forget that the patient tends to reproduce the earliest object rela-tionships and to transmit these nuclear experiences in the relationship with the analyst. For example, the patient can make the transference–countertransference relationship useless and so transform it into yet another failure of the environment. For this reason, it is important not to interpret the obstacles placed in the way of the analytic relationship as resistance to the analysis before the analyst can get close to the primitive suffering parts that still exist.

In this connection, it is interesting to point out that cognitivists (Cohen, 1984; Cohen & Squire, 1980; Schachter, 1987, 1992a, 1992b) have distinguished between different types of memory: explicit memory, which consciously collects facts and information about the past, and implicit memory, which contains changes produced by pre-vious experiences without the intentional process of retrieving them. Implicit memory is the first to develop. At the same time, neuropsy-chological studies confirmed the complete independence of these two systems of memory and that their functioning is based in different nerve centres (DiGiulio, Seidenberg, O'Leary, & Raz, 1994; Glickstein & Yeo, 1990; LeDoux, 1995; Mishkin, Malamut, & Bachevalier, 1984; Saint-Cyr & Taylor, 1992).

Following these studies on memory, psychoanalysts tried to find the connection between the concept of implicit memory and the trans-formation processes operating in psychoanalytic work (Fonagy, 1995; Joseph, 1989). Memories of the type of relationships and the care given during the early period of life cannot be collected by explicit memory, given the newborn's immaturity, but are stored in implicit memory and are related to the development of the inner representations of the subsequent interrelational experiences. According to Sandler and Joffe (1969), the early experiences of the self with others belong to the "non-experiential realm". This realm can become known only through a new phenomenal event in a subsequent subjective experience, and only then does it become explicit. The psychoanalytic process might first show and then change the early models of implicit memory through the interaction in a new relational model with the analyst.

Irene (chapter 8) exemplifies this: she did not seem to see me, and in this way she denied that I really existed. Her need to avoid the interpersonal relationship started becoming an idea in her mind only when she had the real experience of shaking hands at the beginning and end of the sessions. This was a bodily gesture that could assume a symbolic meaning only in our meeting through my interpretations. The process of recognizing and changing the latent relational models of implicit memory occurred slowly in the transference relationship, when, as I said, the patient experimented, to her amazement, with a new, different relational model with the analyst (Fonagy, 2001).

In the adults described, the psychic disorders were accompanied by deficits in different aspects of the personality, as Alvarez (1998) points out occurs in borderline and psychotic children. These include a weak sense of self, a weak sense of identity, a reduced ability to love, low self-esteem, and insufficient respect for one's internal objects. The positive part of the personality is underdeveloped, and the persecutory one is overdeveloped.

Irene's dominant symptom (chapter 8) was the feeling of emptiness that referred to both her inner world (anorexia, depersonalization) and the environment (derealization). During the course of the analysis, her feeling of void was followed by the need to fill it (by bulimia, by a therapy carried out with two analysts at the same time, by strong attachment to the sessions). It took a long time before she could reach a balance between her primitive impulses so that her psychic and bodily identity could take shape.

In addition to the variations in the different levels of the personality organization, the analyst is confronted with patients who, due to a poor sense of identity or oscillations within it, remain rigid out of fear of change. This rigidity can also result from the autistic capsules, which strongly resist change and seem impenetrable to outside stimuli (Tustin, 1986). These characteristics bring to mind the rigidity and repetitive behaviour of autistic children.

In the case of Elisa (chapter 7), in addition to the need for containment, I used up a great deal of time and energy in discouraging the obsessive thoughts that had invaded her mind. Our relationship seemed for a long time void of any specific meaning and lacking in emotions. I tried to make myself available as a fixed reference point and a stable container without overly focusing on her excessive rigidity and her tendency to minimize my role.

During the initial phase of the therapy when Renzo (chapter 10) was a child, the presence of obsessive rituals and the absence of any verbal communication initially dominated the scene for a long time. To discourage his tendency to repeat the same actions, it was necessary for me to intervene continually, to introduce novel elements in our relationship, and to give meaning to ritual behaviour. Only later did I direct my attention to helping him remember, make associations, and connect his thoughts. In this way, I was able to give him the idea of continuity that allowed him to preserve and conserve our relationship and the connected thoughts. All these functions, transmitted in an empathic way, allowed Renzo to develop a thinking capacity and a sophisticated sensitivity, which led to the creation of an intense human relationship, unimaginable in the past.

The patient's weak sense of identity is often accompanied by confusion in distinguishing himself from others and by the impossibility of recognizing temporal coordinates. Maintaining the regularity, rhythm, and constancy of the sessions proved to be an important element to strengthen the sense of identity and initiate a relationship of trust.

According to Maiello (2001), the temporal shapes described by Alvarez (1998) and their rhythmical qualities "belong to these deep levels of proto-mental interpersonal experience and have a bridging function in the transition from states of non-mental psycho-physical at one-ness on the way to mental activity and symbolic thinking" (Maiello, 2001, p. 182). The rhythmical aspects of reality may represent a transitional phase between a primitive state of fusion and the rudimentary awareness of separation.

Alvarez (1998) points out that in normal development, internalized objects maintain a dynamic shape over time, and she adds that thinking develops not only in relation to absence, but also with the modulation in presence, which must reassure the newborn so that he can maintain object-constancy even in the absence of the mother. In addition, Alvarez hypothesizes that the internalization of rhythmical experiences can also contribute to the quality of mental life, especially in terms of flexibility and rigidity.

Fonagy, Target, and Gergely (2000) have found that patients with severe personality disorders show a lack of flexibility and adaptation to symbolic thinking or the behaviour of others. Fixed mental patterns and behaviour created rigid response stereotypes, and these patients were unable to modulate their thinking in relation to others. In these cases, the early relational experiences were so frustrating that, as a result, the feelings and the thoughts of others were systematically rejected. This means that the patients inhibited their capacity to mentalize and to think in terms of thoughts and feelings. The deprived child can only disavow the thinking process and block it in order to avoid mental representations that can reawaken painful feelings.

These observations are partially applicable to adult patients with autistic capsules. In the face of such rigidity, the analyst runs the risk of identifying with the patient's stubbornness. She can present herself as equally impenetrable and unchangeable; or she can oscillate between a sadistic position in which she experiences irritation and rejection and a desire to form contact; or she can assume a masochistic position characterized by an infinite patience and immobility. This uncomfortable situation in which the analyst finds herself blocks her feelings and can lead to actings-out. The absence of empathy makes the analyst experience guilt feelings that increase because the therapy does not progress.

Considering the rigidity of the patient's repetitive behaviour, if the analyst remains impenetrable to the patient's communication, she might reproduce in the patient's mind something already experienced regarding a "not-me" insensitive to his own needs. The analyst might therefore really become just as the patient imagines her—that is, a mechanical container of ideas or a dispenser of interpretations. For this reason, the analyst must be flexible and be attentive to the patient's demands and the degree of his depression or despair, without abdicating her role.

Seemingly in opposition to the patient's rigidity and impenetrability, there are coexisting demands for symbiotic or parasitic relationships because of unmet primitive needs. This tendency to establish a symbiosis can be manifested by the continual search for similar elements in the analyst, who feels she will have to correspond to such needs in order not to disappoint the patient's expectations. Since unresolved symbiotic residues may then emerge in the analyst's personality and they tend to form a non-conflictual relationship with the patient, they might hinder his development. It is evident that these oscillations between unconscious requests and responses in the transference–countertransference relationship must be carefully recognized in order to evaluate their effects and the extent to which they can or cannot be therapeutic.

The process of individuation runs parallel to the process of differentiation from the object. However, although the object might be recognized, it may be considered as a part that is not separate from the self. This undifferentiated state might then lead to a parasitic condition that is created as a defence against anguished feelings of catastrophe or experiences of being mutilated. In these situations, it is necessary for the analyst to recognize in such a parasitic tendency the gravity and archaic origin of the underlying feelings of anguish so that this tendency will not be interpreted only as a manipulation to enslave the analyst.

The impression of an indefinite, traumatic past in which he felt something was missing makes such a patient fear that some negative experiences will emerge from the outside environment, as well as from the relationship with the analyst. He imagines a persecutory background in the analytic relationship. It is essential for the patient to feel self-confident and that he can rely on the analyst. Bearing in mind that the patient's emotional deprivation occurred very early and that his anguish was very intense, his opposition and rejection of the analyst should be interpreted as a vital form of self-preservation. Understanding the patient's hatred does not mean colluding with the patient's aggressiveness or denying it, but understanding his suffering and, at the same time, recognizing the strength of his reactions and his need to express feelings of vengeance. The analyst must put herself in the place of the patient, accept his unconscious desires, and understand his need to develop.

In cases where there was an early disastrous experience, Alvarez (1992), following Bion's theory, stresses the need to consider the phenomenon of projective identification not simply as a defence, but also as a mechanism that helps the patient develop. The projection of aggressiveness in others must not, therefore, be considered only as a defence against persecution, but also as an attempt to overcome persecution and as a sign of development. Therefore, the slightest sign of an increase in the patient's ideal self or ideal object must not be interpreted as a flight towards mania.

The analyst usually has to wait patiently and build up the patient's trust and hope in order to make sense of the purpose of the therapy, which is implicit but not recognized by the patient on a conscious level. All these efforts may allow the mechanisms of introjection and projection to gradually start working, thus allowing the patient and analyst to start communicating.

In cases where somatic symptoms represent the only form of communication, we must keep in mind that it is a very primitive form of language, which reduces one's individuality to mere bodily and sensory existence. Given the absence of imagination, somatic symptoms and actings-out prevail in the transference, so the task of the analyst will be to give a name and meaning to the different communications until the patient himself is able to make associations and develop more symbolic thought.

Faced with the monotonous atmosphere characterized by obsessive behaviour or rituals, the analyst must not only decipher the patient's bodily signs and their intentionality but also pay special attention to the messages that emerge from within: her fantasies caused by the real presence and communication of the patient, her own infantile psychic world, bodily sensations, and regressive areas.

I would like to point out that in reconsidering the development of the newborn, Ogden (1989) offers an illuminating explanation of the primitive experience of being, through his concept of the "autistic-contiguous" state. This primitive psychological organization provides a sensory background in the slow acquisition of the sense of subjective identity. During the first phases of the baby's development, as I previously said, the sense of separateness is gradually established within the relationship of the mother–child couple, provided that the mother communicates to her baby the reassurance that bodily separateness is not catastrophic. If this transmission does not occur in a sensitive and flexible way, it may lead to the development of psychogenic autism.

Ogden (1989) adds:

> In the autistic-contiguous position, the relationship to objects is one in which the organisation of a rudimentary sense of "I-ness" arises from relationships of sensory contiguity (that is, touching) that over time generate the sense of a bounded sensory surface on which one's experience occurs. [p. 53]

Similarly, with patients whose sense of identity is inconsistent, the stability of the setting and the active participation of the analyst take on a fundamental importance. In this connection, the case of Irene (chapter 8) is significant since she communicated only through her body. In this way, she transformed the analytic relationship to mere body and skin contact. This implied death, danger, and persecution for her, as well as the recognition of the boundaries of her own body and the separation between us. This mistaken sensation of cutaneous contact signifies an early problem in the use of the object relationship. In this case, before forming an interpersonal relationship, it was necessary to establish links between sensations, states of mind, and perceptions that would allow Irene to be aware of her own personal physical and psychic identity and emphasize my presence. With autistic patients a further danger for the analyst is to conform with the patient's mental laziness, withdraw into personal autistic areas, lose motivation for analytic work, and abandon the function of transformation (chapter 4).

As mentioned earlier, in autism we can hypothesize that since the newborn had experienced a lack of adequate support to satisfy his specific needs for survival at a time when he had no personal instruments to overcome his discomfort, this might have given rise to the denial of the existence of "not-me" and to the freezing of one part of his personality which needed help. Therefore, similarly in adult patients with autistic residues we can recognize the necessity of analogous attitudes such as holding, empathy, and containment. However, these functions alone are not sufficient to make the analytic work fruitful: there must also be an activity of revitalization, which Alvarez (1992) calls "reclamation". This function emerges from the analyst's whole personality, which continually tries to transmit signals of vitality. As Alvarez (1992) says, the autistic child needs an "intelligent, animate object" that can reactivate reduced mental functions and stimulate his thinking process by holding him in an empathic way.

The function of psychoanalytic treatment is not only to reorganize the structures of the representations, but also to solicit mental functioning (Fonagy, 2001). This can occur through the analyst's active involvement, which removes the threat of overwhelming mental anguish that originally led to the abandonment of the mental process (Alvarez, 1992).

Like Alvarez, Gallo (2001) stresses the importance of the analyst's active role in mobilizing the blocked mental functions and in helping the child exist mentally. Through his imagination and attention to the patient's slightest signs of expression, the analyst will actively participate in helping the patient to begin to communicate and formulate thoughts. A further confirmation of this hypothesis is found in different patients, like Irene and Renzo, who acquired a new development of language and verbal structure that enriched their inner world and increased their capacity to relate to others. During the psychotherapy, unexpected intellectual activity emerged that made different areas of study possible for them.

The decision to bring the therapy to an end marks a particularly delicate phase, even when the personality has reached a good equilibrium and a satisfactory development. Since these patients tend to live in a non-temporal dimension in which the present is blurred by a past experienced as traumatic and they cannot imagine a future, the analytic relationship is experienced as suspended in a continuum with no time dimension. Therefore, it is difficult to bring these therapies to a close, since the separation and the acceptance of a limit come up against massive defences. Being alone means falling for ever, and the word "separation" is taken for disappearance. It is necessary to work out the concept of "end" for a long time until the primitive agonies described by Winnicott (1974) no longer emerge.

We can consider that the analytic process has reached its conclusion when, in the place of an apparent insensitivity and lack of object relationship, there gradually emerge feelings connected to the absence of the object, since the ego can tolerate the elaboration of mourning.

Prelude to spring

In work with adults who reveal autistic capsules, the process of individuation requires the acceptance of an initial period in which the analyst tries to create a relationship with the patient, followed by a period in which gradual differentiation can occur between the two participants in order to reach separation.

After recovering the frozen parts of the autistic capsules, I tried to encourage the patients to assume a maternal function of protection and a paternal function of support towards the damaged and frozen part of their self, to enhance the emotional part stemming from the transference experience, and to work out the synthesis between emotions, feelings, and thinking. The analytic experience cannot expect to repair a patient's early deficits when they are identified but, rather, to strengthen the healthy, underdeveloped, and poorly functioning parts so that the patient can give shape to a new identity.

Because the analytic relationship long remains in a pre-symbolic area, communication occurs at a very primitive level. The analyst experiences a situation of human contact that is simple and immediate and uses more sensory impressions or primitive feelings rather than her more familiar analytic baggage. The technical tools, the theoretical knowledge, and intellectual ambitions lose importance in that phase, and the analyst has to resort to her human understanding and capacity to revitalize the blocked mental functions. Only in a second phase can the usual work of interpretation be used, although she must also consider the oscillations in the consistency of the self and adapt to the different levels of communication.

I would like to emphasize that the function of the analyst must be directed to offering a human bond beyond the technical/professional in her therapeutic effort, and she must present herself to the patient as a complete, living person, thereby stimulating the interpersonal relationship in a peculiar way. Her work of inner elaboration puts her personal world in contact with the patient's.

I would like to return to the metaphor of the Arctic plain that runs through this work and compare it to the emotional life of these patients. Despite the long, dark winter, when the ground is covered by sheets of ice, the native population continues its usual activities outdoors. This is possible because of the presence of a soft, diffused twilight during the day and because the temperature is not too cold as dark-coloured objects absorb and retain the heat from the sun. Since the local population has never experienced any other kind of winter or light, they regard it as normal, and during the long polar night they carry out their daily activities normally. For the patients, too, one part of their life was carried out normally but with less inner and external light—that is, with fewer intense feelings and less access to their mental resources.

We all see reality according to our own personal light, which we regard as the only possible one, until we experience the existence of a different perspective. In the Arctic plain, the period of thawing after a long, ice-cold winter is particularly difficult because the thawing of the ice makes it temporarily impossible to define the boundaries between land and water, because of the mud, and this makes ground travel hazardous. At a certain point, water begins to flow in the streams and the first animals emerge from their lethargy. But it is necessary to wait for the summer before the uniform, long white stretch turns into fields of coloured flowers. This transformation takes a long time and lasts throughout the months of spring.

Similarly, during these therapies we can hypothesize that the long period of emotional cold is followed by the thawing of encapsulated parts that contain the vestiges of early experiences. The thawing of these capsules brings about a change in the patient's inner world that at first seems catastrophic due to the sudden change, which seems to open up new horizons.

Feeling alive and active after a long absence from the vital world of feelings and from the use of complete cognitive functions, one faces an unpredictable destiny of emotional exchanges representing an enriching discovery. However, it also implies that the patient recognizes that he has wasted and lost much time in his past, has created a false sense of security around which he structured his life, and has mistakenly interpreted human relationships. Moreover, it also requires considerable courage to face the risk of future emotional relationships.

Because of the re-appropriation of his own feelings, the sense of a separate identity makes the patient feel that something is missing and it makes him experience a sense of nostalgia. These feelings cause suffering and can be difficult to distinguish from his primitive anxieties of emptiness and "non-existence". In these patients, the passage towards a new vision of the inner and outer world takes time and requires the help of a sensitive analyst to make this passage acceptable or familiar.

In his book, *Le temps des glaciations* (1999b), Resnik uses the metaphor of the Ice Age to indicate a crucial period in the life of the psychotic when emotional life became blocked and feelings cooled down. He says that, during analysis, "thawing" represents a critical moment in which the patient thaws and returns to life. Resnik compares thawing to a form of psychic haemorrhage and regards the process of thawing as a "frightening passage from deadly anaesthesia to burning vitality".

The thawing and recovery of autistic capsules in which very early experiences, embryonic emotions, and feelings of potential energy have remained frozen determines a new emotional situation: the possibility of experiencing feelings such as love, desire, and pain when something lost emerges. Since this can disorient the patient, he needs a period of time and much support in order to get used to the situation and to regain his vital energies.

In the cases described here, therapy came to a final conclusion, overcoming such difficulties, following the disappearance of the initial, chronic symptoms and a better understanding of the self. Perceptions, sensations, and feelings could be linked. In such cases, the patient comes to realize that life could have taken a different turn.

Unfortunately in the case of Ambra (chapter 9), as already observed, the reawakening of the frozen emotional parts had revealed more an insufficiency of vital tone in order to change and a sense of disillusion, rather than amazement at the discovery of hidden potential and of a future on which to build. Ambra's weak libidinal impulses, or her fear of facing a depression that might cause her to re-experience the catastrophic agonies of the past, made her unable to negotiate this transformation. The sudden interruption of the therapeutic bond tragically made it impossible to continue in an attempt to integrate the lost parts.

As this work draws to a close, I am becoming more aware of inadequacies, omissions, inaccuracies, repetitions, the absolute certainty of certain statements and the inevitable gap between what I have written now, what I have thought or felt at that time, and what really took place in the therapeutic course of these relationships. Each one of us might experience reality in the twilight of the Arctic plain. Therefore, it is not a question of concluding but of putting forward some premises that can be worked out in the future.

Experiencing a sensation of loneliness and non-communication when faced with the patient's autistic parts leads the analyst to intra-subjective attention in which bodily sensory-dominated ways of being (or not-being) and primitive anxieties prevail over her feelings and thoughts emerging from her associations. This condition of subjective attention to our simplest states of being might help us to adopt a specific method for each patient, to intervene in a specific way, and to provide the spark that triggers the human exchange that is indispensable for analytic work.

Technical instruments, theoretical knowledge, and intellectual ambitions become less important than our closeness to a primitive state of being, and the analyst must rely more on her human understanding, although the basic principles of professional training must be borne in mind.

As Di Chiara points out (1990) when he reconsiders Bion's ideas, the meeting of patient and analyst should be represented by a passion—that is, "an emotional experience felt with warmth and intensity but not with violence" (Bion, 1963, p. 21). In the meeting of patient and analyst, "the primitive levels might contain the mental instruments for the realization of experiences which are essential for psychic and especially mental life" (Di Chiara, 1990, p. 449).

Faced with the profound changes that I witnessed during these long psychotherapies, I was the one who felt the feeling of "awe", because I saw the emergence of vital aspects that had remained hidden by the frozen defensive mantle and appeared non-existent.

As a witness to Renzo's process of individuation during the course of the therapy from childhood to adulthood, I would like to conclude by citing his words from one of the final sessions:

"I am increasingly convinced that everything stems from the anger I experienced as a child, and I think that I am not mistaken if I seem to understand something more about myself every time that I speak with you. Last time, as I was leaving, I said thank you for what you had said to

me, but now I do not know what I was referring to. . . . Yesterday I saw the film Pinocchio, *who at the end was changed from a wooden puppet into a real child. I am sorry that I was not able to be a normal child like other children and was a puppet for so many years. I also met the fairy with the magic wand, but she arrived too late, and only after a long time was I able to use my mind and understand myself: I recognize that only now have I become a real person."*

The atmosphere behind these words of Renzo was full of emotion, nostalgia, and sadness due to the realization of his difficult past, but it was also full of hope because of his new condition of being a thinking and feeling young man.

GLOSSARY

Acting-out/in: a term used in psychoanalysis to signify a specific impulsive act in relation to the dynamics of the treatment outside or inside the analytic session. In this case, it means a basic refusal to acknowledge feelings in the transference which are expressed through an action rather than through a verbal communication. It is thought to be a form of resistance to the work of analysis (Freud, 1914g).

Addictive behaviour: a phenomenon where, as a defence against mental pain, people habitually resort to actings-out like eating, drinking, smoking, and so forth more than usual. They lack an internal representation of the mother as a caretaking introject or of the father with whom to identify in states of tension or conflict (McDougall, 1982a).

Addictive sexuality: a concept introduced by McDougall (1982a) to indicate compulsive and addictive relationships in which sexuality has a drug-like quality and the partner plays a small role in the subject's inner world, being more an object of need than an object of desire.

Adhesive identification: a form of identification more primitive than the introjective and projective ones. It refers to an early attempt to create a rudimentary sense of identity based on the surface of the object. In cases where this fails, projective identification cannot be employed because there is no sense of internal space. Sticking to an object is opposed to projecting into it. Imitation is a kind of adhesiveness to the surface of the other, and separation thus represents a dreadful split (Bick, 1986; Meltzer et al., 1975). Subsequently Bick modified the term "adhesive identification" to "adhesive identity". Tustin (1994) prefers "adhesive equation" to "adhesive identification" because the individual's body is equated with the object in a concrete, sensory way.

Asperger syndrome: a developmental disorder originating in infancy but also present in adolescence and adulthood. It belongs to the autistic spectrum and is considered as a high-functioning or mild autism. Like children described by Kanner (1943), "Asperger children" are socially isolated and egocentric, but they have better language, invent new words or use language in idiosyncratic, bizarre ways, and have special abilities. (Asperger, 1944)

Autism (infantile):   a severe psychic disorder that affects young children in their mental and emotional development. Such children do not engage in emotional relationships with others, do not use language for communicating, do not play, and have strange repetitive behaviour and rituals (Kanner, 1943). Autistic children avoid eye contact; they exist in a world of their own and ignore the existence of the others. Tustin's revised view (1994) considers autism as a developmental aberration rather than a regression to a normal infantile state.

Autistic capsules: a concept related to a psychic area more or less extended in the personality which contains traces of primitive autistic reactions to extreme infantile anxiety and non-elaborated sensory experiences. These encapsulated parts of the personality can remain hidden under neurotic, psychotic, or borderline psychic organization or in psychosomatic personalities. (S. Klein, 1980; D. Rosenfeld, 1992).

Autistic objects: all kinds of objects (usually hard) that autistic children hold without recognizing their symbolic meaning. Autistic objects are particular to each individual child, and they differ from transitional objects because they have a role of protection from separation and escape from danger. They maintain sensations on the surface of the child's body and give him a concrete sensation of continuity and safety (Tustin, 1980).

Autistic shapes: personal and particular shapes that are experienced in the child's body or on his bodily surface and cannot be shared with other people. These "shapeless shapes" are bodily experiences of autistic children and are preserved as parts of their undifferentiated sense of "being" (Tustin, 1984).

Containment: a process referring to the mother's function as a container of the infant's primitive projections (Bion, 1962a). The infant's projected emotions are contained, tolerated, and digested by the mother and then given back to the baby in a more bearable way. This maternal function can be considered as a model for the analyst in the psycho-analytic relationship.

Countertransference: a concept that includes all the analyst's feelings and unconscious reactions to the patient's transference. It represents the analyst's experience in his meeting with the patient. There is a widespread debate regarding the extension of the concept of counter-transference and its use in analytic work, but it was first suggested as a helpful tool for the analyst by Paula Heimann (1950) and by Heinrich Racker (1948).

Depressive position: according to Melanie Klein (1935), a modality of object-relations that is established after the paranoid–schizoid position. The latter position is reached about the fourth month of life and is gradually overcome during the course of the first year. The depres-sive position is characterized by the capacity of the child to see the mother as a whole object and to attenuate the splitting between the bad and good object. The depressive position is characterized by the achievement of symbol formation and the development of the capacity for concern for the object. This makes it possible for the subject to mediate between the symbol and the symbolized. In this way, thoughts and feelings are experienced as one's own, and the subject experiences his own responsibility with respect to his own actions and thoughts. Bion (1962b), however, modified Klein's concept in that he does not consider it as a developmental phase but as a synchronic dimension of the experience in the development of the mind.

Disaffectation: a situation that comes to light in analytic treatment through an unemotional relationship of the patient with the analyst. Such patients seem to be separated from their emotions and to have lost the capacity to be in contact with their inner world. According to McDougall (1982a), the suffering of "disaffected patients" may not be their inability to experience emotions, but an inability to contain and reflect over an excess of affective experiences that occurred in a pre-symbolic period.

Discharge-in-action: a particular response to stressful events in which mental elaboration is avoided because there is a lack of psychic infor-mation regarding the conflict. This attempt to get rid of the pain and the psychic tension through actings-out can determine different mani-festations such as sexual perversions, all types of addictive behaviour, and psychosomatic reactions such as the breakdown of the immune barriers (McDougall, 1982a).

Empathy: a concept related to a peculiar capacity to know the feelings of the other person in order to share them. Racker (1957) considered empathy as a particular kind of countertransference; Ferenczi (Ferenczi & Rank, 1927) regarded it as the insight of the analyst in foreseeing the patient's reaction before intervening. This is a normal activity for sensitive people. In the Kleinian perspective, empathy is a benign form of projective identification (q.v.), which is a process of inserting a part of oneself into someone else's position in order to gain in fantasy their experience. The most important part of this intrusion into someone else is that there is no loss of reality and no confusion of identity, whereas in pathological projective identification, the boundaries between the self and the object are destroyed (Klein, 1959).

Foreclosure: a term introduced by Freud (1911c, 1915e, 1927e) to describe one of the archaic defence mechanisms that attempted to deny or get rid of troubling experience from the psyche. Freud considered that the capacity of the psyche to eject completely an experience from consciousness rather than keeping it in the form of repression (repudiation) was a typical mechanism of psychosis. For Lacan (1956), "foreclosure" describes a process of not-symbolizing what ought to be symbolized; it is a "symbolic abolition". McDougall (1989) uses this term to indicate the capacity to eject from the psyche certain perceptions, thoughts, fantasies, and other events. She considered that foreclosure is operative in adult regression to psychosomatic rather than psychological responses to conflict or psychic pain. There is a dissociation between word-representation and thing-representation, so that the bodily signals of anxiety become the equivalent of thing-representation and are separate from word-representation that would give meaning to the experience.

Introjective identification: a concept related to a process in which the subject transposes objects and their inherent qualities from the external world to his own mind. This process helps to build up one's personal characteristics (Klein, 1946).

Paranoid–schizoid position: according to Klein (1946), the concept of a primitive psychological organization designed to evacuate anxieties of a persecutory type through the defensive use of omnipotent thinking, denial, and creation of discontinuities of experience. Overcoming this position depends on the relative strength of libidinal impulses with respect to the aggressive ones.

Preconceptions: a concept introduced by Bion (1962b) to indicate an innate predisposition to understand structures, qualities, and function of reality at a proto-mental level. Preconceptions are a psychological entity waiting for a realization that will "mate" with it. When the unexperienced preconception mates with the realization, a conception can be formed in the child's mind and from this his thinking can develop.

Projective identification: a primitive form of nonverbal communication. It is a psychological–interpersonal process based on omnipotent fantasy of placing an aspect of the self into another person in such a way that this aspect can be controlled, and possessed, in the other. This can represent a particular form of identification which establishes the prototype of an aggressive object-relation (Klein, 1946). Bion (1959) distinguished two forms of projective identification: a pathological form characterized by omnipotence and violence, and a normal one without that degree of violence and which can distinguish internal reality from external reality. In the pathological form, there is confusion of self with an object. This process can serve defensive purposes, but it also constitutes a fundamental form of communication and object-relatedness.

Reclamation: according to Alvarez (1992), a concept of a vital counter-transference response to the wasting of time, body, and mind by particularly passive or withdrawn patients. This concept introduces notions of vitality and activity of the psychoanalyst who is faced with the inability of autistic patients to reach out and grasp her.

Reverie: a concept referring to the mother's receptivity to her infant's symbolic, asymbolic, or pre-symbolic experience (Bion, 1962b). According to Bion, the mother's reverie is a process of making sense of the infant's states of anxiety and terror: he called this the alpha-function. The mother's mind needs to be in a state of receptiveness to take in the infant's feelings and give them meaning. Reverie can also refer to the analyst's state of receptivity to the patient's unconscious experience.

Rumination, or merycism: a pathological infantile syndrome paradigmatic of the self-enclosed circularity of the pathological autistic process. The infant actively brings into his mouth the swallowed food and then is pervaded by an ecstatic expression (Gaddini & Gaddini, 1959).

Transference: according to Freud (1912b, 1915e), a process in the analytic situation where the infantile model of relationship re-emerges in the relationship with the psychoanalyst. Klein (1952) considers that it includes the projection of the patient's inner objects into the analyst.

REFERENCES

Alvarez, A. (1983). Problems in the use of the counter-transference: Getting it across. *Journal of Child Psychotherapy, 9.*

Alvarez, A. (1985). The problem of neutrality: Some reflections on the psychoanalytic attitude in the treatment of borderline and psychotic children. *Journal of Child Psychotherapy, 11* (1).

Alvarez, A. (1992). *Live Company: Psychotherapy with Autistic, Borderline, Deprived and Abused Children.* London: Routledge.

Alvarez, A. (1995). Motiveless malignity: Problems in the psychotherapy of psychopathic patients. *Journal of Child Psychotherapy, 21* (2).

Alvarez, A. (1996). Different uses of the counter-transference with neurotic, borderline, and psychotic patients. In: J. Tsiantis, A. Sandler, D. Anastasopoulos, & B. Martindale (Eds.), *Countertransference in Psychoanalytic Psychotherapy with Children and Adolescents.* EFPP Clinical Monograph Series. London: Karnac.

Alvarez, A. (1997). Projective identification as a communication: Its grammar in borderline psychotic children. *Psychoanalytic Dialogues, 7* (6). (Symposium on Child Analysis, Part 1.)

Alvarez, A. (1998). Failures to link: Attacks or defects? Some questions concerning the thinkability of oedipal and pre-oedipal thoughts. *Journal of Child Psychotherapy, 24* (2).

Alvarez, A. (1999). Frustrations and separateness, delight and connectedness: Reflections on the conditions under which bad and good surprises are conducive to learning. *Journal of Child Psychotherapy, 25* (2).

229

Alvarez, A. (2000). Moral imperatives in work with borderline children: The grammar of wishes and the grammar of needs. In: J. Symington (Ed.), *Imprisoned Pain and Its Transformation: A Festschrift for H. Sydney Klein.* London: Karnac.

Alvarez, A., & Reid, S. (1999). *Autism and Personality: Findings from Tavistock Autism Workshops.* London: Routledge.

Anzieu, D. (1979). La psychanalyse au service de la psychologie. *Nouvelle Revue de Psychanalyse, 20*: 59–75.

Asperger, H. (1944). Die "Autistischen Psychopathen" im Kindesalter. *Archiv für Psychiatrie und Nervenkrankheiten, 117*: 76–136.

Bailey, A., Phillips, W., & Rutter, M. (1996). Autism: Toward an integration of clinical genetic, neuropsychological and neurobiological perspectives. *Journal of Child Psychology and Psychiatry, 37* (1): 89–126.

Balint, M. (1968). *The Basic Fault.* London: Tavistock.

Baron-Cohen, S. (1988). Social and pragmatic deficits in autism: Cognitive or affective? *Journal of Autism and Developmental Disorder, 18* (3).

Baron-Cohen, S., Allen, J., & Gillberg, C. (1992). Can autism be detected at 18 months? The needle, the haystack, and the CHAT. *British Journal of Psychiatry, 161*: 839–843.

Baranger, W., & Baranger, M. (1969). *Problemas del campo psicoanalítico.* Buenos Aires: Ediciones Kargieman.

Baranger, W., & Baranger, M. (1990). *La situazione psicoanalitica come campo bipersonale.* Milan: Cortina.

Barrow, A. (1988). "Asperger's Syndrome: A Theoretical and Clinical Account." Unpublished doctoral dissertation, Wright Institute Graduate School of Psychology.

Barrows, P. (2001). The use of stories as autistic objects. *Journal of Child Psychotherapy, 27* (1): 69–82.

Barrows, P. (2002). Becoming verbal: Autism, trauma and playfulness. *Journal of Child Psychotherapy, 28* (1): 53–72.

Benedetti, G. (1980). *Alienazione e personazione nella psicoterapia della malattia mentale.* Turin: Einaudi.

Benedetti, G. (1992). *Psychotherapie als existentielle Herausforderung.* Göttingen: Vandenhoeck & Ruprecht. [Published in Italian as: *La psicoterapia come sfida esistenziale.* Milan: Cortina, 1997.]

Bettelheim, B. (1967). *The Empty Fortress.* New York: Macmillan.

Bick, E. (1964). Notes on infant observation in psycho-analytic training. *International Journal of Psychoanalysis, 45*: 558–66. [Also in: M. Harris Williams (Ed.), *The Collected Papers of Martha Harris and Esther Bick* (pp. 240–256). Strath Tay: Clunie Press, 1987.]

Bick, E. (1968). The experience of the skin in early object relations. *International Journal of Psychoanalysis, 49*: 484–486. [Also in: M. Harris Williams

(Ed.), *The Collected Papers of Martha Harris and Esther Bick* (pp. 114–118). Strath Tay: Clunie Press, 1987.]

Bick, E. (1986). Further considerations on the function of the skin in early object relations. *British Journal of Psychotherapy, 2*: 292–299.

Bion, W. R. (1955). Language and the schizophrenic. In: M. Klein, P. Heimann, & R. Money-Kyrle (Eds.), *New Directions in Psycho-Analysis* (pp. 220–239). London: Tavistock.

Bion, W. R. (1959). Attacks on linking. *International Journal of Psychoanalysis, 40*: 308–315. [Also in: *Second Thoughts* (pp. 93–109). London: Heinemann, 1967; London: Karnac, 1984.]

Bion, W. R. (1962a). A theory of thinking. *International Journal of Psychoanalysis, 43*: 306–310. [Also in: *Second Thoughts* (pp. 110–119). London: Heinemann, 1967; London: Karnac, 1984.]

Bion, W. R. (1962b). *Learning from Experience*. London: Heinemann.

Bion, W. R. (1963). *Elements of Psychoanalysis*. London: Heinemann.

Bion, W. R. (1965). *Transformations*. London: Heinemann.

Bion, W. R. (1970). *Attention and Interpretation*. London: Heinemann.

Bollas, C. (1987). *The Shadow of the Object*. London: Free Association Books.

Bollas, C. (1989). *Forces of Destiny*. London: Free Association Books.

Brusset, B. (2002). L'or et le cuivre. In: F. Richard (Ed.), *Le travail du psych-analyste en psychothérapie*. Paris: Dunod.

Cohen, N. (1984). Preserved learning capacity in amnesia: Evidence for multiple memory systems. In: L. R. Squire & N. Butters (Eds.), *Neuropsychology of Memory* (pp. 83–103). New York: Guilford Press.

Cohen, N., & Squire, L. R. (1980). Preserved learning and retention of pattern-analysing skill in amnesia: Dissociation of knowing how and knowing that. *Science, 210*: 207–209.

Corominas, J. (1982). Handicap psichico: Applicazioni della psicoanalisi alla psicoterapia dell'handicap. *Quaderni di Psicoterapia Infantile, 8*: 143–6.

Corominas, J. (1991). *Psicopatologia i desenvolupament arcaics*. Barcelona: Espaxs, Assaig psicoanalitic. [Italian: *Psicopatologia e sviluppi arcaici*. Rome: Borla, 1993.]

Corominas, J. (1994). Possibles vinculations entra organitzacion patologiques de l'adult i problemes del desevolupament mental primari. *Revista Catalana de Psicoanalisi, 12* (1).

Corominas, J. (2000). Nuclei di sensorialità non mentalizzata: Manifestazioni nella clinica psicoanalitica. In: E. Levis (Ed.), *Forme di vita forme di conoscenza*. Turin: Bollati Boringhieri.

Cremerius, J. (1985). *Il mestiere dell'analista*. Turin: Boringhieri.

Cremerius, J. (1991). *Limiti e possibilità della tecnica psicoanalitica*. Turin: Bollati Boringhieri.

Dawson, G., & Lewy, A. (1989a). Arousal, attention, and socioemotional impairments of individuals with autism. In: G. Dawson (Ed.), *Autism: Nature, Diagnosis and Treatment*. New York: Guildford Press.

Dawson, G., & Lewy, A. (1989b). Reciprocal subcortical–cortical influences in autism: The role of attentional mechanisms. In: G. Dawson (Ed.), *Autism: Nature, Diagnosis and Treatment*. New York: Guildford Press.

Delion, P., Beucher, A., Bullinger, A., Carel, A., Charlery, M., Golse, B., Kotras, F., Lechertier, F., Livoir-Petersen, M., & Pouplard, F. (1998). *Les bébés à risque autistique*. Ramonville Saint-Agne: Erès.

Di Cagno, L., Lazzarini, A., Rissone, A., & Randaccio, S. (1984). *Il neonato e il suo mondo relazionale*. Rome: Borla.

Di Chiara, G. (1990). La stupita meraviglia, l'autismo e la competenza difensiva. *Rivista di Psicoanalisi, 36* (2).

DiGiulio, D. V., Seidenberg, M., O'Leary, D. S., & Raz, N. (1994). Procedural and declarative memory: A developmental study. *Brain and Cognition, 25*: 79–91.

Edwards, J., & Lanyado, M. (1999). Autism: Clinical and theoretical issues. In: M. Lanyado & A. Horne (Eds.), *Child and Adolescent Psychotherapy* (pp. 429–444). London: Routledge.

Erikson, E. H. (1950). *Childhood and Society*. New York: W. W. Norton.

Etchegoyen, H. (1986). *The Fundamentals of Psychoanalytic Technique*. London: Karnac, 1991.

Fenichel, O. (1945). *The Psychoanalytic Theory of the Personality*. London: Routledge & Kegan Paul.

Ferenczi, S., & Rank, O. (1923). *The Development of Psychoanalysis*. New York & Washington, DC: Nervous & Mental Disease Publishing Co.

Ferenczi, S., & Rank, O. (1927). Missbrauch der Assoziationsfreiheit. In: *Bausteine zur Psychoanalyse, 2*. Berlin: Internationaler Psychoanalytischer Verlag.

Fonagy, P. (1995). Playing with reality: The development of psychic reality and its malfunction in borderline patients. *International Journal of Psychoanalysis, 76*: 39–44.

Fonagy, P. (2001). Changing ideas of change. In: J. Edwards (Ed.), *Being Alive* (pp. 14–31). Hove: Brunner-Routledge.

Fonagy, P., Target, M., & Gergely G. (2000). Attachment and borderline personality disorder: A theory and some evidence. *Psychiatric Clinics of North America, 23*: 103–122.

Fraiberg, S. H. (1982). Pathological defences in infancy. *Psychoanalytic Quarterly, 1*.

Freud, A. (1936). *The Ego and the Mechanisms of Defence*. London: Hogarth Press, 1937; New York: International Universities Press, 1946.

Freud, S. (1910d). The future prospects of psycho-analytic therapy. *S.E., 11*.

Freud, S. (1911c). Psycho-analytic notes on an autobiographical account of a case of paranoia (Dementia paranoides). *S.E.*, 12.

Freud, S. (1912b). The dynamics of transference. *S.E.*, 12.

Freud, S. (1912e). Recommendations to physicians practising psycho-analysis. *S.E.*, 12.

Freud, S. (1914g). Remembering, repeating and working-through. *S.E.*, 14.

Freud, S. (1915e). The unconscious. *S.E.*, 15.

Freud, S. (1927e). Fetishism. *S.E.*, 21.

Frith, U. (1989). *Autism: Explaining the Enigma*. Oxford: Blackwell,

Frith, U. (1991). *Autism and Asperger syndrome*. Cambridge: Cambridge University Press.

Gaddini, E. (1969). On imitation. *International Journal of Psychoanalysis, 50*: 475–484.

Gaddini, R., & Gaddini, E. (1959). Rumination in infancy. In: L. Jessner & E. Pavensteld (Eds.) *Dynamic Psychopathology in Childhood* (pp. 166–185). New York: Grune & Stratton.

Gallo, M. T. (2001). Deficits in the object and failures in containment. In: J. Edwards (Ed.), *Being Alive* (pp. 102–114). Hove: Brunner-Routledge.

Gillberg, C. (1990). Autism and pervasive development disorders. *Journal of Child Psychology and Psychiatry, 31* (1).

Glickstein, M., & Yeo, C. (1990). The cerebellum and motor learning. *Journal of Cognitive Neuroscience, 2*: 69–80.

Godfrind, J. (1993). *Les deux courants du transfert*. Paris: Presse Universitaire de France.

Goijman, L. (1984). Psychanalyse et psychothérapie psychanalytique: Oppositions et complémentarités. *Revista de psicoanálisis, 51* (2/3).

Green, A. (1990). *La folie privée*. Paris: Gallimard.

Green, A. (1997). Démembrement du contre-transfert. In: J.-J. Baranes, F. Sacco, M. Aisenstein, S. Bolognini, F. Duparc, A. Ferro, A. Ferruta, & F. Guignard (Eds.), *Inventer en psychanalyse* (pp. 131–161). Paris: Dunod, 2002.

Green, A. (2002). La syndrome de désertification psychique. In: F. Richard (Ed.), *Le travail du psychanalyste en psychothérapie* (pp. 17–34). Paris: Dunod.

Grotstein, J. S. (1980). Primitive mental states. *Contemporary Psycho-Analysis, 16*: 479–546.

Grotstein, J. S. (1981). *Do I Dare Disturb the Universe?* London: Karnac.

Grotstein, J. S. (1983). Review of Tustin's *Autistic States in Children. International Review of Psycho-Analysis, 10*: 491–498.

Haag, G. (1985). La mère et le bébé dans les deux moitiés du corps. *Neuropsychiatrie de l'enfance, 33* (2–3): 107–114.

Haag, G., et al. (1995). Grille de repérage clinique des étapes évolutives de l'autisme infantile traité. *Psychiatrie de l'enfant, 38* (2): 495–527.

Hartmann, H. (1939). *Ego Psychology and the Problem of Adaptation*. New York: International Universities Press, 1958.

Heimann, P. (1950). On countertransference. In: M. Tonnesmann (Ed.), *About Children and Children-No-Longer*. London: Routledge, 1989. [First published in the *International Journal of Psychoanalysis, 31.*]

Heimann, P. (1960). Countertransference. In: M. Tonnesmann (Ed.), *About Children and Children-No-Longer*. London: Routledge, 1989. [First published in the *British Journal of Medical Psychology, 33.*]

Hobson, P. (1989). Beyond cognition: A theory of autism. In G. Dawson (Ed.), *Autism: Nature, Diagnosis and Treatment*. New York: Guilford Press.

Hobson, P. (1990). On psychoanalytic approaches to autism. *American Journal of Orthopsychiatry, 60* (3).

Hobson, P. (1993). *Autism and the Development of Mind*. Hove: Lawrence Erlbaum.

Houzel, D. (2001). Bisexual qualities of the psychic envelope. In: J. Edwards (Ed.), *Being Alive* (pp. 44–56). Hove: Routledge.

Joseph, B. (1982). Addiction to near-death. *International Journal of Psychoanalysis, 63*: 449–456.

Joseph, B. (1985). Transference: The total situation. *International Journal of Psychoanalysis, 66*: 447–454.

Joseph, B. (1988). Projective identification: Some clinical aspects. In: J. Sandler (Ed), *Projection, Identification, Projective Identification* (pp. 65–76). London: Karnac.

Joseph, B. (1989). *Psychic Equilibrium and Psychic Change*. London: Routledge.

Kanner, L. (1943). Autistic disturbance of affective control. *Nervous Child, 2*: 217–50.

Kanner, L. (1944). Early infantile autism. *Journal of Paediatrics, 25* (3): 211–217.

Klein, M. (1931). A contribution to the theory of intellectual inhibition. *International Journal of Psychoanalysis, 12*: 206–218.

Klein, M. (1935). A contribution to the psychogenesis of manic-depressive states. *International Journal of Psychoanalysis, 16*: 145–174.

Klein, M. (1946). Notes on some schizoid mechanism. *International Journal of Psychoanalysis, 27*: 99–110.

Klein, M. (1952). Some theoretical conclusions regarding the emotional life of the infant. In: M. Klein, P. Heimann, S. Isaacs, & J. Riviere, *Developments in Psycho-Analysis* (pp. 198–236). London: Hogarth Press, 1989.

Klein, M. (1959). Our adult world and its roots in infancy. *Human Relations, 12*: 291–303.

Klein, S. (1980). Autistic phenomena in neurotic patients. *International Journal of Psychoanalysis, 61*: 395–401.

Lacan, J. (1956). Réponse au commentaire de Jean Hyppolite sur la Verneinung de Freud. *La Psychanalyse, 1*: 46.

LeDoux, J. E. (1995). Emotion: Clues from the brain. *Annual Review of Psychology, 46*: 209–235.

Lechevalier-Haim, B. (2001). Working towards the depressive position in long-term therapy with autistic patients. In: J. Edwards (Ed.), *Being Alive*. Hove: Brunner-Routledge.

Leslie, A. M. (1987). Pretence and representation: The origins of theory of mind. *Psychology Review, 94*.

Maiello, S. (1995). The sound object: A hypothesis about pre-natal auditory experience and memory. *Journal of Child Psychotherapy, 21* (1): 23–24.

Maiello, S. (1997). Going beyond: Notes on the beginning of object relation in the light of "the perpetuation of an error". In: J. Mitrani & T. Mitrani (Eds.), *Encounters with Autistic States*. New York: Jason Aronson.

Maiello, S. (2001). On temporal shapes: The relation between primary rhythmical experience and the quality of mental links. In: J. Edwards (Ed.), *Being Alive* (pp. 179–194). Hove: Brunner-Routledge.

Mancia, M. (1981). On the beginning of mental life in the foetus. *International Journal of Psychoanalysis, 62*.

McDougall, J. (1972). The anti-analysand in analysis. In: *Ten Years of Psychoanalysis in France*. New York: International Universities Press, 1980.

McDougall, J. (1978). *Plea for a Measure of Abnormality*. New York: International Universities Press, 1980.

McDougall, J. (1982a). Alexithymia, psychosomatisis and psychosis. *International Journal of Psychoanalysis and Psychotherapy, 9*: 379–388.

McDougall, J. (1982b). *Theatre of the Mind: Illusion and Truth on the Psychoanalytic Stage*. New York: Basic Books.

McDougall, J. (1989). *Theatre of the Body*. London: Free Association Books.

McDougall, J. (1996). *Eros aux mille et un visage*. Paris: Gallimard.

Meltzer, D. (1986). *Studies in Extended Metapsychology*. Strath Tay: Clunie Press.

Meltzer, D., Bremner, J., Hoxter, H., Waddell, D., & Wittenberg, I. (1975). *Explorations in Autism: A Psycho-Analytical Study*. Strath Tay: Clunie Press.

Miller, L., Rustin, M., & Shuttleworth, I. (1989). *Closely Observed Infants*. London: Duckworth.

Mishkin, M., Malamut B., & Bachevalier, J. (1984). Memories and habits: Two neural systems. In: G. Lynch & J. L. Mc Gaugh (Eds.), *Neurobiology of Learning and Memory*. New York: Guildford Press.

Money-Kyrle, R. E. (1956). Normal counter-transference and some of its deviations. *International Journal of Psychoanalysis, 37*: 360–366. [Also in: *The Collected Papers of Roger Money-Kyrle*. Strath Tay: Clunie Press, 1978.]

Murray, L. (1991). Intersubjectivity, objects relations theory and empirical evidence from mother–infant interaction. *Infant Mental Health Journal, 12.*

Newson, J. (1987). The education, treatment and handling of autistic children. *Children and Society, 1*: 34–50.

Ogden, T. H. (1980). On the nature of schizophrenic conflict. *International Journal of Psichoanalysis, 61*: 513–533.

Ogden, T. H. (1982a). Treatment of the schizophrenic state of non-experience. In: P. L. Giovacchini, & L. B. Boyer (Eds.), *Technical Factors in the Treatment of the Severely Disturbed Patient* (pp. 217–260). New York: Jason Aronson.

Ogden, T. H. (1982b). *Projective Identification and Psychotherapeutic Technique.* London: Jason Aronson.

Ogden, T. H. (1984). Instinct, phantasy and psychological deep structure: A reinterpretation of aspect of the work of Melanie Klein. *Contemporary Psychoanalysis, 20*: 500–525.

Ogden, T. H. (1989). *The Primitive Edge of Experience.* New York: Jason Aronson [reprinted: London: Karnac Books, 1992].

Ogden, T. H. (1997). *Reverie and Interpretation.* London: Jason Aronson.

O'Shaughnessy, E. (1964). The absent object. *Journal of Child Psychotherapy, 1* (2): 134–143.

Parks, S. L. (1983). The assessment of autistic children: A selective review of available instruments. *Journal of Autism and Developmental Disorders, 13* (3): 255–267.

Perry, B., Pollard, L., Blakley, T. L., Baker, W. L., & Vigilante, D. (1995). Childhood trauma, the neurobiology of adaptation and use-dependent development of the brain: How states become traits. *Infant Mental Health Journal, 16*: 271–291.

Racamier, P. C. (1995). *L'inceste et l'incestuel.* Paris: Editions du Collège.

Racker, H. (1948). Contribution to the problem of counter-transference. *International Journal of Psychoanalysis, 34* (1953): 313–324.

Racker, H. (1957). The meanings and uses of counter-transference. In: *Transference and Countertransference* (pp. 158–201). London: Hogarth Press, 1968.

Reik, T. (1937). *Surprise and the Psychoanalyst.* New York: Dutton.

Renik, O. (1993). Analytic interaction: Conceptualizing technique in light of the analyst's irreducible subjectivity. *Psychoanalytic Quarterly, 72* (4).

Resnik, S. (1972). *Persona e psicosi.* Turin: Einaudi, 2001.

Resnik, S. (1986). *L'esperienza psicotica.* Turin: Boringhieri.

Resnik, S. (1987). Les identifications du corps dans la psychose. *Journal de la psychanalyse de l'enfant, 20*: 84–103.

Resnik, S. (1999a). Corps, affection, passions: Réalité corporelle de l'inconscient. *Journal de la Psychanalyse de l'Enfant, 29*: 23–46.

Resnik, S. (1999b). *Le temps des glaciations*. Ramonville Saint-Agne: Editions Erèz.

Rhode, M. (1997). Going to pieces: Autistic and schizoid solutions. In: M. Rustin, M. Rhode, A. Dubinsky, & H. Dubinsky (Eds.), *Psychotic States in Children*. London: Duckworth.

Rhode, M. (2001). The sense of abundance in relation to technique. In: J. Edwards (Ed.), *Being Alive* (pp. 128–140). Hove: Brunner-Routledge.

Richard, F. (Ed.) (2002). *Le travail du psychanalyste en psychothérapie*. Paris: Dunod.

Rosenfeld, D. (1976). *Clínica Psicoanalítica*. Buenos Aires: Galerna.

Rosenfeld, D. (1982). La noción del esquema corporal psicótico en pacientes neuróticos y psicóticos. *Psicoanálisis, 4* (2): 383–404.

Rosenfeld, D. (1984). Hypochondrias, somatic delusion and body scheme in psychoanalytic practice. *International Journal of Psychoanalysis, 65*: 377–388.

Rosenfeld, D. (1990). Psychotic body image. In: B. Boyer & P. Giovacchini (Eds.), *Master Clinicians on Treating Regressed Patients*. Northvale, NJ: Jason Aronson.

Rosenfeld, D. (1992). *The Psychotic*. London: Karnac.

Rosenfeld, D. (1997). Autisme: Des aspects autistiques dans la pharmaco-dépendance et dans les maladies psychosomatiques. *Journal de la psychanalyse de l'enfant, 20*: 168–188. (Paris: Bayard Editions.)

Rosenfeld, H. (1978). "The Relationship between Psychosomatic Symptoms and Latent Psychotic States." Unpublished paper (cited in S. Klein, Autistic phenomena in neurotic patients. *International Journal of Psychoanalysis, 61* (1980): 395–401.

Rosenfeld, H. (1987). *Impasse and Interpretation*. London: Tavistock.

Rustin, M., Rhode, M., Dubinsky, A., & Dubinsky, H. (1997). *Psychotic States in Children*. London: Duckworth.

Saint-Cyr, J. A., & Taylor, A. E. (1992). The mobilisation of procedural learning: The "key signature" of the basal ganglia. In: L. R. Squire & N. Butters (Eds.), *Neuropsychology of Memory* (pp. 188–202). New York: Guilford Press.

Sandler, J. (1960). The background of safety. *International Journal of Psychoanalysis, 41*: 352–356.

Sandler, J., & Joffe, W. G. (1969). Towards a basic psychoanalytic model. *International Journal of Psychoanalysis, 50*: 79–90.

Schachter, D. L. (1987). Implicit expressions of memory in organic amnesia: Learning of new facts and associations. *Human Neurobiology, 6*: 107–118.

Schachter, D. L. (1992a). Priming and multiple sensory systems: Perceptual mechanisms of implicit memory. *Journal of Cognitive Neuroscience, 4*: 244–256.

Schachter, D. L. (1992b). Understanding implicit memory: A cognitive neuroscience approach. *American Psychologist, 47*: 559–569.

Schafer, R. (1968). *Aspects of Internalization*. New York: International Universities Press.

Schore, A. S. (1996). The experience-dependent maturation of a regulatory system in the orbital prefrontal cortex and the origin of development psychopathology. *Development and Psychopathology, 8*: 59–87.

Searles, H. (1965). *Collected papers on Schizophrenia and Related Subjects*. London: Hogarth Press.

Searles, H. (1986). *My Work with Borderline Patients*. Northvale, NJ: Jason Aronson.

Searles, H. (1988). The schizophrenic's vulnerability to therapist's unconscious processes. In: B. Wolstein (Ed.), *Essential Papers on Countertransference*. New York: University Press.

Sigman, M., & Capps, L. (1997). *Children with Autism*. London: Harvard University Press.

Steiner, J. (1993). *Psychic Retreats*. London: Routledge.

Stern, D. N. (1977). *The First Relationship: Infant and Mother*. London: Fontana/Open Books.

Stern, D. N. (1985). *The Interpersonal World of the Infant*. New York: Basic Books.

Stolorow, R. D., & Atwood, G. E. (1996). *Context of Being: The Intersubjective Foundations of Psychological Life*. Mahwah, NJ: Analytic Press.

Sullivan, H. S. (1940). *Conceptions of Modern Psychiatry*. Washington, DC: William Alanson White Psychiatric Foundation.

Sylar, R. M. (1987). *Reminiscences of Four Years in Arctic Alaska*. North Slope Borough: Planning Department, Inupiat History, Language and Culture Division.

Symington, N. (1983). The analyst's act of freedom as agent of therapeutic change. *International Review of Psycho-Analysis, 10*: 283–291.

Tremelloni, L. (1987). The psychotherapeutic treatment of a psychotic child with marked autistic features. *Psychoanalytic Psychotherapy, 3* (1): 11–25.

Tremelloni, L. (1988). Problèmes de technique dans la psychothérapie d'enfants autistiques avec une forte tendance à la passivité. *Journal de la psychanalyse de l'enfant, 5*.

Tremelloni, L. (1999). Eros senza psiche. In: A. Bimbi (Ed.), *Eros e Psiche*. Tirrenia: Edizioni del Cerro.

Trevarthen, C., Aitken, K., Papoudi, D., & Robarts, J. (1996). *Children with Autism: Diagnosis and Interventions to Meet Their Need*. London: Jessica Kingsley.

Tustin, F. (1972). *Autism and Childhood Psychosis*. London: Hogarth Press.

Tustin, F. (1980). Autistic objects, *International Review of Psycho-Analysis, 7*.

Tustin, F. (1981a). *Autistic States in Children*. London: Routledge & Kegan Paul.

Tustin, F. (1981b). Psychological birth and psychological catastrophe. In: J. S. Grotstein (Ed.), *Do I Dare Disturb the Universe?* Beverly Hills, CA: Caesura Press.

Tustin, F. (1984). Autistic shapes. *International Review of Psycho-Analysis, 11*: 279–290.

Tustin, F. (1986). *Autistic Barriers in Neurotic Patients*. London: Karnac.

Tustin, F. (1990). *The Protective Shell in Children and Adults*. London: Karnac.

Tustin, F. (1994). The perpetuation of an error. *Journal of Child Psychotherapy, 20* (1): 3–23.

Wing, L. (1996). *The Autistic Spectrum: A Guide for Parents and Professional*. London: Constable.

Wing, L., & Gould, J. (1979). Severe impairment of social interactions and associated abnormalities in children epidemiology and classification. *Journal of Autism and Developmental Disorders, 9*.

Winnicott, D. W. (1947). Hate in the counter-transference. In: *Collected Papers: Through Paediatrics to Psycho-Analysis*. London: Tavistock, 1958.

Winnicott, D. W. (1948). Paediatrics and psychiatry. In: *Collected Papers: Through Paediatrics to Psycho-Analysis*. London: Tavistock, 1958.

Winnicott, D. W. (1949). Birth memories, birth trauma and anxiety. In: *Collected Papers: Through Paediatrics to Psycho-Analysis*. London: Tavistock, 1958.

Winnicott, D. W. (1951). Transitional objects and transitional phenomena. In: *Collected Papers: Through Paediatrics to Psycho-Analysis*. London: Tavistock, 1958.

Winnicott, D. W. (1960a). The theory of the parent–infant relationship. In: *The Maturational Processes and the Facilitating Environment*. London: Hogarth Press, 1965.

Winnicott, D. W. (1960b). Ego distortion in terms of true and false. In: *The Maturational Processes and the Facilitating Environment*. London: Hogarth Press, 1965.

Winnicott, D. W. (1965a). The concept of trauma in relation to the development of the individual within the family. In: *Psycho-Analytic Explorations*. London: Karnac 1989.

Winnicott, D. W. (1965b). *The Maturational Processes and The Facilitating Environment*. London: Hogarth Press.

Winnicott, D. W. (1965c). The psychology of madness: A contribution from psycho-analysis. In: *Psycho-Analytic Explorations*. London: Karnac, 1989.

Winnicott, D. W. (1971). *Playing and Reality*. London: Tavistock.

Winnicott, D. W. (1974). Fear of breakdown. *International Review of Psycho-Analysis, 1*: 103–107.

INDEX